Timothy Paul Jones's writings are always engaging, compelling, and often humorous. He captivates me with everything he writes. When I read his writing, I have many "Aha!" or "I wish I'd thought of that" moments. This isn't the first great book that Timothy's written, and it won't be the last. Make certain you don't miss it!

—JAMES L. GARLOW, PhD
Senior Pastor
Skyline Wesleyan Church

A gifted scholar who is sufficiently a scholar to write a challenging book that is still simple enough for students—that is both novel and encouraging! Timothy Paul Jones in *Conspiracies and the Cross* has achieved this remarkable feat. Christian students armed with the invaluable information that Dr. Jones has made available in this remarkably readable form will be able to face both skeptical teachers and critical students with confidence.

—DR. PAIGE PATTERSON
President
Southwestern Baptist Theological Seminary
Fort Worth, Texas

Our God tells us not to "call conspiracy all that this people calls conspiracy, and do not fear what they fear, nor be in dread" (Isaiah 8:13). Many Christians have no fear of the devil, but are secretly afraid of the shelves of the neighborhood Barnes and Noble, teeming as they are with faddish "exposés" of the Christian faith. With brilliance, insight, and wit, scholar Timothy Paul Jones shows Christians and seekers why these conspiracy theories are neither new nor convincing. In so doing, Jones prepares Christians to refute not simply this year's crop of conspiracies, but whatever like them that may grow up over the next hundred years. This book will help the Christian reader to fear what is truly fearful, the Lord God of hosts. And, to warn all skeptics, it just might cause you to rethink the possibility that perhaps the Bible is precisely what it claims to be. That may be scarier than the conspiracy theories to some. But it is the beginning of wisdom.

—RUSSELL D. MOORE
Senior Vice President for Academic Administration
Dean, School of Theology
The Southern Baptist Theological Seminary

The church is in danger of answering questions about the Bible that our culture no longer asks. The conversation has shifted from "Is scripture *relevant?*" to "Is scripture *reliable?*" Textual criticism is no longer a topic reserved for quiet seminaries; these scholarly discussions have moved to the cineplex and the online book retailers. The average believer is unequipped to deal with these new challenges to faith in the historic Jesus. In *Conspiracies and the Cross*, Dr. Jones methodically debunks each of these assaults on the Gospels with logic, grace, and humor. Readers will leave this book with the tools needed to assist the skeptics around them as well their own doubts. This is an accessible volume that I hope will find its way into Sunday school classes and college classrooms everywhere.

—Pastor Larry Shallenberger
Author of *Divine Intention: How God's Work in the Early Church Empowers Us Today*

Bamboozled by the confusion about Jesus and the origins of Christianity today? Timothy Paul Jones sets out the facts behind the Gospels with flair, scholarship, and considerable honesty. A must-read for anyone interested in Jesus and the Christian faith.

—Brent Siddall,
Radio host, *TWR Word*
TransWorld Radio UK

Inasmuch as many Browns and Ehrmans and Crossans and Pagelses and Ludemmans and Smiths have undertaken to set in writing their understanding of the things that have been fulfilled among us some two millennia ago, it seemed good to Timothy Paul Jones, having had thoroughly investigated all things from the very first, to write for you, most excellent reader, a vigorous and well-researched defense of the Gospel's truth so that you may know the certainty of those things in which you were instructed and not be deceived by the multifarious conspiracies of our times.

—Radu Gheorghita
Associate Professor of Biblical Studies
Midwestern Baptist Theological Seminary

CONSPIRACIES and the CROSS

TIMOTHY PAUL JONES

FRONT LINE

A STRANG COMPANY

Most STRANG COMMUNICATIONS/CHARISMA HOUSE/SILOAM/FRONTLINE/REALMS/ EXCEL BOOKS products are available at special quantity discounts for bulk purchase for sales promotions, premiums, fund-raising, and educational needs. For details, write Strang Communications/Charisma House/Siloam/FrontLine/Realms/Excel Books, 600 Rinehart Road, Lake Mary, Florida 32746, or telephone (407) 333-0600.

CONSPIRACIES AND THE CROSS by Timothy Paul Jones
Published by FrontLine: A Strang Company
600 Rinehart Road
Lake Mary, Florida 32746
www.frontlineissues.com

This book is published in association with Nappaland Literary Agency in Loveland, Colorado.

Manuscript edited by Killian Creative, Boulder, Colorado.

Unless otherwise indicated, all Hebrew, Aramaic, Greek, and Latin texts are translated by the author from primary source materials.

Pictures from the Schoyen Collection, Oslo and London, are the property of Martin Schoyen and are used by permission of the Elizabeth Gano Sorensen, Schoyen Collection librarian. Pictures from the Center for the Study of New Testament Manuscripts are used by permission of Daniel B. Wallace, director of CSNTM.

Cover Designer: Justin Evans; Executive Design Director: Bill Johnson

Library of Congress Cataloging-in-Publication Data:

Jones, Timothy P. (Timothy Paul)
  Conspiracies and the cross / Timothy Paul Jones.
     p. cm.
  Includes bibliographical references.
  ISBN-10: 1-59979-205-2
  ISBN-13: 978-1-59979-205-7
  1. Jesus Christ--Historicity I. Title.
  BT303.2.J66 2008
  232.9--dc22

                                    2007045939

Printed in the United States of America
08 09 10 11 12 — 9 8 7 6 5 4 3 2 1

Dedicated to my wife...
in whose every embrace
I taste anew God's goodness to me,
surpassing anything that I have ever deserved.

And to our daughter...
growing so quickly
but still yet and forevermore
the delight of her daddy's heart.

Contents

A T ONE TIME, PEOPLE IN WESTERN SOCIETY LIVED IN A CULTURE IN which the Bible was assumed to possess a certain authority. In today's secular culture, many Christians don't feel as if they can necessarily appeal to the Bible as authoritative anymore. As a result, Christians don't know what to say. Some Christians assume that they *have* nothing to say. They feel intellectually naked in their culture, thinking, "If I can't appeal to Scripture, what *can* I appeal to?"

In such a context, many young people come to assume that there is a conflict between their faith and their mind, and they end up choosing *reason* over *faith*—never recognizing that reason and faith were never contradictory in the first place. I want Christians to recognize that they *do* have something to say, even to a secular culture, because there *is* a rational foundation for their beliefs. We are told to love God not just with our hearts but also with our minds, and we are told to give reasons for the hope that is within us. That's why we must prepare ourselves. Even more importantly, that's why we have to prepare our children with intellectual and moral defenses so that they can fend off the attacks that will surely come.

That's precisely what Timothy Paul Jones does throughout this book. In *Conspiracies and the Cross*, Jones has written a lucid, well-informed, and powerful book. It is an inspiration to Christians and a challenge to non-Christians.

—DINESH D'SOUZA
Robert and Karen Rishwain Fellow at the Hoover Institution,
Stanford University
New York Times best-selling author of
What's So Great About Christianity

THE **TROUBLE** WITH **JESUS**

If Christianity is not rooted in things that actually happened in first-century Palestine, we might as well be Buddhists, Marxists, or almost anything else. And if Jesus never existed, or if he was quite different from what the Gospels and the church's worship affirms him to have been, then we are indeed living in cloud-cuckoo-land. The skeptics can and must be answered.[1]

—N. T. WRIGHT, *THE CHALLENGE OF JESUS*

SO FAR, THE TWENTY-FIRST CENTURY HAS BEEN ROUGH ON JESUS.

Near the end of the twentieth century, a cluster of scholars known as "the Jesus Seminar" concluded that fewer than three dozen of the deeds described in the Gospels actually happened. And the Resurrection? Nothing more than pious fiction spawned by hopeful hallucinations, according to the seminar members.[2]

The teachings of Jesus fared little better. According to the Jesus Seminar, out of approximately five hundred sayings attributed to Jesus, fewer than one hundred of them might accurately represent the rabbi's words.[3] One seminar member even claimed that the complete message of the historical Jesus could be summarized in a single sentence: "God says, 'Caesar sucks.'"[4] As the year 2000 loomed closer, these revised views of Jesus began to reemerge each year about the same time as the tulips, cultivating a fresh crop of confusion just in time for each year's Easter celebration.

As the turn of the millennium approached, it was discovered that certain computers somehow lacked the capacity to count past 1999. As a result, the year 2000 was widely expected to usher in a period of widespread chaos. As it turned out, New Year's Eve 1999 came and went with more of a whimper than a bang, and millions of families faced the age-old question, "What are we supposed to do with all these cans of processed-meat product?"

Nearly four years later—about the time the last canned meat casserole came out of the oven—opinions about Jesus suddenly turned *really* strange. *The Da Vinci Code*—a suspense novel from a writer named Dan Brown—unexpectedly rocketed to first place on the best-seller lists and exposed millions of readers to radical reinterpretations of Jesus. Brown's reinterpretations might have remained relatively unknown except for the writer's persistent claim in interviews and on the novel's title page that "absolutely all" of his claims about art, architecture, and historical events were true.[5]

Even though Dan Brown's ideas were considerably more outlandish than most of what the Jesus Seminar had concocted thus far, few of his claims were new. For example, the holy matrimony of Jesus and Mary Magdalene, the central subject of Leonardo da Vinci's supposed code in Dan Brown's book, is an idea that had already made an appearance in a couple of quirky pseudohistories, *Holy Blood, Holy Grail* and *The Templar Revelation: Secret Guardians of the True Identity of Christ*. What about the idea that scandalous truths about Jesus were encoded somewhere in the Dead Sea Scrolls? A book titled *The Dead Sea Scrolls Deception* had suggested that possibility in the 1990s. How about the theory that the most accurate depiction of Jesus can be found in a handful of "lost Gospels" that were excluded from the New Testament? John Dominic Crossan and Elaine Pagels had already pushed these claims in books such as *The Historical Jesus: The Life of a Mediterranean Peasant* and *The Gnostic Gospels*.[6]

> Jesus…is an imaginative theological construct.[7]
> —The Jesus Seminar (1996)

> Jesus was viewed by His followers as a mortal prophet…a great and powerful man, but a *man* nonetheless.[8]
> —DAN BROWN, *The Da Vinci Code* (2003)

HOW CHRIST CONSPIRACIES TURNED TRENDY

Despite the fact that the theories promoted in *The Da Vinci Code* were far from new, the best-selling novel brought ideas that had once remained on the desks of skeptical scholars and conspiracy buffs to the attention of millions of readers. In the aftermath of *The Da Vinci Code*, Christ conspiracies suddenly turned trendy, and radical reinterpretations of Jesus glutted the shelves of mainstream bookstores. "Speculative histories were out there before Dan Brown wrote," commented *Publishers Weekly* editor Lynn Garrett, "but they didn't make the best-seller lists and their authors didn't go on *The Daily Show*."[9] The editorial director of one publishing house summarized the newly popularized genre of speculative biblical history this way: "Dan Brown didn't invent it, but he made it sexy."[10]

Ever since Dan Brown "made it sexy," conspiracies about Jesus and the Gospels have multiplied not only in frequency but also in strangeness. One of the resulting reinterpretations of the life of Jesus boasted the title *The Jesus*

Papers: Exposing the Greatest Cover-Up in History. This book claimed to contain inside information about a scandalous, long-suppressed letter from the hand of Jesus Himself.[11] In this supposed letter, Jesus—who, by the time He gets around to writing the note, has somehow survived the Crucifixion and now resides with Mary Magdalene in the suburbs of Jerusalem—explains that He never intended anyone to think He was the unique Son of God.

Another reexamination of the biblical records—*Misquoting Jesus: The Story Behind Who Changed the Bible and Why,* from religious scholar Bart Ehrman—suggested an entirely different set of reasons to doubt the accuracy of the New Testament. According to Ehrman, the ancient biblical texts were copied so poorly and edited so thoroughly that the meanings of entire biblical books have changed.[12]

Then came a document known as the Gospel of Judas. In 2006, several scholars released a new reconstruction of a long-lost Gospel that claimed the turncoat disciple known as Judas Iscariot as its author. A *National Geographic* documentary about this reconstruction suggested that the newly restored Gospel provided "new insights into the disciple who betrayed Jesus"[13]— insights that directly contradicted the New Testament Gospels. There was a movie titled *The God Who Wasn't There.*[14] According to the producer of this film—as well as a handful of recent books, such as Timothy Freke's *The Jesus Mysteries*—Jesus most likely never existed at all.[15]

In spring 2007, the speculations careened in even crazier directions. In the space of a few weeks, a Texas pastor named Jose Luis de Jesus Miranda pronounced himself to be "the Antichrist" as well as "the Second Coming of Christ, that messiah they've been waiting for,"[16] and a sensational documentary entitled *The Jesus Family Tomb* declared that archaeologists had unearthed a burial box that once held the bones of Jesus—a proposition that, if true, could present a bit of a problem for the whole idea of Jesus having been resurrected never to die again.[17] In the weeks that followed, one *TIME* magazine correspondent referred to this flurry of sensational theories as the result of "OTMSBBS: one-too-many-speculative-Bible-books syndrome."[18]

Then came the march of the militant atheists. In the space of a few months, three best sellers—Richard Dawkins's *The God Delusion*, Sam Harris's *Letter to a Christian Nation*, and Christopher Hitchens's *God Is Not Great*—attacked Christianity head-on.

Here's how Christopher Hitchens summed up his attitude toward Christian faith: "I'm not an atheist. I'm an anti-theist. . . . I can't stand people of faith."[19] Hitchens referred to the stories of Jesus in the New Testament as "crude carpentry, hammered together long after its purported events, and full of improvised attempts to make things come out right."[20]

According to Dawkins's *The God Delusion*, the Judeo-Christian God is "arguably the most unpleasant character in all fiction...a petty, unjust, unforgiving control freak; a vindictive, bloodthirsty ethnic cleanser; a misogynistic, homophobic, racist, infanticidal, genocidal, filicidal, pestilential, megalomaniacal, sadomasochistic, capriciously malevolent bully."[21] And what about Jesus? "A huge improvement over the cruel ogre of the Old Testament," Dawkins declares, but the death of Jesus Christ is "sadomasochistic and repellent. We should...dismiss it as barking mad."[22]

So why can't we simply disregard such vicious attempts? Because these works *have* had an effect on people.

Only 9 percent of middle-aged adults and 14 percent of adults in their early thirties identify themselves as atheists or agnostics. Yet, when it comes to the people who have grown up in the shadow of such claims about Jesus—persons presently in their late teens and early twenties—nearly *20 percent* openly refer to themselves as atheists or agnostics. Put another way, one out of every five college-aged students has rejected not merely *Jesus* but the very possibility of knowing God at all! [23]

Despite the many differences in opinion about Jesus, one fact remains certain: nearly two thousand years after His followers first affirmed that He was alive, Jesus of Nazareth is still hot news.

> Maybe we have enough evidence to say that our understanding of what happened back then was too simple. Dan Brown didn't invent it, but he made it sexy.[24]
>
> —MICHAEL MAUDLIN,
> HarperSanFrancisco editorial director (2007)
>
> I am attacking God, all gods, anything and everything supernatural, wherever and whenever they have been or will be created.[25]
>
> —RICHARD DAWKINS,
> professor at Oxford University (2006)

KNOW MORE

agnostic (from Greek, *a*- ["not"] + *-ginoskein* ["to know"]): an individual who believes that it is not possible to know whether God is real.

atheist (from Greek, *a*- ["not"] + *-theos* ["God"]): an individual who denies the reality of God.

NOTHING TO FEAR

All these claims had God the Father perched on the edge of His celestial throne, I'm sure. Perhaps the Father even spent a few nights pacing the streets of gold, wondering whether His eternal plans were teetering on the verge of failure. Surely—after the supposed discoveries of the Messiah's moldering remains and of a disclaimer letter from the hand of Jesus Himself—the divine kingdom was doomed to collapse.

Unless, of course, God knew about the Christ conspiracies long before their authors were even conceived.

Unless, when all the evidences are examined with an open mind, a reasonable foundation for embracing the New Testament as an accurate historical record still remains.

And unless these reconstructions don't have nearly as much merit as the media seem to ascribe to them.

If so, I have no reason to fear such theories, and, even after a decade of exploring dozens of these supposed conspiracies, that's precisely what I've come to believe: *There is no reason to fear these skeptical reconstructions of Jesus.* When subjected to actual historical evidences, each conspiracy crumbles beneath the weight of its own overblown claims.

TWO ROTTEN REASONS TO BELIEVE IN JESUS

Why, then, is this book necessary? If these reconstructions are readily refutable, why spend so much time responding to them? Why not simply ignore the Christ conspiracies?

Here's why the Christ conspiracies can't be overlooked: *The strongest faith is a faith that knows not only what we believe but also why.* In the past five years or so, I've spoken with thousands of people—most of them firm believers in the biblical perspective on Jesus—about the historical foundations of their faith. In the process, I've heard multitudes of well-meaning Christians provide the same two reasons for their faith in Jesus.

The first reason runs something like this: "I just know Jesus is alive because I've felt His presence—that's the only proof I need!" The other one is usually stated in these terms: "The Bible is God's Word; so, if the Bible says it, I believe it, and that settles it."

I respect these believers' sincerity; I really do. But may I be blunt for just a moment? *These are rotten reasons to believe in Jesus.*

Just because you've felt something that you identified as God's presence *doesn't* mean that what you felt was true.

And how do you *know* that the Bible is God's Word? Is it simply because the Bible claims to be inspired by God? Unless there's a firmer foundation for the truth of Scripture than the Bible's own claims about itself, the fact that "the Bible says it" doesn't settle *anything*.

Sure, the apostle Paul referred to the Hebrew Scriptures as "God-breathed," and a letter ascribed to Simon Peter placed New Testament writings in the same inspired category as the Old Testament (2 Timothy 3:16; 2 Peter 3:16–17), but the Quran—the holy book of the Islamic faith—claims divine inspiration for itself too.[26]

So why couldn't a devout Muslim make a similar statement about the Quran: "The Quran says it, I believe it, and that settles it"? Yet, if *both* the Christian Scriptures and the Quran are divinely inspired, God must suffer from a serious multiple-personality disorder, because the claims of the two books cannot be reconciled with each other. According to the Quran, for example, Jesus was a human prophet who may not have died at all.[27] Yet, according to the New Testament, Jesus died on a cross and rose from the dead three days later (1 Corinthians 15:3–4; 2 Corinthians 13:4). Accepting a book as sacred truth because it claims to be God's Word simply doesn't work.

What about the inward, personal awareness that Jesus is present and alive?[28] Doesn't *that* prove the truth of the Christian Gospel? What could possibly be wrong with faith of this sort—a faith that's based on an individual's personal experience with Jesus?

In truth, this foundation for faith is even flimsier than the first one. Why? Think about it this way: based on supposed personal experiences with God, cult leader Jim Jones claimed that he was the reincarnation of both Jesus Christ and the Buddha (as well as Vladimir Ilyich Lenin!),[29] Jose Luis de Jesus Miranda declared himself to *be* the second coming of Christ as well as the Antichrist, and forty-one Heaven's Gate cult members committed suicide in 1997 so that their souls could catch a ride on an outbound UFO.[30]

If the foundation for my faith is my own personal experience with the divine, what's the difference between my claim that Jesus Christ rose from the dead and De Jesus Miranda's claim that he *is* both Christ and Antichrist? Or between my trust in Jesus and someone else's belief that an Internet utility known as the Mystical Smoking Head of Bob can answer life's most perplexing questions, for that matter? (And, no, the Mystical Smoking Head of Bob is *not* simply one more by-product of my hyperactive imagination. It's really out there, it has three eyes, and it can deliver prophetic oracles in Pig Latin.[31] When I asked the Mystical Smoking Head if this book would become a best seller, it told me, "Etterbay otnay elltay ouyay ownay." I took that to be a positive sign.) In the final analysis, our experiences are inadequate foundations for our faith because even if our experiences are indeed real, *we don't always interpret the meaning of our experiences correctly*, which is how people like Jim Jones and Jose Luis de Jesus Miranda end up making themselves out to be messiahs.

Think about it this way: misinterpretations of our experiences occur even when those experiences don't directly involve God. For example, a few weeks ago, my wife told me, "No, nothing's wrong," and I made the ridiculous assumption that nothing was wrong. I made this assumption primarily because this was precisely what she said. What I somehow misinterpreted was the *meaning* of this verbal experience, which was, "Yes, there has been a problem. The problem has been caused by you, but you will need to grovel for several minutes before I will even consider telling you the precise nature of said problem." (I misinterpret these sorts of clues quite often, to tell you the truth.) If I so badly interpret the meaning of my experiences with my beloved spouse, it would be a bit ridiculous to base what I believe about God on my interpretation of my personal experiences.

And what about the claims of ancient writers that the biblical documents were divinely inspired? Well, *any* author can claim that a certain writing is the sacred Word of God. I could even make such a statement about *this* book, though I most likely won't. (The publisher and the Mystical Smoking Head of Bob both agreed that this would be a bad idea. Plus, it wouldn't be true.) In the simplest possible terms, I need a foundation for faith that runs deeper than my own less-than-reliable interpretations of my experiences or the Bible's own claims about itself.

So do you, and so does anyone who claims to believe what the Bible says.

> The Lord—that is, the Messiah—recognize as holy in your hearts to be ever prepared to offer defense of the hope that is in you to anyone who asks you for such a word.
> —Simon Peter, 1 Peter 3:15 (around a.d. 60)

FINDING a FIRMER FOUNDATION

Perhaps that's why so many people's souls are starving for some connection to Jesus that's more substantive than what they've typically heard in churches. They are longing for some foundation for their beliefs that's firmer than either their own fleeting feelings or the Bible's internal claims. They want to trace their understanding of Jesus back to facts and artifacts from Jesus and from the people who knew Him.

And that's precisely why so many of the Christ conspiracies seem so appealing.

Take a second look at a few of the most popular conspiracies: *The Jesus Family Tomb* suggests that archaeologists have handled the very bones of Jesus. *The Jesus Papers* reveals the contents of an alleged letter from Christ's own hand. Some of the documentaries that referenced the Gospel of Judas imply that the reconstructed manuscript of this Gospel provided fresh, first-hand insights into the identity of Jesus Christ. *The Da Vinci Code* claims that a few of Jesus's first followers had passed a series of earth-shattering secrets from one generation to another, encrypting these truths in codes and paintings and clandestine societies.

Do you see the pattern?

In the most popular conspiracies, the supposed scheme is rooted in some external evidence that the authors claim they can trace to Jesus Himself—a letter that He wrote, a box and a tomb where His body decayed into dust, a code from His first followers, a Gospel from His betrayer.

Yet, what if the reports about Jesus that emerged nearest to the time of Jesus Himself can't be located in any Christ conspiracy? What if *no* fact or artifact that claims to confirm these conspiracies actually comes from firsthand witnesses of Jesus Christ? And what if the facts about Jesus that actually *can* be traced to eyewitnesses of Jesus are most likely the ones now found in the New Testament, not the ones supposedly encrypted in lost letters and tombs and secret societies?

As I have examined the historical evidence, that's precisely what I have come to believe: the truths about Jesus that are most likely traceable to the eyewitnesses are the ones that I find today in the New Testament. What's more, I've found that this conclusion rests on far firmer evidence than my own feelings about Jesus or the Bible's own claims about itself. It finds its footing in reasonable reconstructions of real, historical records.

Here's my desire for you as you read *Conspiracies and the Cross*: By the time you finish this book, I hope that you'll not only believe the New Testament's claims about Jesus but also that you'll know *why* those claims make the best sense of the historical evidence. I want you to be able to spot the weaknesses not only in past Christ conspiracies but also in the supposed fresh revelations about Jesus that will inevitably emerge in the future. I want you to know *what* you believe about Jesus and *why*.

So why do I possess such a passion for helping people to understand how we can know that the New Testament writings tell the truth about Jesus? Truth be told, this passion arose even before my status as a pastor, professor, and author created a vested interest in the accuracy of the New Testament documents. My passion was born on a cast-off couch in the library of a small Kansas college where a seventeen-year-old student sat, staring out a darkened window, searching for some semblance of truth.

HOW TRUTH FOUND ME

A few fluorescent lights still flickered in the corners of the library, nearly hidden behind towering bookshelves. Other than the areas around those four fixtures, the main room of the library was utterly dark. The head librarian had told workers to leave these bulbs illuminated, vainly anticipating that some hapless college student might creep into the stacks after hours to steal a book. From my perspective, this scenario didn't seem particularly likely. Until examination week, most of my fellow students would remain blissfully ignorant of the library's existence. Besides, the library's list of missing items confirmed that most students saw no need to wait until the lights were turned off to filch their favorite books.

After locking the lobby doors, I sank into a well-worn couch. An uneven stack of books on the table in front of me tossed oblong shadows across a tiled floor. The pile included tomes about dying deities, the canon of Scripture and textual criticism, rabbinic Judaism, and the history of atheism. Somewhere in that mix were also some early Christ conspiracies—there was Hugh Schonfield's *The Passover Plot*[32] as well as a duo of books entitled *The Messianic Legacy* and *Holy Blood, Holy Grail* from some British writers whose words seemed quite believable to me at the time.[33]

During the past month, while working the lonely five-hour shift before the library closed each evening, I had struggled through nearly all of these books. With each page, I seemed to choke on ever-deepening doubts about my faith. "Two months into my first semester of Bible college," I whispered as I stared at the haphazard stack of books, "and I don't even know what I believe anymore."

It wasn't as if my professors were attacking the Bible; they weren't. Yet, with each lecture and reading, my assumptions about Scripture—assumptions that I had held since childhood—had crumbled into hopeless fragments. When I took my seat on the first day of New Testament Survey, I had thought that the Greek and Hebrew manuscripts employed by the translators of the King James Version had been preserved perfectly from the time of the apostles until today. As far as I knew, all the most familiar elements of Christian faith—a dying deity, the Resurrection, baptism, and the Lord's Supper—were unique to Christianity. Until that moment, I may not always have *lived* my beliefs, but I had never doubted them.

Now, I knew that the ancient world was filled with stories of sacramental meals and ceremonial washings, dying deities and resurrected redeemers. Long before Jesus tumbled into a feeding trough in some obscure corner of the Roman Empire, the Persians venerated Mithras, a deity who—according to some scholars—was born of a virgin and whose birth was celebrated by shepherds and wise men. There were Egyptian divinities worshiped thousands of years before Jesus who were believed to have died and risen from the dead—Osiris and Adonis, Attis and Horus—and when it came to the end of Jesus's life, there were possibilities for His final fate besides the biblical claims of the Resurrection and Ascension. Some scholars claimed that He didn't die on the cross at all;

others suggested that the stories of the Resurrection were intended to be taken only as hopeful symbols—not as witnesses to any historical reality.

In another class, I learned that the original manuscripts of the New Testament had disintegrated into dust more than a thousand years ago and that no two remaining copies of these documents were identical. Then, I ran across a volume that included dozens of Gospels that I had never heard about—odd, esoteric Gospels that claimed to come from Thomas and Mary and Philip and James. What if these Gospels actually told the truth about Jesus?

Nothing had prepared me for these revelations, and I knew that no one in my church or at home was prepared to deal with such doubts, either. Two months into my first semester of college, I found myself no longer able to embrace the Bible blindly as divine truth. I needed to know *why*. Why did so many elements of Christian faith seem to be borrowed from other religions? What if the Resurrection was merely a symbol or, worse yet, a mythical delusion? And what about all those other Gospels?

My professors would probably have been glad to help me, but I was too timid to admit my doubts to them. So, I began to read—not casually flipping through an occasional interesting text, but obsessively consuming book after book during my late-night shifts as a student librarian. By the time I found myself sinking into the couch and crying in the shadows of so many conflicting opinions, I had devoured dozens of volumes from every conceivable perspective, and still I didn't know what to believe.

I did the only thing I knew to do. I kept at it. I kept reading everything I could find, searching for some distant glistering of truth. Finally, near the end of my second semester of college, the clouds of doubt began to clear—not all of them and not all at once, but bit by bit faith reemerged.

It wasn't the same sort of faith that I had possessed when the semester began. In truth, my faith had grown in the darkness. Now, it was deeper, richer, and better equipped to understand what it means to embrace the Bible as God's Word. After seven months of seeking truth, truth finally found me. Sure, I still had some questions, and I struggled for several years with the idea that the Bible could be completely true, but before that school year ended, I saw that the biblical perspective on Jesus Christ made the most sense of the historical records. For the moment, that was enough.

Through the writings of C. S. Lewis, I saw that the presence of some reflections of Christian faith in other religions doesn't mean that Christianity is false. To the contrary, it means that there is, in every system of faith and every human heart, a yearning—however vague—for one true God who enters into death and triumphs over it.[34]

From the works of Bruce Metzger, especially *The Canon of the New Testament* and *The Text of the New Testament*,[35] I learned how—despite the hundreds of thousands of variants in the Greek New Testament—it's almost always possible to determine the original reading of the text. What's more, I learned that none of these points of textual uncertainty undermines any crucial element of Christian faith.

F. F. Bruce's *The Canon of Scripture* and *The New Testament Documents: Are They Reliable?*[36] convinced me that the authors of the Gospels weren't recording symbolic myths or legends. They were intentionally writing historical documents. The authors' purposes, to be sure, were theological, but their theology was rooted in real events that had happened in the context of human history. And all those other Gospels? I discovered that many of them emerged after the New Testament Gospels and that their authors were typically disinterested in the actual, historical events of Jesus's life.

Still, I recall the aching emptiness that knotted my stomach during those months of doubt. I remember the frustration I felt when I realized the answers I had heard in church simply weren't enough. Most of all, I will never forget the joy that surged in my soul as a pattern of thoughtful trust replaced the blind belief that I had embraced for far too long. That's why I'm so passionate about *Conspiracies and the Cross*. I know that blind belief in Jesus isn't enough. I remember the soul-satisfying joy of moving from blind belief to thoughtful trust, and I want you to experience that joy too.

HOW MANY CONSPIRACIES?

Believe it or not, there is some good news about the Christ conspiracies. Here it is: *there aren't very many of them.*

I know, I know—I already hear the protests from a few astute readers: "But I went to the bookstore yesterday and browsed for a few minutes beneath the sign that said 'Bible.' There were dozens of conspiracy theories about Jesus, and when I looked at an online bookseller, there were hundreds of them! *Hundreds!* How can you claim that 'there aren't very many'?"

To be sure, there *are* hundreds of volumes that radically reconstruct the life of Jesus. Yet each one includes at least a few of the same claims as other supposed conspiracies. For example, Michael Baigent suggests in *Holy Blood, Holy Grail* and *The Jesus Papers* that Jesus survived the Crucifixion. Yet, for the most part, Baigent simply rehashes claims that have circulated for centuries. Similar claims can be found not only in contemporary conspiratorial chronicles such as Barbara Thiering's *Jesus and the Riddle of the Dead Sea Scrolls*[37] but also in the writings of several eighteenth- and nineteenth-century skeptics.[38] It's even possible that the Quran—the holy book of the Islamic faith—promoted this possibility in the seventh century A.D.[39]

When it comes to other Christ conspiracies, the situation is no different.

None of the conspiracies are completely new, and most of the reconstructions simply recycle skeptical theories from generations past. In the final analysis, despite the hundreds of titles that continue to flood the shelves of local bookstores, there are fewer than a dozen Christ conspiracies. In this book, I'll take a look at these theories about Jesus, carefully scrutinizing each supposed conspiracy in light of the historical evidences.

I'm not certain what led you to pick up *Conspiracies and the Cross*. Perhaps you're a seeker, searching for truth. Perhaps you're a believer, looking for a firmer foundation for your faith. Maybe you're simply confused about the identity of Jesus Christ. Wherever you find yourself, I do not demand that you agree with me; I simply ask you to join me. Join me as I journey through the remnants of long-faded civilizations, listening for the voices that still echo in fragments of papyrus and stone. Take an honest and open-minded look with me at each bit of historical evidence, and decide for yourself where truth is most likely to be found.

The CHRIST CONSPIRACIES

CONSPIRACY NUMBER ONE	
No one knows who wrote the Gospels	The New Testament Gospels and the traditions of the Resurrection emerged too late to represent eyewitness testimony.
CONSPIRACY NUMBER TWO	
How the lost Gospels got lost	Early-church leaders eliminated many books from the New Testament; some of these "lost scriptures" were the sacred texts of the first Christians.
CONSPIRACY NUMBER THREE	
It was all about power	Early Christian leaders selected sacred books and essential beliefs to protect the church's power structures—not to testify to historical truth about Jesus. Other books and beliefs were violently suppressed.
CONSPIRACY NUMBER FOUR	
Who misquoted Jesus?	The Gospels and other New Testament writings were copied so poorly and edited so thoroughly that the meanings of entire books have changed.

CONSPIRACY NUMBER FIVE	
Gospel truth or gospel fiction?	With few exceptions, the acts and sayings in the New Testament Gospels do not represent actual, historical happenings. Decades after the death of Jesus, believers fabricated words and deeds—including the story of the Resurrection—to fit the needs of their communities.
CONSPIRACY NUMBER SIX	
The mysterious case of the mythical Messiah	Jesus never existed at all. Decades after His supposed death of Jesus, believers fabricated the Gospel stories from pagan myths.
CONSPIRACY NUMBER SEVEN	
Codes in the Gospels, secrets in the scrolls	The Dead Sea Scrolls and perhaps even the New Testament books include encoded secrets about Jesus—information that, if properly understood, could completely change everything that Christians believe.
CONSPIRACY NUMBER EIGHT	
Jesus, Mary, and the Holy Grail	Jesus married Mary Magdalene and founded a physical dynasty—and this long-suppressed information may be entwined with the legend of the Holy Grail.
CONSPIRACY NUMBER NINE	
The dogs beneath the cross	Jesus was never buried, and He was never raised from the dead. Dogs and other wild animals consumed His body.
CONSPIRACY NUMBER TEN	
No place for the evidence	History deals with what probably happened. Since miracles are always improbable, the resurrection of Jesus cannot be considered as a historical event, regardless of how much historical evidence supports it.

Conspiracy Number One

NO ONE KNOWS WHO WROTE THE GOSPELS

WHAT'S the CONSPIRACY?

THE NEW TESTAMENT GOSPELS DO NOT REPRESENT EYEWITNESS TESTI-mony about Jesus. They are anonymous, secondhand witnesses to the life of Jesus.

WHO SAYS SO?

- The Jesus Seminar
- Bart Ehrman, *Jesus: Apocalyptic Prophet of the New Millennium*, *Misquoting Jesus*, and *Lost Christianities*
- Timothy Freke and Peter Gandy, *The Laughing Jesus: Religious Lies and Gnostic Wisdom*

How do you know who wrote the New Testament Gospels?

Oh yes, I know the names that your New Testament places above the Gospels—Matthew, Mark, Luke, and John—but in the earliest Gospel manuscripts, those titles didn't appear on the first page. In fact, until some time in the second century A.D., there were most likely no titles on the Gospels at all!

So how do you know who wrote these books?

For that matter, how did early Christians know?

Or did they? Some skeptics claim that the early Christians *didn't* know who wrote the New Testament Gospels or that even if they did know, this information was forgotten long ago. In any case, according to these skeptics, the Gospel authors *couldn't* have been Matthew, Mark, Luke, or John—or *any* eyewitness of the events reported in the Gospels, for that matter. Here's what one popular scholar has to say about the status of the titles:

> The Gospels that came to be included in the New Testament were all written anonymously; only at a later time were they called by the names of their reputed authors, Matthew, Mark, Luke, and John.... None of them contains a first-person narrative ("One day, when Jesus and I went into Capernaum..."), or claims to be written by an eyewitness or companion of an eyewitness.[1]

Scholars continue to call these books Matthew, Mark, Luke, and John as a matter of convenience; they have to be called *something*, and it doesn't make much sense to call them George, Jim, Fred, and Sam.[2]

A couple of critics even claim that Christians didn't recognize Matthew's, Mark's, Luke's, and John's accounts of Jesus's life as authoritative until a church leader declared these four Gospels to be genuine a century and a half after the time of Jesus. According to this historical reconstruction, a church leader named Irenaeus wrote the following excerpt at some point around A.D. 180:

> [Irenaeus] suddenly produces four Gospels which tell the story of Jesus as an historical narrative. He claims to have four eyewitness accounts of the life of Jesus, which he attributes to Matthew, Mark, Luke, and John, and he rejects all other Christian Gospels as spurious. No one before Irenaeus had ever claimed that there were only four genuine Gospels.[3]

Is it really reasonable, however, to discount so readily the names of Matthew, Mark, Luke, and John?

Is it possible that the Gospels might actually represent eyewitness testimony about Jesus?

Are we really so bad off when it comes to identifying the authors of the New Testament Gospels?

Now, it's important to consider at this point that the truth of the four New Testament Gospels *doesn't* depend on whether Matthew, Mark, Luke, and John actually wrote these books. In other words, the Gospels might represent historical truth even if these four authors *didn't* write the books that bear their names.

At the same time, even though anonymous Gospels *could* accurately chronicle the historical events of the life of Jesus, I don't think we have to settle for anonymous Gospels. Maybe you agree with me, and perhaps you don't, or maybe you simply aren't sure. Whatever you believe about the origins of the Gospels, take a careful look with me at the historical evidences for who might have produced these texts. First, we'll look at *when* the Gospels were written. Then, we'll take a look at *how* we can determine who probably penned these texts.

CONSPIRACY NUMBER ONE

The New Testament Gospels and the traditions of the
Resurrection emerged too late to represent eyewitness
testimony.

The TRUTH BEHIND the CONSPIRACY

The New Testament Gospels began to circulate no later than
the late first century A.D. From the time that the Gospels
first circulated in the churches, Matthew, Mark, Luke, and
John were recognized as their primary sources.

CLUES to CRACK the ANONYMITY CONSPIRACY

Let's suppose that you wanted to discover *when* I wrote this book. (I know, I know; that probably isn't a fragment of information that's kept you awake at night, but stay with me for a few moments, OK?) What would you do? How would you find out which months I meandered from one coffee shop to another, trying desperately to look as though I was doing something significant?

To begin with, you might flip through the first few pages of *Conspiracies and the Cross* and locate a copyright date. Supposing that the date you found there was 2008, you would probably guess that I wrote these words at some point before the end of 2008. (Either that, or I wrote the book in the future and somehow found my way back to the present; however, given the fact that I can't even find my own car in the parking lot without using the remote key to sound the horn, this seems highly unlikely.) Then, you might glance through the endnotes near the back of the book and notice the dates of the works I quoted as I wrote the book. As you read the endnotes, what you'd find is that the newest resources cited in *Conspiracies and the Cross* were published in 2007.

From these facts, you might quickly and correctly conclude that I completed this book in 2007. (Then again, before you reached that point, you might have recognized that people who regularly spend their time reading endnotes and copyright pages tend to have fairly empty social calendars—that, or they end up as writers, meandering from one coffee shop to another, trying desperately to look as if they're doing something significant.) If you wanted to confirm this conclusion, you might meander through a few of my city's finest coffee shops, show my picture to a barista or two, and ask questions such as, "Have you seen this person before? When did he remain in this location long after his presence officially qualified as loitering? Did he seem as if he was trying desperately to look as though he was doing something significant?"

But what if a book was written at a time when publishers and printing presses didn't exist—only scribes who copied manuscripts by hand? What if these scribes didn't include publication dates in the opening pages of their books? And what if no one had invented copyright pages or endnotes? For that matter, what if coffee shops hadn't even been contrived yet? How could you decide when a book was written?

KNOW MORE

codex, codices (from Latin word meaning "block"): stacks of vellum or papyrus, folded and bound for the purpose of creating a book

papyrus, papyri (from Greek *papyros*): plant from which ancient people manufactured paper. Papyrus plants are nearly twelve feet tall and have a stem as thick as your wrist. The stems were sliced lengthwise in thin strips. Two layers of these slices were placed on top of each other—with the grain of each piece running perpendicular to the one beneath it—then beaten together and dried to make paper.

That's precisely the dilemma that we face when we try to determine when the ancient Gospels were written. For more than one thousand years, scribes copied these documents by hand, and the earliest Gospel manuscripts included no dates.[4] Some early Gospel manuscripts don't even include references to their authors, perhaps because those portions of the manuscripts decayed over the years or maybe because the manuscripts didn't include such ascriptions in the first place. How is it possible, then, to determine when the New Testament Gospels were written?

CLUE NUMBER 1: **A fragment from the New Testament Gospels survives from the late first or early second century.**

To begin with, we might search the texts for *internal clues*. The authors of the Gospel according to Luke and John insist that they based their accounts on eyewitness testimony. In the case of Luke's Gospel, the author claims to have received information about Jesus from eyewitnesses (Luke 1:2). In the case of John's Gospel, the author insists that he *was* an eyewitness (John 19:35). Still, if I want to make an honest assessment of the reliability of the New Testament Gospels, I can't automatically assume that these authors were telling the truth. After all, many "lost Gospels" claim to come from eyewitnesses too. The opening sentence of the Gospel of Thomas runs something like this:

"These are the hidden sayings that the living Jesus spoke and Didymus Judas Thomas recorded." In the case of the New Testament Gospels, the internal clues are important, but these clues are not conclusive.

To gain a firmer foundation for the dates of the New Testament Gospels, let's focus on some *external clues*. Specifically, let's look at the earliest surviving fragments of the New Testament Gospels, the remnants of documents that ancient scribes duplicated from earlier copies or perhaps from original manuscripts.[5]

The oldest of these fragments is a tiny scrap of papyrus—only two inches wide and fewer than four inches tall—from the Gospel according to John. This fragment is sometimes referred to as "John Rylands Papyrus 457," "Papyrus 52," or more simply, "P52."[6] The Greek words on the front side of P52 come from John 18:31–33. The fragment's reverse side records a few words from John 18:37–38. Despite its small size and few words, P52 is one of the most significant surviving fragments of the New Testament. Its importance is rooted, however, not so much in *what* it says but in *when* it was copied.

So how can we know when Papyrus 52 was copied?

Well, even though every person's handwriting is different, each era of history tends to develop distinct styles of writing. If you examine the records of marriages and births in a nineteenth-century family Bible, for example, you'll notice distinct flourishes and letter formations that you probably *won't* find in a family Bible from the 1980s. In earlier times—before the invention of printing presses, typewriters, or word processors—formal handwriting tended even *more* strongly to develop distinct styles.

The distinct styles of writing that mark certain eras enable scholars to assign approximate dates to ancient manuscripts. Suppose that scholars aren't quite certain *when* a manuscript was copied. To determine when the document came into existence, they might compare the handwriting style of the less-certain manuscript with the writing styles in manuscripts that have well-established dates—provincial records, for example, or dated letters. The idea is that manuscripts from similar time periods will have similar handwriting styles. If the writing style in the less-certain manuscript is similar to the style of a well-attested manuscript, both documents were probably copied in the same approximate time period.

So what does all of this have to do with P52?

Here's what we discover when P52 is compared with other ancient fragments of papyrus: The style of writing found on P52 is most similar to a bit of papyrus from Fayyum, a desert region in the northern reaches of Middle Egypt.[7] This fragment, known as Papyrus Fayyum 110, is a personal letter from a farmer named Lucius Gemellus. In the letter, Gemellus shares some thoughts with his slave Epagathos about the fertilization and irrigation of the olive orchard.[8] The content of this letter isn't particularly exciting, unless, of course, you've been particularly worried about the precise mixture of water and manure to toss on those olive trees in your backyard. Yet the strong similarities between the handwriting in this fragment and P52 are *extremely* significant, because Gemellus dated this letter in the year that we know as "A.D. 94"—though, of course, that wasn't what Gemellus called it! For him, it was the fourteenth year of the reign of Emperor Domitian. This places the papyrus fragment that is most similar to P52 near the end of the first century. Further comparisons reveal some similarities between the script of P52 and scripts that were common during the reign of Emperor Hadrian in the early second century.

So what do these comparisons tell us about the Gospels?

In the late first or early second century, a scribe in central Egypt—far from Asia Minor, where John's Gospel seems to have originated—copied a codex of the Gospel according to John. The scrap of papyrus that we know as Papyrus 52 is a remnant from this ancient codex. *So, in the early years of the second century A.D.—perhaps even earlier—the Gospel according to John was already in circulation throughout the Roman Empire.* What's more, if the Gospel according to John was already circulating in central Egypt in the late first or early second century, this account of Jesus's life must have been compiled at some point in the latter half of the first century, at a time when eyewitnesses of Jesus's ministry were still alive.

Other ancient fragments of John's Gospel have survived too—Papyrus 66, for example, and Papyrus 90, both copied in the late second century. The Gospel according to John isn't the only Gospel that's found among the first- or second-century papyri. Some early remnants from a copy of Matthew's Gospel have also survived. These fragments—from a codex that's been designated "the Magdalen Papyrus" or "Papyrus 64"—were unearthed in Egypt.[9] What do we learn when these fragments are compared with other pieces of papyri? Papyrus 64 seems to have been copied sometime in the late second century.[10] Then there are the papyri known as Papyrus 4, Papyrus 75, Papyrus 103, and Papyrus 104. P4 preserves some portions of the Gospel according to Luke that were copied in the second century, P75 comes from a late second-century codex that once included Luke's and John's Gospels, while P103 and P104 include more second-century fragments from the Gospel according to Matthew. These fragments of papyrus clearly suggest that by the middle of the second century A.D., Matthew's Gospel and Luke's Gospel were being widely distributed in the Roman Empire, while John's Gospel was in circulation by the late first or early second century. If these Gospels were circulating throughout the imperial provinces by the mid-second century, their authors must have composed them no later than the early 100s.

What about the Gospel according to Mark? Well, the authors of the Gospel according to Matthew and Luke seem to have used Mark's Gospel as one of their sources. (Notice, for example, how often Luke's Gospel shares word-for-word content with Mark's Gospel and even follows the order of events in Mark's Gospel. Most likely, the Gospel according to Mark was one of the accounts that, according to the opening verses of Luke's Gospel, "many have undertaken to compose" [Luke 1:1–2].) If that's the case, the Gospel according to Mark was in circulation even earlier than the Gospel according to Matthew and Luke.

Here's what the earliest surviving fragments of the New Testament Gospels establish for us: *Every New Testament Gospel was completed by the early second century; John's Gospel was finished no later than the late first century and was circulating throughout the ancient world by the late first or early second century.* From the papyri alone, it's clear that the Gospel according to John, at the very least, was completed while eyewitnesses of Jesus might still have been alive. So, the New Testament Gospels were written sometime between the A.D. 30s— during the governorship of Pontius Pilate, when Jesus was crucified—and the early 100s.

KNOW MORE

The New Testament was originally written in Greek, though some portions may have originally circulated in Aramaic, a language that looks similar to Hebrew. The authors of the Old Testament wrote in Hebrew and, occasionally, in Aramaic.

QUICK GUIDE

EARLY COPIES OF THE NEW TESTAMENT GOSPELS		
Document	Summary of Contents	Approximate Date of Composition
Papyrus 52 (John Rylands Papyrus 457)	Fragment from John 18:31–33, 37–38	Late A.D. 90s or early 100s
Papyrus 90	Fragment from John 18:36–19:7	A.D. 100s
Papyrus 66	Fragments from John 1:1–21:17	A.D. 100s
Papyrus 4	Fragments from Luke 1:58–2:7; 3:8–4:2; 4:29–35; 5:3–8; 5:30–6:16	A.D. 100s

Document	Summary of Contents	Approximate Date of Composition
Papyrus 64 and 67 (Magdalen Papyrus)	Fragments from Matthew 3:9–15; 5:20–28; 26:7–33	Late A.D. 100s
Papyrus 75	Fragments from Luke 3:18–John 15:8	Late A.D. 100s
Papyrus 103	Fragment from Matthew 13:55–56; 14:3–5	Late A.D. 100s
Papyrus 104	Fragment from Matthew 21:34–37, 45	Late A.D. 100s

 **First-century witnesses place the New Testament Gospels in the first century A.D.**

I think it's possible to place dates on the New Testament Gospels that are even *more* precise than the papyrus fragments can establish, though. Let's suppose for a moment that two separate witnesses agreed about the origins of the New Testament Gospels. Then, suppose that both witnesses received their knowledge in the first century A.D. through eyewitnesses of Jesus's ministry or close associates of the eyewitnesses. As it turns out, that's precisely what we find when we look at some writings from the first two centuries of Christian faith. The names of these two personages were Papias of Hierapolis and Polycarp of Smyrna. Let's look together at each of these witnesses and see what they tell us!

Papias of Hierapolis: The first testimony comes from Papias, a pastor in the southwestern portion of the area known today as Turkey. Papias was probably born in the middle of the first century, around the time of Paul's second missionary journey. In the late first or early second century, Papias became the leading pastor of a church in the city of Hierapolis. Philip, a deacon from the Jerusalem church (Acts 6:5; 8:4–8), spent the last years of his life in Hierapolis. It was from Philip's daughters—the ones mentioned in Acts 21:8–9—and from associates of the apostolic eyewitnesses[11] that Papias received the following information:[12]

> I won't hesitate to arrange alongside my interpretations whatever things I learned and remembered well from the elders, confirming the truth on their behalf.... The elder said this: Mark, who became Peter's interpreter, wrote accurately as much as he remembered—though not in ordered form—of the Lord's sayings and doings. For [Mark] neither heard the Lord nor followed after him, but later (as I said) he followed after Peter,

who was giving his teachings in short anecdotes and thus did not bring forth an ordered arrangement of the Lord's sayings; so, Mark did not miss the point when he wrote in this way, as he remembered. For he had one purpose: To omit nothing of what he had heard and to present no false testimony in these matters.... And Matthew, in the Hebrew dialect, placed the sayings in orderly arrangement.[13]

Although Papias recorded these traditions around A.D. 110,[14] he seems to have received them well before the end of the first century.[15] If Papias of Hierapolis was familiar with Matthew's and Mark's Gospels before the end of the first century, both Gospels must have been completed in the first century, while eyewitnesses of the events were still alive. It's very possible that Papias also recorded traditions about Luke's and John's Gospels, but—since the writings of Papias have survived only in fragmentary form—those testimonies have been lost.

Polycarp of Smyrna: If Papias alone had made these claims, perhaps we could pass over them as the product of one man's pious imagination. But Papias *doesn't* stand alone in this testimony. Another pastor—a man named Polycarp, born around A.D. 70—received the same information about the Gospels apart from Papias.

As a young man, Polycarp was a student of John, the follower of Jesus. As an adult, Polycarp became pastor of a church in the village of Smyrna. Here's what Polycarp learned from the eyewitnesses and passed on to one of his pupils:

Matthew composed his Gospel among the Hebrews in their language, while Peter and Paul were preaching the Gospel in Rome and building up the church there. After their deaths, Mark—Peter's follower and interpreter—handed down to us Peter's proclamation in written form. Luke, the companion of Paul, wrote in a book the Gospel proclaimed by Paul. Finally, John—the Lord's own follower, the one who leaned against his very chest—composed the Gospel while living in Ephesus, in Asia.[16]

So it wasn't only Papias who knew the New Testament Gospels in the late first or early second century. Polycarp was familiar with them too—and not only Matthew's and Mark's Gospels but also the Gospels according to Luke and John.

Taken together, the testimonies of Papias and Polycarp clearly suggest that from the first century forward, Christians valued the four New Testament Gospels and connected these Gospels to eyewitnesses or close associates of eyewitnesses. As such, all four Gospels must have been completed before the end of the first century A.D., at a time when eyewitnesses were still alive.[17]

> I can still describe the very spot in which blessed Polycarp sat as he taught; I can still describe how he exited and entered, his habits of life, his expressions, his teachings among the people, and the accounts he gave of his interaction with John and with others who had seen the Lord. As he remembered their words— what he heard from them about the Lord and about his miracles and teachings, having received them from the eyewitnesses of the "Word of Life"—Polycarp related all of it in harmony with the Scriptures.... Continually, by God's grace, I still recall them in faith.[18]
>
> —IRENAEUS OF LYONS, church leader (late A.D. 100s)

KNOW MORE

In the book that bears the name "Matthew," Matthew is presented as a "publican" or "tax collector."[19] It's doubtful that any early Christian would have fabricated this bit of vocational trivia. The very idea that Jesus asked a tax collector to follow Him must have been a bit embarrassing. When the Gospels were written, Roman governors expected tax collectors to stockpile personal wealth by cheating people—and most tax collectors apparently fulfilled this expectation. There was one skill that tax collectors did possess. They could read and write. Tax collectors were, in fact, known to carry *pinakes*, hinged wooden tablets with a thick wax coating on each panel.[20] Tax collectors used styli of metal or bone to etch notes in the wax—notes that, in some cases, were later translated and rewritten on papyrus.[21] Papyri from Egypt prove that tax collectors also wrote receipts and registers for citizens in their villages.[22]

Christians connected the names of Matthew, Mark, Luke, and John with the Gospels from the time that these Gospels first circulated.

What's more, Christians clearly connected the four Gospels with the names of Matthew, Mark, Luke, and John from the time that these Gospels first began to circulate. How do we know this? Well, the first editions of these Gospels don't seem to have included titles. At first, each Gospel was probably known simply as "the Gospel," and this worked fine until churches ended up with more than one of them! As congregations began to receive the four Gospels in the late first and early second centuries, they began to give names to distinguish each document.

Here's a somewhat skeptical reconstruction of how this process played out:

> [The New Testament Gospels] were written thirty-five to sixty-five years after Jesus' death...not by people who were eyewitnesses, but by people living later....Where did these people get their information from?...After the days of Jesus, people started telling stories about him in order to convert others to the faith.[23]...When...Christians recognized the need for *apostolic* authorities, they attributed these books to apostles (Matthew and John) and close companions of apostles (Mark, the secretary of Peter; and Luke, the traveling companion of Paul). [24]

In other words, according to skeptics such as Bart Ehrman, Christians didn't connect the Gospels to Matthew, Mark, Luke, and John because these individuals actually *wrote* the Gospels. He believes that early believers fabricated these connections to make the documents seem more authoritative.

There's a serious problem with this reconstruction, though.[25] By the late first and early second century, the Gospels had spread throughout the Roman Empire.[26] If second-century Christians had simply added names to each Gospel to make that Gospel seem authoritative, what would have happened? (Remember, there was no centrally recognized authority to force congregations to connect a certain name to each Gospel—no executive director, no denominational board, no international convention of Christians.[27] It wasn't as if one pastor could stop by an office and e-mail fellow pastors about how to name a certain Gospel!) Here's what might have occurred: One church would have dubbed a Gospel with the name of Andrew, for example, while another congregation ascribed the same Gospel to Peter or Thaddeus or Bartholomew. As a result, each Gospel might have a half-dozen—or more!—different names, depending on where your ship happened to land.

That's not even close to what we find when we look at the ancient manuscripts.

Here's what we *do* find: Once titles begin to appear in the manuscripts, *every titled manuscript of the Gospel that we know as Matthew identifies Matthew as the source.* This happens not only with the Gospel according to Matthew but also with the other New Testament Gospels. Although the precise form and wording of the titles may vary, every titled manuscript of the Gospel according to Mark identifies Mark as the Gospel's author—and the same pattern also characterizes manuscripts of the Gospel according to Matthew, Luke, and John.

How did this happen?

Here's the explanation that seems to make the most sense: When churches received each Gospel, they also received information about that Gospel's origins, telling them whose eyewitness testimony this Gospel represented. These "oral traditions" are what we find recorded in the writings of Papias and Polycarp's pupil Irenaeus. Because they received clear oral traditions when they received each book, when Christians began adding titles to these manuscripts, every congregation connected each Gospel to the same author. Why? They already knew where each Gospel came from. Nothing less can explain the early consistency of the titles.

KNOW MORE

Every known manuscript of the Gospel according to Matthew is written in Greek. Yet Papias and Irenaeus report that Matthew wrote his Gospel first and that he wrote in *Hebrew*. As a result, many scholars believe the apostle Matthew originally wrote Jesus's teachings in *Aramaic*, a language that's closely related to Hebrew. Later, someone—perhaps Matthew or someone associated with Matthew—merged these teachings with portions of Mark's Gospel to form the Gospel according to Matthew as we know it,[28] in the Greek language.[29] Such practices were not unheard of in the first century: Flavius Josephus wrote two histories of the Jewish-Roman War, one in Aramaic and the other in Greek. As with Matthew's Gospel, the Aramaic version didn't circulate widely and, thus, has not survived.[30] The book of Tobit—found in Roman Catholic and Eastern Orthodox Bibles—was also thought for many years to have circulated only in Greek. Recently, fragments of separate Hebrew and Aramaic versions of this book have been discovered among the Qumran scrolls.[31]

CRACKING THE ANONYMITY CONSPIRACY

So it seems that from the time when the texts first began to circulate, the content of the New Testament Gospels was known to stem from Matthew, Mark, Luke, and John. If indeed Matthew, Mark, Luke, and John *were* the sources of the books that bear their names, each New Testament Gospel represents eyewitness testimony about Jesus.

What's recorded in the Gospel according to Mark is the testimony of Simon Peter, recalled and preserved by John Mark. Luke's Gospel integrates written and oral sources gathered by Paul's personal physician. The materials that are unique to the Gospel according to Matthew came from Matthew, a tax collector who deserted a profitable profession to follow Jesus. And the stories in the Gospel according to John? It seems that they originated from John Bar-Zebedee—one of Jesus's first followers—or perhaps one of John's students who recorded his teacher's testimony. That's how the earliest surviving sources describe the origins of the Gospels that bear the names of Matthew, Mark, Luke, and John, and there's little reason to doubt what these sources have to say. If these sources are, in fact, correct about how the Gospels emerged, the content of each New Testament Gospel can be traced to the testimony of people who walked and talked with Jesus of Nazareth.

HOW TO PREPARE FOR FUTURE CHRIST CONSPIRACIES

Research the origins of the books in your New Testament. Begin with a simple book such as *Talk Through the Bible* by Bruce Wilkinson and Kenneth Boa, but don't stop there! Research the perspectives found in texts such as Robert Gundry's *A Survey of the New Testament* and *An Introduction to the New Testament* by Donald Carson and Douglas Moo. Then, compare what you've learned with what you find in skeptical sources such as Bart Ehrman's *A Brief Introduction to the New Testament* and *The New Testament: A Historical Introduction to the Early Christian Writings*.

HOW THE LOST GOSPELS GOT LOST

WHAT'S the CONSPIRACY?

E ARLY CHURCH LEADERS ELIMINATED MANY BOOKS FROM THE NEW Testament; some of these "lost Gospels" were the sacred Scriptures of the first Christians.

WHO SAYS SO?

- The Jesus Seminar
- Dan Brown, *The Da Vinci Code*
- Timothy Freke and Peter Gandy, *The Laughing Jesus: Religious Lies and Gnostic Wisdom*
- Elaine Pagels, *Beyond Belief*

Here's another claim that appears in many popular books about Jesus: The original retellings of Jesus's life aren't found in the Gospel according to Matthew, Mark, Luke, or John. There were other Scriptures—"lost Gospels"—that may have predated the New Testament Gospels. These "lost Gospels" reveal, according to one scholar, "diversity in the Christian movement that later, 'official' versions of Christian history…suppressed."[1]

The LOST GOSPELS CONSPIRACY

Ah, yes…mysterious forms of Christian faith that "the 'official' versions" of Christianity somehow "suppressed."

Sounds like a Christ conspiracy to me.

What if it's true?

What if the earliest Gospels *were* excluded and suppressed in favor of the Gospels according to Matthew, Mark, Luke, and John? For persons who accept the New Testament perspective on Jesus as the truth, here's the dilemma: *These excluded Gospels portray Jesus in ways that differ radically from the perspective of the New Testament Gospels.*

For example, according to the New Testament Gospels, Jesus was fully human yet fully God (Mark 2:5–7; John 1:14–18; 20:28); even though He was divine, He suffered, died, and rose from the dead (Mark 15:1–16:8). That's not always the picture that the so-called "lost Gospels" paint when it comes to Jesus, though. In some alternative Gospels, Jesus seems to have been a mere mortal;[2] in others, Jesus was completely spiritual,[3] so spiritual, in fact, that He only *seemed* human. Simply put, if the "lost Gospels" get the story of Jesus right, the New Testament Gospels have somehow gotten the story wrong. With this in mind, let's look at a couple of the most popular "lost Gospels" to see what they have to say.

GOSPEL OF THOMAS—THE EARLIEST SOURCE OF INFORMATION ABOUT JESUS?

One "lost Gospel" boasts the title the Gospel of Thomas. This Gospel and several others—including the Gospel of Philip and the Gospel of Truth— were unearthed in 1945 near an Egyptian village known as Nag Hammadi. A farmer named Muhammad 'Ali al-Samman found the ancient scrolls while searching for fertilizer. He and his brothers returned home with the thirteen papyrus books, where his mother used a few of the papyri as kindling in their stone oven! [4]

One popular book refers to these Nag Hammadi documents as "the texts of the original Christians"[5] and implies that the Nag Hammadi Gospels were written *before* the New Testament Gospels. If these claims were true, the Gospel of Thomas might provide an earlier portrait of Jesus than the New Testament Gospels.

So what does Jesus do in the Gospel of Thomas?

In the Gospel of Thomas, Jesus doesn't pull off any miracles, He doesn't die on the cross, and He doesn't rise from the dead. Much of the time, He seems to wander around with His disciples, randomly spouting cryptic aphorisms such as, "Split a piece of wood, and there am I! Lift a stone, and you will find me!…Lucky is the lion eaten by a human, so that the lion becomes human. But cursed is the one eaten by the lion because the lion still becomes human." From these citations, it would seem that the Jesus of the Gospel of Thomas spent a lot of time running from lions and hiding behind rocks and trees. In the process, Jesus ends up sounding less like a Jewish Messiah intent on changing the world and more like a Jedi Master with an odd fixation on feral cats.

In all fairness, not everything in the Gospel of Thomas has to do with playing hide-and-seek or avoiding human-eating lions. Nearly half of the teachings in Gospel of Thomas also appear in the New Testament Gospels. Even with these similarities, however, the Jesus of the Gospel of Thomas doesn't seem to be God incarnate—or even a human miracle worker, for that matter. In this Gospel, Jesus is a wise teacher...well, that and an amazing hide-and-seek partner.[6]

Yet here's what scholars such as Marvin Meyer and Elaine Pagels have suggested about the Gospel of Thomas:

> Is it possible that the Gospel of Thomas might tell us a great deal...about Jesus and his teachings? Could this be an early source—maybe even our earliest source—of Jesus's teachings, collected in an unedited, unvarnished form?...Professor Helmut Koester came to conclude that the Gospel of Thomas perhaps could be dated as early as the mid-first century—about twenty years after Jesus's death—which would make it the earliest Gospel we know, and certainly one of the most important.[7]

"Our earliest source...of Jesus's teachings, collected in an unedited, unvarnished form"? That's what's suggested about the Gospel of Thomas. Since the Gospel of Thomas doesn't clearly mention miracles or resurrection, some scholars who view the Gospel of Thomas as an earlier source of information about Jesus assume that the earliest Christians didn't believe in Jesus's miracles or physical resurrection—or, at least, these supernatural elements weren't all that significant to the earliest believers. Jesus was, according to these critics, simply a wandering sage who inspired people to pursue a new way of life. One scholar describes the resulting vision of Jesus in this way: "Before church dogma...before the honorific titles bestowed upon Jesus, there was Jesus the Jewish man of wisdom."[8]

The problem is, if Jesus was merely a "Jewish man of wisdom," He's still dead.

If Jesus is still dead, any trust that you place in Jesus is—in the words of the apostle Paul—"empty, and you are still in your sins....If in this life alone we have lived in expectation of the Messiah, we of all people are most desperately in need of mercy" (1 Corinthians 15:17, 19).

KNOW MORE

Coptic (ancient language)—A descendant of ancient Egyptian dialects, the Coptic language thrived in Egyptian religious communities in the third and fourth centuries A.D. These communities included not only Christian monastic communities but also Gnostic sects. Many "Gnostic Gospels"—including the Gospel of Judas; the Gospel of Thomas—have survived in Coptic versions. Because the Coptic alphabet comes from Greek, Coptic looks similar to Greek, and many Greek loanwords appear in Coptic documents.

KNOW MORE

Nag Hammadi documents: a collection of more than forty Gnostic documents, unearthed in the mid-1940s near Nag Hammadi, a village in Upper Egypt. Significant texts found at Nag Hammadi include the Gospel of Thomas, the Coptic Apocalypse of Paul, the Coptic Apocalypse of Peter, the Apocryphon of John, the Dialogue of the Savior, the Coptic Gospel of the Egyptians, the Gospel of Philip, and Gospel of Truth.

QUICK GUIDE

THE NAG HAMMADI LIBRARY

According to *The Da Vinci Code,* the Nag Hammadi texts are "the earliest Christian records. Troublingly, they do not match up with the gospels in the Bible."[9]

It is true that the Nag Hammadi documents do not "match up with the gospels in the Bible." The documents found at Nag Hammadi are *not,* however, "the earliest Christian records." The documents in the New Testament were written between A.D. 40 and 100. The *oldest* document at Nag Hammadi is probably the Gospel of Thomas, and the surviving form of this text dates from the early to mid-second century at the earliest. Most of the texts at Nag Hammadi were composed between the late second and early fifth centuries A.D.

Many current theories about Jesus rely on these texts. To help you sort through the conspiracies, here is a complete listing of the Nag Hammadi documents with a summary of the contents and the approximate date of the original composition of each one.

Document	Summary of Contents	Approximate Date of Composition
Acts of Peter and the Twelve	Tale of a pearl merchant who turns out to be Jesus; not to be confused with the Christian document Acts of Peter from the late second century	A.D. 150–250

Document	Summary of Contents	Approximate Date of Composition
Apocalypse of Adam	Adam tells Seth how he and Eve became more powerful than their Creator; no explicit mention of any Christian themes or characters	A.D. 160–300
Allogenes	Refers to Gnostics as members of the race of Seth (*allogenes* means "from another race")	A.D. 300–350
Apocalypse of James 1	Supposed dialogue between Jesus and James the brother of Jesus	A.D. 200–300
Apocalypse of James 2	Supposed dialogue between Jesus and James the brother of Jesus, ending with James's martyrdom	A.D. 150–180
Apocryphon of James	Mildly gnostic letter, claiming to come from James the brother of Jesus	A.D. 140–160
Apocryphon of John	Presents the deity of the Old Testament and creator of the physical world as an evil demigod	A.D. 160–200
Asclepius	Greek philosophical tractate	Uncertain
Authoritative Teaching	Gnostic tractate, urging persons to avoid physical pleasures	A.D. 150–200
Book of Thomas the Contender	Supposed "secret words" spoken by Jesus to Thomas and recorded by Matthias	A.D. 150–225
Concept of Our Great Power	Gnostic description of salvation and of the end of the world	A.D. 300–390
Coptic Apocalypse of Paul	Describes Paul's supposed ascension through several levels of the heavens	A.D. 160–260, perhaps later
Coptic Apocalypse of Peter	Describes Jesus as if He possessed no physical body	A.D. 250–300
Coptic Gospel of the Egyptians	Presents Jesus as the reincarnation of Seth, third son of Adam and Eve	A.D. 200–300
Dialogue of the Savior	Found only in fragments, which present a consistently negative view of sexuality and of women	A.D. 150–200
Discourse on the Eighth and Ninth	Guide for Gnostics to experience the mystical realm	A.D. 150–200

Document	Summary of Contents	Approximate Date of Composition
Epistle of Peter to Philip	Supposed letter, followed by a gnostic discourse concerning the nature of Jesus Christ	A.D. 180–220
Eugnostos the Blessed	Presentation of gnostic cosmology; some elements may be pre-Christian	Uncertain
Exegesis on the Soul	Short story, recounting the gnostic myth of the soul's fall from the heavens	A.D. 200–250
Gospel of Philip	Collection of gnostic sayings from several previous writings, apparently reflecting the teachings of Valentinus	A.D. 160–250
Gospel of Thomas	List of sayings of Jesus; some are authentic, but others were fabricated later	A.D. 100–150 or later in its present form
Gospel of Truth	Gnostic reworking of the Creation and of the ministry of Jesus	A.D. 150–180
Hypostatis of the Archons	Mythological presentation of Gnostic cosmology	A.D. 250–350
Hypsiphrone	Fragments of text describe the descent of a heavenly figure similar to Sophia	Uncertain
Interpretation of Knowledge	Valentinian reinterpretation of the teachings of Jesus and Paul	A.D. 160–200
Marsanes	Descriptions of gnostic experience and rituals	A.D. 200–300
Melchizedek	Fragments of text seem to provide a Gnostic reinterpretation of the Old Testament account of Melchizedek	A.D. 200–300
Origin of the World	Presentation of gnostic theology	A.D. 290–330
Paraphrase of Shem	Fragments presenting a negative view of sexuality	Uncertain
Prayer of Thanksgiving	Brief prayer of gratitude for having received gnosis	A.D. 150–250
Prayer of the Apostle Paul	Brief prayer with similarities to Three Steles of Seth and Gospel of Philip	A.D. 160–300
Republic (Plato)	Gnostic adaptation of the philosopher Plato's classic work	Uncertain

Document	Summary of Contents	Approximate Date of Composition
Sentences of Sextus	List of wise sayings	Uncertain
Sophia of Jesus Christ	List of supposed questions from the apostles, to which Jesus provides gnostic answers; probably an adaptation of Epistle of Eugnostos	Uncertain, some portions may stem from the late first or early second centuries
Teachings of Silvanus	Unlike other Nag Hammadi documents, not a gnostic text; emphasizes spiritual growth through self-denial	A.D. 160–220
Testimony of Truth	Polemic against competing gnostic groups	A.D. 180–220
Thought of Norea	Depicts a feminine savior, apparently the counterpart of the biblical figure Seth	A.D. 180–240
Three Steles of Seth	Includes many gnostic hymns and prayers	A.D. 220–260
Thunder, Perfect Mind	A divine female figure, Thunder, sings hymns about herself, not clearly gnostic, Jewish, or Christian in origin	Uncertain
Treatise of the Great Seth	Supposedly the words of Jesus to a group of gnostic believers; Simon of Cyrene is crucified instead of Jesus	Uncertain
Treatise on the Resurrection	Brief letter denying the future physical resurrection of believers	A.D. 180–200
Trimorphic Protennoia	Gnostic description of the descent of "the First Thought" from God into the world	A.D. 160–200
Tripartite Tractate	Gnostic description of salvation history and cosmology	A.D. 200–250
Valentinian Exposition on Baptism, Anointing, and the Eucharist	Gnostic reinterpretations of Christian rituals	A.D. 150–180
Zostrianos	Description of gnostic cosmology	A.D. 260–300

GOSPEL OF Q—A LOST SOURCE OF INFORMATION ABOUT JESUS?

Some scholars who are fond of the Gospel of Thomas also proclaim the importance of another early Gospel. This Gospel is known by the mysterious moniker Q. The abbreviation Q comes from the German noun *Quelle* or "source." In the nineteenth century, German scholars dubbed this Gospel "Q" because they believed the sayings in Q served as a shared source for the Gospel according to Matthew and Luke. Here's how Marcus Borg, a Jesus Seminar scholar, has described the lost Gospel Q:

> Written in the 50s of the first century, only a couple of decades after the death of Jesus, Q is significantly earlier than the four Gospels of the New Testament.... It provides evidence for an early Christian community that did not make the death and resurrection of Jesus central to its message. Q, quite simply, is the closest that we can come to the historical Jesus.... It was later writers who added the details about Jesus' life that became the bedrock of Christian belief. Jesus in the Lost Gospel Q is neither Christ nor the Messiah but rather the last in a long line of Jewish prophets.[10]

Another Jesus Seminar fellow puts it this way: "Q... is the earliest written record we have from the Jesus movement, and it is a precious text indeed.... Q puts us as close to the historical Jesus as we will ever be."[11] According to these scholars, Q is an unembellished list of the sayings that were first attributed to Jesus.

The lost Gospel Q has gained quite a bit of notoriety in recent years. It even made an appearance in Dan Brown's novel *The Da Vinci Code*. In the process of describing this supposed lost Gospel of Q, characters in *The Da Vinci Code* also imply that the fourth-century emperor Constantine worked with church leaders to eliminate the "lost Gospels"—a popular variation of this conspiracy theory:

> More than *eighty* gospels were considered for the New Testament, and yet only a relative few were chosen for inclusion—Matthew, Mark, Luke, and John among them.... Because Constantine upgraded Jesus' status almost four centuries *after* Jesus' death, thousands of documents already existed chronicling his life as a *mortal* man.... Constantine commissioned and financed a new Bible, which omitted those gospels that spoke of Christ's *human* traits and embellished those gospels that made Him godlike. The earlier gospels were outlawed, gathered up, and burned.... The legendary "Q" *Document* [is] a manuscript that

even the Vatican admits they believe exists. Allegedly, it is a book of Jesus' teachings, possibly written in His own hand.[12]

Dan Brown's characters also claim that the Gospels found at Nag Hammadi and among the Dead Sea Scrolls constitute the "earliest Christian records." What's more, *The Da Vinci Code* adds a couple more "lost Gospels" to the list—the Gospel of Philip and the Gospel of Mary (which *The Da Vinci Code* dubs "a Gospel in Magdalene's words").

Then there's the Gospel of Judas, the lost Gospel that was so highly publicized in 2006—a document that, according to one advertisement from *National Geographic*, provides "new insights into the disciple who betrayed Jesus."[13] Some of these "new insights" include the possibility that Judas was a favored disciple and that Jesus specifically ordered Judas to betray Him.[14]

If these "lost Gospels" *do* tell us how the earliest Christians understood Jesus, what the New Testament Gospels tell us about Jesus is something less than truth. Simply put, if the "lost Gospels" are right, the person whom Christians worship as the living Lord was either a spiritual myth or a mere man—a human being who lived, who died, and whose body disintegrated into dust.

The NEW TESTAMENT GOSPELS—LATER LEGENDS of the LIFE of JESUS?

Interestingly, even writers who agree that the Gospel of Thomas, Q, and other suppressed texts provide the earliest information about Jesus disagree sharply about the precise *meaning* of the life of Jesus in these writings. Robert Funk and some others in the Jesus Seminar have suggested that the original retellings of Jesus's life portray Jesus as an inspiring Jewish teacher. Marcus Borg, another member of the Jesus Seminar, claims Jesus was "a spirit person, subversive sage, social prophet, and movement founder" whose core value was compassion for the oppressed.[15] According to Elaine Pagels, the Jesus of the Gospel of Thomas was a teacher who encouraged each follower "not so much to *believe in Jesus*...as to *seek to know God* through one's own, divinely given capacity."[16] John Dominic Crossan—yet another Jesus Seminar fellow—has classed Jesus as an iconoclastic teacher, a societal dropout in the tradition of a band of Greek philosophers known as "Cynics."[17]

Although these scholars can't seem to agree on who Jesus *was*, they each seem to be quite certain who He *wasn't*: *Jesus wasn't who the New Testament Gospels claim that He was.* A couple of writers go so far as to make the sweeping claim that the "the original Christians" didn't even view Jesus "as an historical man who 'suffered for our sins'"; instead, they saw Him as a mythical symbol of each person's capacity to find God within herself or himself.[18] And where—according to these writers—can contemporary people discover the truth about how the "original Christians" viewed Jesus? You guessed it: in the "lost Gospels"—in these supposed earlier Gospels that didn't make it into the New Testament.

Do these Gospels *really* represent earlier traditions than the New Testament Gospels, as some critics claim? To find out, let's look first at the best evidence for when the New Testament Gospels were written. Then we'll look at the "lost Gospels" to see how they compare.

> CONSPIRACY NUMBER TWO
>
> Early-church leaders eliminated many books from the New Testament; some of these "lost scriptures" were the sacred texts of the first Christians.
>
> The TRUTH BEHIND the CONSPIRACY
>
> Early church leaders *did* reject many writings that claimed to provide information about Jesus, but there is no evidence that these "lost Scriptures" were the sacred texts of the "original Christians."

CLUES TO CRACK THE LOST GOSPELS CONSPIRACY

CLUE NUMBER 1: The "lost Gospels" didn't come from the earliest Christians.

Now, let's take a look at the earliest "lost Gospels" and see how they stack up against the New Testament Gospels.[19] In the first place, there are fewer than twenty "lost Gospels" that even *might* come from the first or second century A.D., a far cry from the claim in *The Da Vinci Code* that "more than *eighty* gospels were considered" as potential authoritative accounts of the life of Jesus.

Several of these "lost Gospels" adapted one or more New Testament Gospels. The Gospel of the Ebionites and the Gospel of the Nazoreans, for example, are second-century rewrites of Matthew's Gospel that were edited—or, according to an ancient theologian named Epiphanius of Salamis, "mutilated"—by certain sects to fit their distinctive theology.[20] Likewise, around A.D. 140, a teacher named Marcion trimmed the portions from Luke's Gospel that emphasized Jesus's human nature to produce his Gospel of the Lord. Other "lost Gospels," including the Gospel of Philip, the Gospel of Mary, and the Dialogue of the Savior, model many of their statements on sayings previously known from the Gospels according to Matthew, Mark, and Luke.[21] Since they draw from the New Testament Gospels, these Gospels must have emerged *after* the New Testament Gospels. So, even though these Gospels boast names such as "Philip" and "Mary," these individuals were clearly *not* the sources behind these documents.

Others of the "lost Gospels" clearly reflect theological discussions of later time periods. For example, the Gospel of Truth comes from the community of Valentinus, a mid-second-century teacher who proclaimed that Jesus was not truly human. Since Valentinus was active around A.D. 150, the Gospel of Truth must have been written at that time or later.[22] Similarly, the Gospel of the Egyptians focuses on forms of self-denial—such as abstaining from sexual relations with the goal of transcending all distinctions between female and male—that became most prevalent in the late second century.[23] At one point in the Gospel of the Egyptians, Salome asks Jesus when she will receive a fuller knowledge of God. To this, Jesus supposedly replies, "When the male with the female is neither male nor female"[24]—a phrase that fits most naturally among the second-century supporters of an offshoot of Christianity known as Gnosticism.

The Gospel of Judas may represent the views of another gnostic sect, the "Cainites." Cainites were fond of reworking familiar biblical narratives—stories about Cain, Esau, and Korah in the Hebrew Scriptures, for example—so that the villains became heroes. That's what happens in the most popular reconstruction of the Gospel of Judas: Jesus Himself commands Judas Iscariot to betray Him. In the end, Judas becomes a heroic martyr when the other disciples stone him to death. These sorts of fractured Bible stories became popular among gnostics in the mid to late second century, so if this reconstruction is correct, it would seem that the Cainite gnostics created the text no earlier than the mid-second century, probably later. Another reconstruction of the Gospel of Judas points out that the text refers to Judas as *daimon*, a term that *can* mean "spirit" but which more commonly means "demon." If this reconstruction is accurate, the Gospel of Judas would seem to represent a second-century expansion of the stories of Judas found in the New Testament Gospels—an expansion that was intended to critique orthodox Christianity.[25] In either case, the claims about this Gospel in the news media—"a story that could challenge our deepest beliefs,"[26] the commercials claimed—represented unsubstantiated clamoring. The Gospel of Judas emerged more than a generation after the latest New Testament writings.

Unlike many "lost Gospels," the Gospel of Peter isn't a gnostic work at all. This Gospel retells the death and resurrection of Jesus, even agreeing with the New Testament Gospels that Mary Magdalene was one of the earliest witnesses to the Resurrection—although the Gospel of Peter adds a talking cross to the scene at the tomb. Still, the attitude of the Gospel of Peter toward Jews strongly suggests a second-century date. Unlike the New Testament Gospels, the Gospel of Peter seems to pin the primary blame for the crucifixion of Jesus on the Jewish people. When the Roman governor Pontius Pilate washes his hands, for example, the Gospel of Peter explicitly points out that the Jewish leaders refused to do the same. According to Gospel of Peter, "the Jews were glad" when Jesus died, but they lamented soon afterward, "We are cursed because our sin. The judgment and end of Jerusalem are close at hand."[27] Such negative views of the Jews correspond most closely to the sentiments of some church members in the mid-second century.

At least one supposed "lost Gospel" isn't an ancient document at all—it's most likely a recent hoax.[28] In 1960, a professor named claimed that while cataloging manuscripts at a monastery in the Judean desert in the 1950s, he found an eighteenth-century copy of a letter from the second-century church leader Clement of Alexandria.[29] This letter, written in Greek, mentions a Secret Gospel of Mark, a version of the New Testament Gospel that included an extra paragraph between Mark 10:34 and 10:35. This extra paragraph declares, in part:

> In the evening, the youth came to him, wearing linen cloth around his naked body. He spent the night with Jesus, and taught him the mystery of God's kingdom.[30]

Despite Morton Smith's claims to the contrary, several clues suggest that Smith created this paragraph as part of an elaborate hoax. In the first place, even though Smith provided photographs of this letter, the letter itself has suspiciously turned up missing.

Furthermore, even though the handwriting looks like eighteenth-century cursive Greek, there is a "forger's tremor" in the handwriting—a series of small irregularities that occur when someone is trying to imitate another person's writing style. A few words have even been retouched to make them look *more* like eighteenth-century handwriting. Perhaps most intriguing, Morton Smith's supposed second-century letter refers to falsehoods being mingled with truth as impurities being blended with salt—a metaphor that assumes the existence of granular salt as you probably use at your table today. The problem is that in the third century, salt came in chunks that couldn't be mixed or mingled at all. In fact, salt wasn't available in free-flowing granules until the early 1900s when a corporation added an anticaking additive to their product. What was the name of this corporation? *Morton* Salt![31] Factors such as these have led several researchers to conclude that Morton Smith played an elaborate prank on fellow scholars and that the Secret Gospel of Mark is a hoax.[32]

So what about the Gospel of Thomas and Q? When did these "lost Gospels" come into existence? Were they really the Gospels of the first Christians? In the first place, many people are surprised to discover that Q isn't a Gospel at all! Q is a scholarly hypothesis that explains how the Gospel according to Matthew and Luke came to include so many identical teachings that *don't* show up in Mark's Gospel. The idea is that the authors of Matthew's and Luke's Gospels must have worked from a common early Christian writing that recorded teachings attributed to Jesus. While this theory does seem to fit the available evidence, it's a theory with no physical proof—no Q document has ever been found. Even if such a document *did* exist, its contents would be far from scandalous. The contents of a Q document would simply be the teachings of Jesus that the Gospel according to Matthew and Luke happen to share!

The case of the Gospel of Thomas is a bit more complex. The Gospel of Thomas is a list of sayings and brief teachings that are attributed to Jesus. More than half of these teachings appear in one or more of the New Testament Gospels—the parable of the soils, for example, and Jesus's declaration that "the kingdom of God is among you" (compare Mark 4:2–9; Luke 17:21; Gospel of Thomas 3:3; 9:1–5). The simple style and arrangement of the sayings in Gospel of Thomas have suggested to many scholars that this Gospel emerged *before* the New Testament Gospels. Still, the earliest mention of the Gospel of Thomas is found in a late second-century writing from a church leader named Hippolytus of Rome, and even this reference is uncertain.[33] The earliest known fragments of Gospel of Thomas come from the late second century.

Most important, the compiler of the Gospel of Thomas seems to have known one or more of the New Testament Gospels. Here's one example of why this is likely: In Mark's Gospel—which nearly all scholars would date *before* the Gospel according to Luke since Mark's Gospel seems to have served as one of Luke's sources—an awkward clause closes a parable about a lamp: "For nothing is hidden if not to be revealed" (Mark 4:22). Luke's Gospel smooths this sentence so that it reads, "For nothing is hidden that will not be revealed" (Luke 8:17). If—as some critics claim—the Gospel of Thomas was written *earlier* than the New Testament Gospels, we'd expect the form of this teaching in the Gospel of Thomas to be closer to Mark's less refined wording than to Luke's polished clause, but that's not what we find when we read the Gospel of Thomas.

In fact, the Gospel of Thomas is closer to the smoothed wording of the Gospel according to Luke,[34] and this isn't the only point at which the Gospel of Thomas follows later traditions instead of earlier ones. This suggests that the surviving form of the Gospel of Thomas emerged after Mark's Gospel—and probably after Luke's Gospel, for that matter. Though some portions of the Gospel of Thomas do date from the first century, the Gospel of Thomas as we have it seems to have been compiled *after* the New Testament Gospels. This would make the earliest reasonable date for the surviving version of the Gospel of Thomas to be sometime in the second century, after the deaths of the eyewitnesses of Jesus's ministry.[35]

The few "lost Gospel" fragments that could represent first-century traditions do not contradict the New Testament Gospels in any way.

A few tiny fragments of unidentified Gospels *might* represent first-century traditions about Jesus—but these texts are too fragmentary to be certain about their origins or their portrayal of Jesus. In any case, none of these tidbits of text directly contradict any essential truth in the New Testament Gospels. Most of them seem to represent variations of stories already found in the New Testament.

The earliest of these fragmentary Gospels comes from a second-century document known as "the Egerton Gospel" or "Papyrus Egerton 2."[36] These pieces of papyrus record two encounters between Jesus and the Pharisees that are paralleled in John 5:39–46 and Mark 12:13–17, a miracle story very similar to the healing that's recorded in Mark 1:40–45, and a paragraph that's too fragmented to reconstruct with any confidence. The Egerton papyrus demonstrates that at a very early stage, believers in Jesus wanted to preserve records not only of what Jesus *taught* but also of what He *did*. They viewed Jesus not only as a teacher but also as a divine healer.

Two papyrus fragments discovered near Oxyrhynchus in Egypt also seem to come from ancient retellings of Jesus's life and teachings. One of them, Papyrus Oxyrhynchus 840, was apparently written in the late second or early third century, long after the New Testament Gospels. It includes a minor historical misstatement that people in the first century A.D. would have recognized as mistaken.[37] The other set of fragments, Papyrus Oxyrhynchus 1224, is so patchy that it's impossible to be certain about its original contents; the document seems to record an incident at a meal with some Pharisees (compare Mark 2:15–17) and some sayings of Jesus such as, "Pray for your enemies," and "The one who is not against us is for us" (compare Matthew 5:44; Mark 9:40). Another text—discovered near the region of Fayyum in Egypt and known as the Fayyum Fragment—fuses Mark 14:26–31 with Matthew 26:30–35, where Jesus says to Simon Peter, "Before the rooster crows twice, you will deny me three times." Since this fragment merges the wording of two New Testament Gospels, it must have been written after these Gospels.

Gnosticism (from Greek, *ginosko*, "I have knowledge"): sect that emerged within or parallel to the Christian movement in the first and second centuries A.D. Gnostics claimed to possess secret knowledge about God that was unavailable to others. Gnostics viewed the physical world and its Creator—usually identified with the God of the Old Testament—as evil. For Gnostics, Jesus Christ was not God in human flesh. He was a divine spirit in what appeared to be a human body; His mission was to free people from the constraints of the physical world.

CRACKING THE LOST GOSPELS CONSPIRACY

So, were the "lost Gospels" actually the sacred texts of the earliest Christians? Were these rejected books written before the New Testament Gospels?

Not as far as I can tell.

With few exceptions, the "lost Gospels" were compiled and composed decades after the accounts in the New Testament, at a time when the eyewitnesses were no longer living. The "lost Gospels" weren't cut out of the sacred texts of the earliest Christians; they were never part of these Christians' sacred texts to begin with.

To be sure, it is possible that early Christians summarized the sayings of Jesus in a document such as Q. Some early traditions that survive in writings such as the Gospel of Thomas probably emerged in the first century. Considering that half of the teachings in the Gospel of Thomas also appear in the eyewitness accounts found in the New Testament Gospels, this shouldn't surprise us. It's possible that fragments such as Papyrus Egerton 2 represent real traditions about Jesus that come from the first century.

Still, all the best evidence suggests that the earliest Christians shared the understanding of Jesus that's reflected in the Gospels according to Matthew, Mark, Luke, and John. Nothing from the "lost Gospels" can overshadow the strong evidence from the fragments of ancient papyri and from the words of ancient believers. From these witnesses, it is clear that the earliest Christians viewed Jesus not only as a wise teacher and prophet but also as a miracle worker and risen Lord. What's more, even in the earliest centuries of Christian faith, these believers embraced the New Testament Gospels—not the "lost scriptures"—as the most reliable retellings of the life and ministry of Jesus.

So how does this Christ conspiracy fare when compared to evidence from the first centuries of Christianity? When we examine the ancient witnesses, this conspiracy cracks beneath the weight of the historical evidence. The "lost Gospels" provide fascinating glimpses into the minds of believers and heretics throughout the first few centuries of Christian faith. But what these texts cannot consistently provide is reliable, eyewitness testimony about Jesus of Nazareth. That testimony is found in the book that's known to us as the New Testament.

HOW TO PREPARE FOR FUTURE CHRIST CONSPIRACIES

As more archaeological excavations occur, more "lost Gospels" will be found—and more sensationalized reports will race through the media, claiming that long-lost facts about Jesus have finally come to light. The next time you see such stories in newspapers or on the television screen, plan to do some research. First, find out if this "lost Gospel" actually contradicts any New Testament writings. After you've compared the content of the "lost Gospel" with the New Testament Gospels, discover *when* the manuscripts were copied as well as *when* the original document was probably written. Compare these dates with the dates of the New Testament Gospels. Most likely, you'll find that these "lost Gospels" cannot be reliably traced to eyewitness testimony about Jesus.

QUICK GUIDE
THE "LOST GOSPELS"

Document	Summary of Contents	Approximate Date of Composition
Gospel of Thomas	List of Jesus's teachings, mingled with some early gnostic elements	Early to mid A.D. 100s, perhaps later, with some portions surviving from the first century
Papyrus Egerton 2	Fragments of four episodes from the life of Jesus, three of which are paralleled—with different wordings—in the New Testament Gospels	Early to mid A.D. 100s
Papyrus Oxyrhynchus 1224	Fragments from Jesus's teachings as well as an account of a banquet, similar to narratives found in New Testament Gospels	Early to mid A.D. 100s

Document	Summary of Contents	Approximate Date of Composition
Gospel of the Hebrews	Hebrew Gospel, lost except for brief quotations from early church leaders. One of the surviving quotations preserves a record of the resurrection of Jesus and of an appearance to James	Early to mid A.D. 100s
Gospel of Peter	Fragments of a lost Gospel, surviving portions recount the death, burial, and resurrection of Jesus; seems to represent a separate testimony to the Resurrection, not directly paralleled in the New Testament Gospels	Early to mid A.D. 100s
Fayyum Fragment (Papyrus Vindobonensis Greek 2315)	Fragment that recounts Jesus's prediction that Peter will betray Him, paralleled in Matthew's and Mark's Gospels. Wording combines and derives from Matthew's and Mark's narratives.	Mid A.D. 100s
Gospel of the Egyptians	Not to be confused with the much later Coptic Gospel of the Egyptians, this text urges self-denial in a manner reminiscent of mid to late second-century Gnosticism	Mid A.D. 100s, perhaps later
Secret Book (Apocryphon) of James	Gnostic text that may include some traditions from the first century, though these elements have been heavily mingled with gnostic traditions	Mid A.D. 100s
Gospel of the Ebionites	Version of Gospel according to Matthew, edited to fit the theology of a Jewish sect known as the Ebionites	Mid A.D. 100s, perhaps earlier

Document	Summary of Contents	Approximate Date of Composition
Gospel of the Nazoreans	Version of Gospel according to Matthew, edited to fit the theology of a Jewish sect known as the Nazoreans	Mid A.D. 100s, perhaps earlier
Gospel of the Lord	Version of Gospel according to Luke, edited to fit the theological leanings of a sect led by Marcion, who denied the humanity of Jesus and who declared that the God of the Old Testament and the God of the New Testament were two separate deities	Mid A.D. 100s
Papyrus Oxyrhynchus 840	Fragment of an otherwise unknown Gospel, incorrectly refers to high priest as a "Pharisee," suggesting a date long after the destruction of Jewish temple in A.D. 70 and far from Jerusalem	Mid to late A.D. 100s
Gospel of Mary	Gnostic Gospel in which Mary—assumed to be Magdalene, though the Gospel does not state this—is central	Mid to late A.D. 100s
Dialogue of the Savior	Gnostic creation myth	Mid to late A.D. 100s
Gospel of Truth	Valentinian gnostic text	Mid to late A.D. 100s
Gospel of Judas	Retelling of the actions and fate of Judas Iscariot, probably from the Cainite Gnostics	Mid to late A.D. 100s
Gospel (or Vision) of the Savior (Papyrus Berolinensis 22220)	Fragments from gnostic account of a supposed vision of Jesus that draws from New Testament Gospels and Gospel of Peter.	Late A.D. 100s
Infancy Gospel of James	Christian fiction, imagining the early years of Jesus's life	Late A.D. 100s, perhaps slightly earlier

Document	Summary of Contents	Approximate Date of Composition
Infancy Gospel of Thomas	Christian fiction, imagining the early years of Jesus's life	Probably late A.D. 100s, perhaps mid-100s
Acts of John	Supposed retelling of events from the life of the apostle John; seems to deny humanity of Jesus	Late A.D. 100s
Gospel of Philip	Gnostic reflections, supposedly gathered by the apostle Philip	Late A.D. 100s or early 200s
Secret Gospel of Mark	Hoax perpetrated by Morton Smith	A.D. 1958

Conspiracy Number Three

IT WAS ALL ABOUT POWER

WHAT'S the CONSPIRACY?

EARLY CHRISTIAN LEADERS SELECTED SACRED BOOKS AND ESSENTIAL beliefs to protect the church's power structures, not to testify to the historical truth about Jesus. Other beliefs and books were suppressed, sometimes violently.

WHO SAYS SO?

- Dan Brown, *The Da Vinci Code*
- Elaine Pagels, *The Gnostic Gospels*

Suppose you became a Christian in the second century A.D.

You'll be making this supposition several times as you read this book. So, why not really get into it? Grab yourself some sandals and a toga, or at least a bathrobe. Then learn some useful Greek or Latin phrases, like, *Quantum materiae materietur marmota monax si marmota monax materiam possit materiari?* which means, "How much wood could a woodchuck chuck if a woodchuck could chuck wood?" Or how about this one: *Visne saltare? Viam Latam Fungosam scio!* That's Latin for, "Want to dance? I can do the Funky Broadway!"—which is certain to make you the life of the party. You may even have to yell, *Non plaudite! Modo pecuniam jacite!* ("Don't clap! Just throw me the money!")

Now, back to the second century A.D.: You've heard the story of a deity who died on a cross and rose from the dead. Through baptism, you've openly identified yourself with His followers. Now you want to learn more about this deity, yet you quickly realize that some people who call themselves "Christians" understand Jesus very differently from the Christians in your congregation. One nearby group that claims the name *Christian* also claims that Jesus wasn't actually a human being—He was a spirit that only *seemed* human!

How would you decide who was right?

As a twenty-first century Christian, the most reasonable reply seems to be, "Read your New Testament!"—or, if you still want to go with Latin, *"Legere Novum Testamentum tui!"* The problem is that most Christians in the second century *couldn't* read.[1] Even if you were one of the privileged few who possessed the capacity to read, you wouldn't personally own a Bible. Your only "Bible"

46

would have been found in an *armarion*—a specially constructed cabinet with niched shelves for scrolls and codices—that remained in the home where your congregation most often gathered. The *armarion* would have sheltered a *Septuagint* scroll and a couple dozen other sacred scrolls or codices.

Some of these texts would have been identical to the twenty-seven books that you find in a New Testament today—but not all of them. Certainly, the four Gospels, the Acts of the Apostles, Paul's letters, and probably John's first letter would have had a place in the *armarion*. Yet the cabinet would probably have lacked a few writings—the letter to the Hebrews or the second epistle that's ascribed to Peter, for example, or a couple of John's letters. Each of these letters would have been copied by scribes in other congregations—yet these scribes might also have duplicated a couple of books that you'd never find in a New Testament today. A quirky allegory titled *The Shepherd* could have made an appearance in your *armarion*, or perhaps the Gospel of Peter, the Acts of Paul, or even a letter from a Roman pastor named Clement.

Do you sense the dilemma that faced first- and second-century Christians? How could they maintain the faith of the first Christians in the shadow of so many competing claims? How did they decide on the books and the beliefs that we call "Christian" today? To discover the answers, let's first take a careful look at the claims of several scholars who are a bit skeptical about the process. Before the chapter ends, we'll also find ourselves taking a time-travel trip through three second-century cities to observe the actual process that resulted in the documents we call "the New Testament" today.

KNOW MORE

Septuagint (from Latin, *septuaginta*, "seventy"): Greek translation of the Jewish Scriptures, completed between the third and the first century B.C. The designation Septuagint stems from a spurious legend that seventy—according to some versions of the story, seventy-two—scholars worked separately to translate the Septuagint, and that after seventy-two days, all the scholars emerged with identical translations.

THE POWER CONSPIRACY

From the previous chapters, at least one reason why the "lost scriptures" and "lost Christianities" were lost should be clear: early Christians couldn't consistently connect these writings and teachings to eyewitnesses of Jesus's life.

Yet what if there were other motivations at work when these decisions were made? What if the church's primary point *wasn't* the preservation of historical truth about Jesus? What if the real impulse behind these selections was certain men's determination to preserve their own power?

That's precisely what a handful of popular writers want you to believe.

Here's what some critics claim about why alternative Gospels were excluded from the New Testament: *The "lost Gospels" were eliminated—cut out of the church's authoritative writings—because church leaders preferred the portrayal of Jesus found in the Gospels that came to be known by the names Matthew, Mark, Luke, and John.* Why did these church leaders prefer the portrayal of Jesus in the Gospels according to Matthew, Mark, Luke, and John? *Because they wanted to use the New Testament Gospels to preserve and to expand their power in the churches.*

In *The Da Vinci Code*, Dan Brown places these words on the lips of a fictional scholar to describe the rise of four New Testament Gospels and of belief in the deity of Jesus:

> It was all about power.... The early Church literally *stole* Jesus from His original followers, hijacking His human message...and using it to expand their own power.... The modern Bible was compiled and edited by men who possessed a political agenda—to promote the divinity of the man Jesus Christ and use His influence to solidify their own power base.[2]

"It was all about power," Dan Brown's fictional scholars claim. Yet these fictional scholars aren't the only characters to ascribe such motives to early Christians. Real-life scholars make these claims too.

Elaine Pagels, a popular scholar and professor at Princeton University, has put it this way: "When I entered the Harvard doctoral program...I was astonished to hear... [about] file cabinets filled with 'gospels' and 'apocrypha' written during the first centuries, many of them secret writings of which I'd never heard."[3] Why hadn't Elaine Pagels heard about these writings at any previous time? Because early church leaders "suppressed" them—at least that's Dr. Pagels's perspective on the matter. Pagels proposes her hypotheses in a text titled *The Gnostic Gospels*, a best-selling book that has received widespread critical acclaim and numerous awards, including a National Book Award and the National Book Critics Circle Award.

Dr. Pagels's portrayal of why certain Gospels were suppressed runs something like this:

■ Church leaders wanted to centralize power in *one* supreme overseer (or "bishop"). So, they preserved the Gospels that confessed belief in *one* God even as they suppressed Gospels that portrayed multiple gods.[4]

■ Church leaders wanted to centralize power in the hands of certain overseers—overseers who lived in cities where apostles who claimed to have seen the resurrected Lord had once lived. So they suppressed Gospels that included spiritual visions of Jesus while preserving the Gospels that clearly presented a physical resurrection.[5]

■ Church leaders wanted to exclude females from all leadership roles, so they suppressed the writings that described God as Mother while exalting writings that portrayed God as Father.[6]

What happened when people refused to give up their alternative Gospels? According to Pagels—citing an early church leader named Clement—"Carried away with his argument, Clement warns that whoever disobeys the divinely ordained authorities, 'receives the death penalty!'"[7] In truth, it isn't Clement but Pagels who has gotten "carried away" with this quotation. At this point in the text, Clement's primary point isn't what should happen to heretics; he's describing what happened in the ancient Jewish temple when sacrifices were not properly offered.[8]

These patterns, Pagels implies, provided a pretext to concentrate primary power in Rome, the city where Simon Peter spent his final years.[9] Since Simon Peter was remembered as one of the first witnesses of physical resurrection, the elevation of the bodily resurrection to a key doctrine supposedly provided his successors with unique power in the churches.

If the picture painted in *The Gnostic Gospels* is correct, the main impulse for recognizing the authority of certain Christian writings *wasn't* because these writings conveyed historical truth about Jesus. The prime motivation was power, and the driving force was politics.[10]

KNOW MORE

orthodox (from Greek *orthos* ["right" or "straight"] + *doxa* ["perception," eventually "good repute" or "worship"]): beliefs that conform to Christian faith as presented in the documents known today as the New Testament. Scholars who emphasize the diversity of beliefs in the early Christian movement sometimes replace this term with "proto-orthodox"—literally, "before orthodox."

heretical (from Greek *haireisthai*, "to choose one's own way"): in Christian theology, a belief that deviates from the essential message of Jesus Christ proclaimed by the apostles and recorded in the documents known today as the New Testament. This category would include such early sects as:

■ Docetists, who denied the full humanity of Jesus

■ Ebionites, who denied the deity of Jesus

■ Adoptionists, who believed that Jesus was adopted by God the Father and *became* divine at His baptism

■ Marcionites, who denied that the God of the Old Testament was also the God revealed in Jesus

■ Gnostics who viewed the physical world as inherently evil and who reinterpreted biblical texts to fit this presupposition. Most Gnostics were also Docetists.

bishop (translation of Greek *episkopos*, "overseer"): Christian leader, specifically ordained to preserve divine truth among God's people. "Bishop" and "overseer" translate the same Greek word, *episkopos*. Among the earliest Christians, "bishop" or "overseer" seems to have described the same function as "elder" (*presbyteros*) or "pastor" (*poimen*). By the early second century A.D., *bishop* or *overseer* had become a separate office, ranking higher than elders or pastors.[11]

There wasn't a New Testament in existence at the beginning of the second century A.D. or even by the end of that century, although by that time, some theologians, nervous about what they considered to be the "truth," were attempting to create one. Despite these theologians' best efforts, Christians had to wait almost two more centuries for an agreed-upon text.[12]
—MICHAEL BAIGENT, *The Jesus Papers* (2006)

HOW CONSTANTINE CREATED THE BIBLE—OR DID HE?

What's more, according to other popular scholars, Christians in the first and second centuries had no standard for determining which books and beliefs were authoritative. These decisions emerged many decades after Jesus and His disciples wandered the dusty roads of Judea and Galilee. A couple of critics even claim that *no one* recognized the New Testament Gospels as authoritative until a late second-century pastor named Irenaeus of Lyons declared Matthew, Mark, Luke, and John to be the authentic accounts of Jesus's life.[13]

Richard Dawkins, author of *The God Delusion*, seems to subscribe to this scenario: "The four gospels that made it into the official canon," Dawkins contends, "were chosen, more or less, arbitrarily, out of a larger sample of at least a dozen including the Gospels of Thomas, Peter, Nicodemus, Philip, Bartholomew, and Mary Magdalen."[14]

Other scholars claim that what Christians regarded as "Scripture" wasn't settled until the fourth century A.D., after Emperor Constantine involved himself in church affairs.[15] One member of the Jesus Seminar has flatly declared, "The event that triggered the creation of the Christian Bible was the conversion of Constantine and the sudden reversal of imperial status experienced by the Christian churches."[16]

Dan Brown's fictional Leigh Teabing made this point with these words:

> The Bible is a product of man, my dear. Not of God.... History has never had a definitive version of the book.... The Bible, as we know it today, was collated by the pagan Roman emperor Constantine the Great.... Jesus' establishment as the "Son of God" was officially proposed and voted on by the Council of Nicaea.[17]

KNOW MORE

Council of Nicea (historical event, A.D. 325) Ancient gathering of church leaders in the village of Nicea, located near the modern city of Iznik in northwestern Turkey. According to the claims of conspiracy theorists such as Michael Baigent as well as characters in Dan Brown's *The Da Vinci Code*, "Jesus' establishment as 'the Son of God' was officially proposed and voted on by the Council of Nicea... [and] a relatively close vote at that." Before the Council of Nicea—these theorists suggest—"Jesus was viewed by His followers as a mortal prophet... a great and powerful man, but a man nonetheless." According to *The Da Vinci Code*, Constantine convened the council because Christians and pagans were fighting one another and he wanted "to unify Rome under a single religion. Christianity." Unfortunately for these theorists, such claims are riddled with historical blunders:

■ In the first place, the purpose of the Council of Nicea
was neither to unify the empire under one religion nor
to declare Jesus divine. The council's purpose was to seek
consensus regarding what the Scriptures taught about Jesus.

■ The two factions at the Council of Nicea were not Christians and pagans; they were two different groups that both
claimed to be Christian. A pastor named Arius—whose
followers became known as "Arians"—had claimed that
Jesus was a created being, not eternal God in human flesh.
In response, more than three hundred church overseers
summarized their shared commitment to a tenet that Christians had embraced since the first century A.D., the belief
that Jesus was uniquely God.

Finally, the vote at the Council of Nicea wasn't "close" as
Dan Brown contends: out of approximately three hundred
church leaders at the Council of Nicea, only two refused to
sign the Creed of Nicea, a document that described Jesus as
"true God from true God." According to a letter written by
an eyewitness, "though some...confessed that they believed
things contrary to the God-inspired Scriptures,...more
than 300 overseers unanimously confirmed one and the
same faith, which according to the truth and the legitimate
interpretation of God's law is the faith."

Another critical scholar also places the consensus about the books of the
New Testament in the fourth century A.D. This scholar points to a letter from
a leading pastor named Athanasius of Alexandria—written in A.D. 367—as
the critical turning point:

We are able to pinpoint the first time that any Christian of record listed
the twenty-seven books of our New Testament as *the* books of the
New Testament—neither more nor fewer. Surprising as it may seem,
this Christian was writing in the second half of the fourth century,
nearly three hundred years after the books of the New Testament
had themselves been written. The author was the powerful bishop of
Alexandria named Athanasius. In the year 367, Athanasius wrote his
annual pastoral letter to the Egyptian churches under his jurisdiction,
and in it he included advice concerning which books should be read as
Scripture in the churches. He lists our twenty-seven books, excluding

all others. This is the first surviving instance of anyone affirming our set of books as the New Testament. And even Athanasius did not settle the matter. Debates continued for decades, even centuries.[18]

—W. H. C. Frend, *The Rise of Christianity*

CONSPIRACY NUMBER THREE

Early Christian leaders selected sacred books and essential beliefs to protect the church's power structures—not to testify to historical truth about Jesus. Other books and beliefs were violently suppressed.

The TRUTH BEHIND the CONSPIRACY

Essential beliefs about Jesus—as well as standards for what types of texts were authoritative for Christians—were established while the apostolic eyewitnesses were still alive, decades before any supposed disputes over power structures.

THE POWER CONSPIRACY

If these reconstructions have rightly rendered the history of Christianity, the books that you find in your New Testament were not recognized as authoritative until the fourth century A.D.—more than three centuries after Jesus taught His disciples along the shores of Lake Galilee. And the driving motives behind the selection of these books? Well, the motives don't seem to have been particularly pure. Church leaders wanted to consolidate power in the hands of a few male bishops. So, according to some of these reconstructions, church leaders chose books and beliefs that would bolster this power. What about the books and beliefs that challenged this emerging power structure? They were violently suppressed, only to resurface in recent years after having spent decades buried in distant lands and forsaken in scholars' file cabinets.

Writings censored because they challenged an emerging power structure?

Apocryphal books concealed in scholars' file cabinets because no one wants to admit the scandalous story that they share?

A worldwide organization that nearly succeeded in suppressing the truth about its sordid history?

Sounds like a conspiracy to me.

There are parts of this reconstruction that warrant a second look, though. Take a look with me at the history behind the conspiracy. Let's track down a broader perspective on what happened in the first centuries of Christianity as well as some truths that may be more surprising than any conspiracy the critics could conceive.

CLUES TO CRACK THE POWER CONSPIRACY

Let's look first at Elaine Pagels's reconstruction of early Christian history. Remember her claims? According to Pagels, early Christian belief in the bodily resurrection of Jesus was not based upon a historical event. The Resurrection— she implies—did not become a crucial belief until *after* the apostles' deaths.

Before this time, according to Pagels, some Christians saw the resurrection of Jesus as a physical reality while others defined *resurrection* in terms of ecstatic visions of a spiritual Jesus that could appear to anyone. The bodily resurrection of Jesus—Pagels concludes—didn't become an essential belief until a few church leaders began to stress this sort of resurrection. And what was the main motive behind the move toward requiring faith in a physical resurrection? It was to secure the power of certain bishops who believed that they were "successors to the apostles."

 **Christians recognized the bodily resurrection of Jesus as an essential belief while the apostles were still alive.**

So what's the problem with the perspective that Pagels presents?

According to Pagels, belief in a physical resurrection provided leverage to increase the power of leaders in apostolic cities after the apostles were no longer present. So, if Pagels's reconstruction is right, here's what we *ought* to find in the historical records: recognition of the physical resurrection of Jesus as an essential belief should have emerged *during* or *after* the struggles regarding which overseers possessed the most power, at some point *after* the deaths of the apostles.[19]

That isn't even close to what we find in the historical records.

The first controversy over which overseers possessed the most power seems to have occurred around A.D. 155.[20] This was when the overseer of the Roman church demanded that all Christians observe Easter on the same date.[21] Even then, many overseers—especially in Asia Minor—ignored the Roman overseer's demands with no apparent misgivings. What about the "lost scriptures" that Elaine Pagels cites as evidence of an alternative view of the resurrection? The earliest of these writings—the Gospel of Mary, a supposed letter from Peter to Philip, and a letter from an unknown author addressed to someone named Rheginos—comes from the mid to late second century A.D. So, not only the *controversies* but also the *documents* that provide primary proof for Pagels's hypothesis come from the mid 100s A.D. or later!

When did recognition of the bodily resurrection of Jesus begin to be viewed as an essential belief? *It happened in the first century A.D., while the apostles were still alive.* The Acts of the Apostles—written in the mid to late first century[22]—declares that David "foresaw and spoke concerning the Messiah's resurrection...that His flesh did not experience decay" (Acts 2:31). The Gospel according to Mark, penned in the A.D. 60s, repeatedly points toward a physical resurrection (Mark 8:31; 9:9–10, 31; 10:34). Around A.D. 49, Paul described his Lord in these terms: "Jesus the Messiah and God the Father, the one *having raised Him from the dead*" (Galatians 1:1, emphasis added), assuming that his readers shared this belief.[23] In 1 Corinthians 15, Paul recorded a snippet of oral history that circulated in Judea in the months following the crucifixion of Jesus.[24] Here too Paul explicitly affirms the physical resurrection of Jesus:

> For I passed on to you what I also received:
> That the Messiah died on behalf of our sins according to the
>   Scriptures,
> And that He was buried,
> And that He rose on the third day according to the Scriptures,
> And that He was seen by Cephas,
> Then the Twelve;
> Then He was seen by more than five hundred brothers at once...
> Then He was seen by James,
> Then by all the apostles.
>
> —1 CORINTHIANS 15:3–7

These descriptions do not depict mere spiritual visions of Jesus following His death. They clearly imply a *bodily resurrection* that occurred in a particular place at a particular point in human history.[25] From the first stages of Christian faith, Christians proclaimed the physical resurrection of Jesus as a crucial belief. "If the Messiah has not been raised," Paul declared to the Corinthians in A.D. 55, "our proclamation is empty and so is your trust" (1 Corinthians 15:14).

All of these references to the bodily resurrection of Jesus—with the exception of Mark's Gospel—circulated among the churches *while the apostle Peter and other eyewitnesses were still alive.*[26] The Gospel according to Mark probably began to circulate soon after Simon Peter's martyrdom in Rome.[27] So, the church's recognition of the bodily resurrection as an essential belief clearly *preceded* any attempts to push for unique authority among certain successors of the apostles. When arguments over power began to plague the Roman church in the second century, Christians had already recognized the physical resurrection of Jesus as a crucial element to their confession of faith for several decades.

That's why Ignatius of Antioch, writing a letter to the church in Smyrna near the end of the first century, could declare with absolute certainty:

> Even after the resurrection, [Jesus] was in the flesh. Indeed, when he came to Peter and his friends, he said, "Take hold of me! See that I am no disembodied spirit!" At once, they touched him, and they too were convinced. That's why they disregarded death itself and proved to be the victors.[28]

Despite Pagels's conspiratorial claims, belief in the bodily resurrection of Jesus originated with the first eyewitnesses and continued long beyond their deaths.

What's the central problem with Elaine Pagels's claim that church leaders exalted certain Gospels—Gospels that highlighted the bodily resurrection of Jesus—to centralize the power of the apostles' successors in certain cities? The problem with this claim is that Christians began to view the bodily resurrection of Jesus as an essential belief before anyone *could* have succeeded the apostles, because the apostles were still alive! And the documents that proclaim spiritual visions in place of physical resurrection? They emerged a century after Christians confessed their faith in the one who "died on behalf of our sins...and...rose again on the third day" (1 Corinthians 15:3–4).

> The flaw in Pagels' logic is [that] *she uses an effect produced by an orthodox belief to explain the origin of the belief itself.* She might as well argue that Elvis fans made up his existence because they liked his music so much.... Pagels declares in her conclusion that "it is the winners who write history—their way." Ironically, she seems to miss the fact completely that orthodoxy "won" because history was on its side.[29]
>
> —SOPHIA DE MORGAN,
> "Gnostic Gnonsense," in *Answering Infidels*

CLUE NUMBER 2: Belief in one God and in God the Father originated in the Jewish faith, not in second-century church politics.

What about Dr. Pagels's other claims? According to Pagels, early Christian bishops demanded belief in God the Father so that they could justify their exclusion of women from leadership, and they compelled faith in one supreme deity to bolster the power of one supreme bishop over the churches. So, from Pagels's perspective, Christians who believe in monotheism and in the fatherhood of God find their foundation *not* in any facts about God but in the political machinations of ancient bishops. In truth, these supposed connections between theology and politics are even weaker than her claims about the bodily resurrection. The idea of one God who fathers His people was rooted in more than *one thousand years* of Jewish faith, not in any first- or second-century decision to centralize power in one male overseer! (For references to one God in the Hebrew Scriptures, see Deuteronomy 4:35–39; 6:4; 1 Kings 8:60; Isaiah 45:5, 14, 18, 21–22; 46:9; for references to God as the Father of His people, see Psalm 89:26; Isaiah 9:6.)

Here's a far more plausible reconstruction of what happened in the church's early centuries: *From the earliest stages of their faith, Christians regarded the bodily resurrection of Jesus as a crucial belief.* This event was, after all, the experience that triggered their trust in the first place, but the idea of a bodily resurrection repulsed many first-century Greco-Roman people.[30] Influenced by the ancient philosopher Plato, these cultured Romans viewed the physical body as "the soul's prison,"[31] a burden to be escaped at death. This was quite a contrast to the Jewish perspective that the human body, as part of God's good creation, could experience redemption and restoration at the end of time.

As Christianity spread among non-Jewish people, the idea of bodily resurrection became an embarrassment for many Christian teachers. (Remember what happened when Paul mentioned resurrection to a group of Greek philosophers? "When they heard of resurrection from the dead, some jeered at him" [Acts 17:32].) As such, some teachers began to downplay the bodily resurrection of Jesus, replacing the idea of resurrection with spiritual visions of Jesus that could occur at any time. In other words, they changed Christian faith to fit the preferences of their culture. Some teachers even tried to incorporate other pieces of the pagan culture into Christian faith—the mother goddess, for example, and multiple divine beings instead of one God.[32]

The writings of these teachers *were* rejected, yet it wasn't because of anyone's lust for power. The "suppression" of these texts had everything to do with preserving the faith of the first Christians and little, if anything, to do with centralizing the church's power structures in certain cities or among certain overseers.

CLUE NUMBER 3: **Books and beliefs that could not be connected to apostolic eyewitnesses did not become authoritative in the early church.**

The motivations behind the creation of the New Testament canon were *not* primarily political—that much is clear—but if it wasn't political power that drove the decisions, what was it? How did the process of selecting certain texts while eliminating others actually happen? How did the twenty-seven texts that we call "the New Testament" end up between the covers of your Bible? To find out, we'll need to take a quick trip through time. Don't worry about the cost, though. The cost of your ticket was included in the price of the book. (Lucky for you, huh?) You will, however, have to bring your own pretzels and peanuts; it was hard enough for the publisher to fit a time machine in each book without including snacks too.

Your trip through time will include three primary stops in three different places: the city of Rome, the northeastern shore of the Mediterranean Sea, and, finally, the desert plains just outside the city of Carthage in North Africa.

Are you ready to go?

If so, fasten your seat belt, don't even think about using your seat cushion as a flotation device, and prepare for takeoff. Keep your hands and feet in the book at all times, and if anyone asks *why* you have your feet stuck in a book, just ignore them or say, *Utinam barbari bracis tuum invadant,* which means, "May the barbarians invade your shorts." That will convince them that you're really not so weird after all.

KNOW MORE

So how were the Old Testament books chosen? The Jewish people understood their Bible—the collection of books that Christian call "the Old Testament"—to include three sections: Torah, Nevi'im, and Ketuvim. Together, these three sections are known as "Tanakh." Torah, or "Instructions," referred to Genesis, Exodus, Leviticus, Numbers, and Deuteronomy. The Nevi'im, or "Prophets," were the books of Joshua, Judges, 1 and 2 Samuel, 1 and 2 Kings, Isaiah, Jeremiah, Ezekiel, and the twelve Minor Prophets. Ketuvim, or "Writings," came to mean three poetic books (Psalms, Proverbs, Job), five festival scrolls (Song of Solomon, Ruth, Lamentations, Ecclesiastes, Esther), as well as Daniel, Ezra, Nehemiah, 1 Chronicles, and 2 Chronicles. There was early, widespread agreement among Jews concerning which books belonged in Torah and Nevi'im. Which books belonged in Ketuvim wasn't settled until the second and third centuries A.D. In the end, the books that were included in the Old Testament were (1) written in Hebrew, (2) used in Jewish worship, (3) reflected in the divine law and covenant given through Moses at Mount Sinai, and (4) completed before the time of Ezra, since Ezra was believed to have been the scribe who gathered the holy books of the Jewish faith.

FIRST STOP: ROME—MID-SECOND CENTURY A.D.

You can't help but be excited as your time machine tumbles into the city of Rome. (See map on page 178.) After all, this is *the* city—seat of the Roman Empire, residence of the Caesars, the place where all roads lead, the last place on earth where Peter and Paul lived, the Eternal City. Citizens and slaves, vagrants and wide-eyed visitors congest the stone-paved streets. The stench is nearly unbearable to twenty-first-century nostrils. You are accustomed to deodorants, daily baths, and sewer systems that flow somewhere besides in the streets. These people are not. You consider telling them how bad their armpits smell—that would be *Fetere sub lacertum vestri* in Latin, in case you ever need to know—but you decide that, since there are so many of them and so few of you, tactfulness is in your best interest.

You slip through a small gate and escape the teeming throng. A slave beside the gate nods toward a broad villa. As you wander between the colonnades, you hear a voice within, speaking with great deliberation. Peeking into a central gathering place, you glimpse the master of the household standing in front of a cabinet—an *armarion*—that has been specially constructed to hold papyrus codices.

As the master speaks, he carefully examines each codex. Near his feet, his scribe sits cross-legged, transcribing his master's words. You lean closer, straining to hear the words that the master is entrusting to his scribe's pen:

> The third book of the Gospel is "according to Luke." After the ascension of the Messiah, Paul took Luke with him....Luke—the physician—composed this Gospel in his name, just as it has been told. He himself had not seen the Lord in the flesh; still, he personally investigated certain events, and he begins to relate his account from John's birth. The fourth of the Gospels is the one of John, one of the disciples.[33]

The master moves on, glancing at each codex and describing each text. He lists most of the books that appear in your New Testament, though he seems to leave out a few. As he examines one particular codex, the master stops and pores over several papyrus pages. When he speaks, he weighs each word with utmost care:

> Hermas composed *The Shepherd* quite recently—in our times, in the city of Rome, while his brother Pius the overseer served as overseer of the city of Rome. So, while it should indeed be read, it ought not to be read publicly for the people of the church—it is counted neither among the prophets (for their number has been completed) nor among the apostles (for it is after their time).[34]

The present time period is most likely the reign of Emperor Marcus Aurelius—the years that we know today as the A.D. 160s and 170s.[35] What about the papyrus that now rests in the lap of this second-century scribe? A man named Ludovico Muratori will one day discover a Latin copy of this document, and it will become known as "the Muratorian Fragment."

What's important about the Muratorian Fragment isn't merely the fact that it includes an early list of authoritative books for Christians. What the fragment provides in its references to a book titled *The Shepherd* is a snapshot of how and why certain books were excluded from the New Testament. *The Shepherd*, penned by a man named Hermas, is a quirky allegory filled with visions that are mediated through a divine being in a shepherd's outfit. In the second and third centuries, the book was a best seller among Christians—well, not really, but it *would have been* a best seller if such concepts had existed at that time.[36] *The Shepherd* became so popular in the second century that some people wanted to read the book in times of worship, alongside the four Gospels, the apostles' epistles, and the Jewish Scriptures.

The Muratorian Fragment tells us why *The Shepherd* came to be cut out of the sacred collection that Christians read during times of worship: *The Shepherd* couldn't be placed among the Hebrew prophets because the era of Old Testament prophecies had ended ("their number has been completed"). Yet the book didn't fit among the authoritative Christian writings, either, because with the deaths of the apostolic eyewitnesses, that era had ended too ("it is after their time"). Though *The Shepherd* might continue to be read as a devotional text ("it should indeed be read"), the book could not be considered an authoritative text for Christians ("it ought not to be read publicly for the people of the church").

So what truths can we pick up from our first stop? At least as early as the mid-second century, the standard for determining which writings were authoritative in the church was whether the book represented eyewitness testimony about Jesus. Writings that came after the deaths of these witnesses could not be regarded as universally authoritative in the churches, regardless of how popular these texts might become. Here's what's also clear from the Muratorian Fragment: even though Christians disagreed for several hundred years about seven or so writings, the core of the New Testament—including the four Gospels, Acts, Paul's letters, and at least John's first letter—was accepted as authoritative no later than the mid-second century, probably earlier.

QUICK GUIDE

EARLY LISTS OF NEW TESTAMENT WRITINGS

The Muratorian Fragment *(mid-second century A.D., Rome)*	Eusebius of Caesarea's Church History *(early fourth century A.D., Palestine and Asia Minor)*	Athanasius of Alexandria's Easter Letter *(late fourth century A.D., Alexandria, Egypt)*
ACCEPTED	ACCEPTED	ACCEPTED
Matthew	Matthew	Matthew
Mark	Mark	Mark
Luke	Luke	Luke
John	John	John
Acts	Acts	Acts
Romans	Romans	Romans
First and Second Corinthians	First and Second Corinthians	First and Second Corinthians
Galatians	Galatians	Galatians
Ephesians	Ephesians	Ephesians
Philippians	Philippians	Philippians
Colossians	Colossians	Colossians
First and Second Thessalonians	First and Second Thessalonians	First and Second Thessalonians
First and Second Timothy	First and Second Timothy	First and Second Timothy
Titus	Titus	Titus
Philemon	Philemon	Philemon
First John	Hebrews	Hebrews
Second and Third John (listed as one)	First Peter	James
Jude	First John	First and Second Peter
Revelation	Revelation*	First, Second, and Third John
Wisdom of Solomon		Jude
		Revelation
DISPUTED	DISPUTED	DISPUTED
Apocalypse of Peter	James	
	Jude	
	Second Peter	
	Second and Third John	

The Muratorian Fragment (mid-second century A.D., Rome)	Eusebius of Caesarea's Church History (early fourth century A.D., Palestine and Asia Minor)	Athanasius of Alexandria's Easter Letter (late fourth century A.D., Alexandria, Egypt)
REJECTED Laodiceans Alexandrians The Shepherd of Hermas	REJECTED Apocalypse of Peter Acts of Paul The Shepherd of Hermas Epistle of Barnabas Teaching of Twelve Apostles Gospel of Peter Gospel of Thomas Gospel of Matthias Gospel of the Hebrews Acts of Andrew Acts of John	REJECTED All others

* Indicates that this listing *may* have placed this writing in the list of disputed books

KNOW MORE

canon (from Greek *kanon*, "measuring stick," also a description for measurements that allowed one sculptor's work to be duplicated by another sculptor[37]): writings that adherents of a certain religious faith treat as uniquely authoritative. Looking back on the church's history,[38] the fourth-century writer Eusebius of Caesarea noticed three standards in the church's recognition of certain texts as authoritative. Each text had to be:

Genuine: The text must have originated with the apostolic eyewitnesses or close associates of the eyewitnesses. This standard effectively "closed" the canon so that books written after the apostolic era could not be added.

True: The text must agree with the known teachings of the eyewitnesses.

Well authenticated: The overseers who were closest to the apostles—both geographically and chronologically—must have viewed the book as authoritative, genuine, and true.[39]

According to Eusebius of Caesarea, the four Gospels, the Acts of the Apostles, Paul's thirteen letters, John's first letter, the first letter that bears Peter's name, and the Revelation of John were "acknowledged as genuine by all," that is, they had always been viewed as authoritative texts for believers in Jesus.[40]

SECOND STOP: ANTIOCH OF SYRIA—A.D. 199

The time machine is turning eastward for our second stop, hurtling over the Ionian Sea, Greece, and Asia Minor. The landing is a bit rocky, but when landing along the northeastern shore of the Mediterranean Sea, rocks are pretty much impossible to miss. Standing on the stony coastal road that extends north from Antioch of Syria, you notice someone striding toward you, barely visible in the morning mist. The man's pace is brisk. As you begin to walk beside him, he eyes you with suspicion.

"Do you worship Jesus as Messiah and God as do I?" you ask him.

The man breathes a sigh of relief.

"I do. I am Serapion, overseer of God's people in this place."

"Where are you headed?" you ask.

"Rhossus, to meet with the church's elders."

"What for?"

"The church in Rhossus was in turmoil when I became overseer here. When I asked them about the problem, some said that it started over a Gospel that was 'inscribed with Peter's name.' I told them, 'If that's all that threatens to produce hard feelings among you, let it be read.' Then, I read this Gospel for myself. Most things in this Gospel came from the Savior's right word, but some things were false! I have already sent a letter to the elders. Now I go to set things straight in person." With this, Serapion quickly bypasses you and disappears around a bend in the road.

By our reckoning, the year is A.D. 199. Serapion's situation is sketchy, but it provides a fascinating glimpse into the formation of the New Testament. Here's a snippet of text from Serapion's actual letter:

We receive Peter and the other apostles even as we receive Christ—but the writings that circulate falsely under their names, we have consistently rejected, knowing that we never received such writings as these. When I was with you I assumed you were all connected to the right faith. So, without reading the Gospel that was inscribed with Peter's name, I said, "If that's all that threatens to produce hard feelings among you, let it be read." Now, I've learned from information given to me that their minds were lurking in a cave of heresy! I will make a point of coming to you again; so, brothers, expect me speedily.... I borrowed the writing, and I was able to work through it. What I found was that most things in it came from the Savior's right word, but some things were additions.[41]

What can we pick up from Serapion's experiences? Even at the end of the second century, Christians remained open to using previously unknown texts, but *only* if they could clearly trace these texts to apostolic eyewitnesses of Jesus.[42] What did church leaders do when they weren't certain whether a text represented eyewitness testimony? They compared the writing to the writings that they had already "received"—to the texts that were universally known to represent apostolic testimony about Jesus.

By the late second century, this corpus of "received" texts seem to have included four Gospels, the Acts of the Apostles, the letters of Paul, John's first letter, and perhaps a few other documents. When Serapion compared the Gospel of Peter with these undisputed documents, he saw some difficulties. These difficulties suggested to Serapion that this Gospel couldn't have originated with Simon Peter. Specifically, Serapion found several passages in the Gospel of Peter that could be construed to suggest that Jesus merely *seemed* human.

In this way, Serapion of Antioch quickly identified the Gospel of Peter as a falsely ascribed text. As such, he declared that the book shouldn't be read publicly in the churches. Despite Serapion's rejection, the Gospel of Peter remained popular devotional reading among Christians for several centuries. In fact, more ancient papyri remain from the Gospel of Peter than from the Gospel according to Mark, yet, except for those few months in Rhossus, only the scantest evidence exists to suggest that Christians ever read the Gospel of Peter alongside the four New Testament Gospels in their times of worship.

> We receive Peter and the other apostles even as we receive Christ—but the writings that circulate falsely under their names, we have consistently rejected, knowing that we never received such writings as these.
>
> —SERAPION OF ANTIOCH, letter to Rhossus (A.D. 199)

```
KNOW MORE
```

Here's how the Gospel of Peter describes the resurrection of Jesus: "The soldiers...saw the sky open, and two men descending from there. The men, shining brightly, came near the tomb. The stone pushed before the entrance rolled away of its own accord, moving aside. The tomb being opened, the young men entered. When the soldiers saw these things, they awakened the centurion and the elders—for they too were guarding the tomb. While they were explaining what they had seen, they saw three men come out of the tomb, two of them supporting the other and a cross coming behind them. The heads of the two reached toward the heavens, but the head of the one being led reached beyond the heavens. They heard a voice from the heavens, saying, 'Have you proclaimed to those that are asleep?' And a voice came from the cross, 'Yes.'"[43] What are the *differences* and the *similarities* between this story and the resurrection accounts in Matthew, Mark, Luke, and John? Does anything about this account actually *contradict* Matthew, Mark, Luke, or John, or does this Gospel simply *expand* the original story?

LAST STOP: CARTHAGE, NORTH AFRICA—A.D. 200

The last leg of your trip takes you southwest. This time, the landing isn't so rocky. As you emerge into the sunlight, mirages swirl and twirl amid sand and scrubby bushes. In the distance, you glimpse several dense clusters of squarish homes and domed bathhouses. This is the city of Carthage. Just past the city, the Mediterranean Sea stretches northward, deep blue and nearly motionless. The dome of a low-slung basilica punctuates one string of houses. Peering through a slit in the wall of this public meeting place, you see a well-dressed man standing in the center of a huddle of listeners. He gestures toward a scroll that has been spread on a delicately carved table. The man speaks with great elegance and skill, each flourish of his hand carefully measured to convey his passion, "In Asia, the elder who composed that writing—as if he could add to Paul's fame from the storehouse of his own fame!—confessed, after being convicted, that he did it out of love for Paul, and he was removed from office."[44]

The speaker's name is Tertullian. He is the author of dozens of treatises on the Christian faith and serves the churches in the city of Carthage as an overseer. The present controversy began when some church members—involved in a dispute over baptism—appealed to a text known as the Acts of Paul.

Now, I must admit that if the Acts of Paul had made it into the New Testament, the book could certainly have energized your church's times of worship. In this book, Paul and a woman named Thecla travel around the Roman Empire, defeating dark powers and proclaiming a lifestyle of total self-denial. Personally, my favorite part of the book is when Paul baptizes a lion that's eighteen feet tall!

> Paul found a lion whose height was twelve cubits and whose size was like that of a horse. And he met Paul and they saluted each other as though they knew each other. And the lion said to Paul: "Good to meet you, Paul, servant of God and apostle of the Lord Jesus Christ! I have one thing, which I ask you to do to me." Paul said to him: "Speak; I will hear." And the lion replied, "Make me to enter into the great things of the Christians."[45]
> —Unknown ex-pastor in Asia Minor,
> Acts of Paul (around A.D. 180)

The problem with the Acts of Paul is that the text is pure fantasy. Confronted with church members who were citing the Acts of Paul as authoritative, Tertullian researched the book's origins and discovered that the text didn't represent eyewitness testimony about Jesus or even about Paul. The entire work represented one pastor's fictional retelling of Paul's journeys. What happened when the author's literary whims were exposed? The pastor-turned-novelist was shamed and deprived of his ordination.

What do we learn from this episode? In the first place, writing novels that involve immersing eighteen-foot-tall lions could lead to losing your job. More to the point, the incident makes it clear how seriously early Christians took the task of determining whether the church's authoritative texts contained historical truth. Otherwise, why would this pastor who wrote simply "out of love for Paul" have been deprived of his position in the church? Furthermore, the words of Tertullian remind us how strongly Christian leaders focused on the question, Did this text truly come from an apostolic eyewitness? If a text didn't meet this standard, it could not function as an authoritative text in the churches.

Well, with this final stop in North Africa, your trip is over. Unfortunately for you, the time-travel voucher that was included in the purchase price of this book was only a one-way ticket. So, you may want to start making plans to hitchhike home from Carthage. Have fun!

CRACKING THE POWER CONSPIRACY

So, what factors actually formed the New Testament and the faith of the early church? Conspiratorial reconstructions suggest that church leaders selected texts that preserved and expanded their own political powers. If so, what shaped the early church were books and theological beliefs that were chosen with the goal of control. The problem is that the core beliefs of the earliest Christians—belief in a bodily resurrection, for example, and the existence of only one God—were well established *before* the deaths of the apostles.

Were there some political intrigues in the early church? Certainly! Were certain texts excluded from the church's authoritative books? Of course. Were some alternative Scriptures suppressed in the early church? In some sense, yes, but this "suppression" didn't turn physical until the fourth century A.D., when Emperor Constantine began to use political power to influence the church's policies.[46] By this time, the core of the New Testament was already established. Were there times when people's motives were not particularly pure? Most likely. Yet throughout this process, the primary standard for truth wasn't the word of powerful overseers, and it wasn't anyone's desire to preserve personal power.

The standard ran something like this: *Testimony that could be connected to eyewitnesses of the risen Lord was treated as uniquely authoritative.* That's why *The Shepherd of Hermas*, the Gospel of Peter, and the Acts of Paul slipped into obscurity while the twenty-seven books in your New Testament stood the test of time. Over time, Christians came to the conclusion that these twenty-seven books could be reliably connected to apostolic eyewitnesses of the risen Lord Jesus. What's most significant about this process is that twenty or so of the New Testament texts were *never* questioned. The eyewitnesses of Jesus were always known to have been the sources behind these books.

So, what about the conspiracy theory that the early church's political struggles were what molded our Bible as well as our most essential beliefs? I think that we can consider that conspiracy *cracked*. What molded not only the beliefs but also the Bible of the first Christians was an intense desire to know the eyewitness truth about Jesus.

"The Bible didn't arrive by fax from heaven," one character in *The Da Vinci Code* claimed, and, in this, he was correct. The Bible *didn't* arrive on Earth in a single transmission, sent directly from some divine facsimile device, but the New Testament didn't come to us through Emperor Constantine or Athanasius of Alexandria either. The New Testament documents were inspired, written, and recognized as authoritative over several centuries, yet a definite standard governed the entire process, and this standard wasn't the word of a powerful emperor or bishop. It was a dogged determination to make certain that every authoritative text had its source in someone who witnessed the actual events.

HOW TO PREPARE FOR FUTURE CHRIST CONSPIRACIES

Suppose you hear about a book or a discovery that points to political intrigues in the early church. First, look carefully at *when* it happened. Chances are, the intrigues occurred long *after* the first century A.D. when Christians recognized certain crucial beliefs about Jesus. Even if the intrigues may have occurred in the first century, remember this: The central question is *not,* Were there some political actions and motivations in the early church? There *were.* The real question is, Does reliable evidence exist to suggest that the truths taught among the earliest Christians reflected eyewitness knowledge of Jesus? The answer to this question is a resounding *yes.*

WHO MISQUOTED JESUS?

WHAT'S the CONSPIRACY?

THE GOSPELS AND OTHER NEW TESTAMENT WRITINGS WERE COPIED so poorly and edited so thoroughly that the meanings of entire books have changed.

WHO SAYS SO?

- Bart Ehrman, *Misquoting Jesus: The Story Behind Who Changed the Bible and Why*

- Christopher Hitchens, *God Is Not Great*

- Dan Brown, *The Da Vinci Code*

Let's suppose that you wanted a second copy of this book. Actually, while we're thinking such happy thoughts, let's suppose that you needed a *couple thousand* more copies of *Conspiracies and the Cross*. Once you've placed that purchase on your credit card, you'll be ready to begin the next paragraph.

Now, as you glance through each of your two thousand copies of *Conspiracies and the Cross*, you're apt to notice an astounding pattern: *every copy of the book is pretty much identical.* That's right! The same words appear on the same pages in every copy of the book! Amazing, huh?

Well, truth be told, that fact probably *doesn't* amaze you for one simple reason: you were born after 1450. (I know, I know; some of you are scratching your heads at this point, wondering, "Wow! How did he do that? How could he ever have guessed that I was born after 1450?" Let's just say that I have excellent sources.)

So what happened in 1450?

Around that time, a German goldsmith and printer named Johannes Gutenberg invented the first printing press with movable metal type—an invention that permitted the mass duplication of books and documents. The downside of such a contraption was the potential for mass reproduction of typesetting *errors*. Take the case of the so-called "Wicked Bible," for example. In 1631, a typesetter accidentally—or maybe *not* so accidentally—omitted the word *not* from Exodus 20:14. As a result, hundreds of Bibles circulated in England with the Sixth Commandment reworded to read, "Thou shalt commit adultery." In

1716, another typesetter reversed two letters, and—according to *that* Bible—Jesus commanded a man whose sight He had recently restored, "Go and sin on more" (John 5:14). That was popular advice, I'm sure.

The *benefits* of Gutenberg's invention have far outweighed any problems, though. Prior to the invention of a printing press with movable metal type, scribes copied manuscripts by hand, and errors inevitably worked their way into manuscripts. Occasionally, prior to Gutenberg's era, woodworkers carved manuscript pages from wood, or metalsmiths forged printing-press plates in single pieces, but these sorts of plates wore out quickly, and one tiny error could render an entire plate permanently unusable.

After Johannes Gutenberg revolutionized the printing process, everything changed. Once Gutenberg's contraption caught on, it became possible to create hundreds—even thousands—of identical copies of any manuscript. Using his skills as a goldsmith, Gutenberg alloyed the right metals to form long-lasting type. Drawing from his skills as a printer, he mixed high-quality ink and built a press that workers could operate efficiently.

But wait...

If Gutenberg didn't invent the printing press until 1450, does that mean the words of the New Testament were copied *by hand* for more than a thousand years?

Yes, that's right.

For nearly a millennium and a half, scribes hand copied the New Testament manuscripts with only the light of lamps and candles and without the benefit of glasses or contact lenses.

Scribes reproduced the manuscripts of the New Testament generation after generation, using quills, pieces of papyrus or parchment, and ink that was a mixture of charcoal, water, and ground gum.

How, then, could the Christian Scriptures possibly have been copied correctly? Is it conceivable that errors have crept into the text over the years? Is it possible that the texts were even edited at some point to fit the beliefs and agendas of powerful church leaders?

That's precisely what some writers want you to think.

KNOW MORE

Around A.D. 200, Tertullian of Carthage claimed that the churches of Corinth, Philippi, Thessalonica, Ephesus, and Rome still possessed Paul's original letters.[1] In time, the documents became worn, so they were replaced and discarded.[2]

CONSPIRACY NUMBER FOUR

The Gospels and other New Testament writings were copied so poorly and edited so thoroughly that the meanings of entire books have changed.

The TRUTH BEHIND the CONSPIRACY

The overwhelming majority of supposed "changes" in manuscripts of the Greek New Testament are not even noticeable in any English translation. None of the changes that *are* noticeable affect any essential belief about God.

The COPYIST CONSPIRACY

One of the first best sellers to make such a case was Dan Brown's *The Da Vinci Code*: "The Bible," one protagonist explains, "was compiled and edited by men who possessed a political agenda."[3] Emperor Constantine, *The Da Vinci Code* contends, compelled his scribes to embellish the New Testament to make Jesus appear "godlike," but Dan Brown's claims are mingled with so much poor research that it was difficult to determine whether this portion was truth or fiction.

Then, in 2006, a book about textual criticism from a well-respected scholar became "one of the unlikeliest best sellers" of the year. The book was entitled *Misquoting Jesus: The Story Behind Who Changed the Bible and Why*. After Jon Stewart mentioned *Misquoting Jesus* on his show, this treatise shot to the No. 1 slot on Amazon.com—quite a feat for a book that's mostly concerned with an obscure field of research known as "textual criticism."

The author of this unexpected best seller was Bart D. Ehrman, chair of the Department of Religion at the University of North Carolina at Chapel Hill. As a youth and young adult, Ehrman had professed faith in Jesus Christ and attended evangelical churches. In the 1980s, Ehrman rejected his former faith. Now he describes himself as "a happy agnostic."[4]

So what's the problem with his little tome on textual criticism?

Mingled with a lot of excellent information about New Testament manuscripts, *Misquoting Jesus* is filled with jabs that seem to tear down the authenticity and authority of the texts that Ehrman seeks to reconstruct. Here's what the cover copy of *Misquoting Jesus* claims about how the New Testament was copied: "Many of our cherished biblical stories and widely held beliefs concerning the divinity of Jesus, the Trinity, and the divine origins of the Bible itself stem from both intentional and accidental alterations by scribes."[5]

Some of these changes are, Ehrman contends, so significant that they "affect the interpretation of an entire book of the New Testament."[6]

What's the proof for such claims? How can skeptics be so certain that the copying of the Scriptures was so thoroughly bungled? Here's what Ehrman has to say:

> Not only do we not have the originals [of the Greek manuscripts of the New Testament], we don't have the first copies of the originals.... What we have are copies made later—much later.... These copies differ from one another in so many places that we don't even know how many differences there are. Possibly it is easiest to put it in comparative terms: there are more differences among our manuscripts than there are words in the New Testament.... We have only error-ridden copies, and the vast majority of these are centuries removed from the originals and different from them...in thousands of ways.[7]

That's one reason why the Bible now seems to Ehrman to be "a human book from beginning to end."[8] Ehrman continues:

> If one wants to insist that God inspired the very words of scripture, what would be the point if we don't *have* the very words of scripture? In some places...we simply cannot be sure that we have reconstructed the original text accurately. It's a bit hard to know what the words of the Bible mean if we don't even know what the words are.... It would have been no more difficult for God to preserve the words of scripture than it would have been for him to inspire them in the first place... The fact that we don't have the words surely must show, I reasoned, that he did not preserve them for us. And if he didn't perform that miracle, there seemed to be no reason to think that he performed the earlier miracle of inspiring those words.[9]

Supposedly, Bart Ehrman makes this provocative case "for the first time."[10]

KNOW MORE

If you have a difficult time understanding *how* texts end up changed as they are copied, try this experiment: Gather about a dozen people together, and give each person a piece of paper and a writing utensil. Ask persons in the group to copy exactly what you say as you say it. Then, slowly read aloud a chapter or so from a Scripture that isn't particularly familiar, and don't stop—no matter what! Afterward, crumple all the copies and randomly rip small holes in them, discarding the smallest bits of paper. Mix the wadded pieces of paper in a box with some dry sand. (If you have a house cat and you want the results of this experiment to get *really* interesting, leave the box on your living room floor for a few days and see what happens.) A few weeks later, regather the same group of people. Give them the box and ask them—without using their Bibles—to reconstruct the original text. After they've created their reconstruction, read the text from your Bible and see how close the reconstruction runs to the original text.

After you've analyzed the text, consider these thoughts with the group: The New Testament manuscripts were copied by hand for more than one thousand years. Yet, when all manuscripts and fragments are considered together, there is more than 99 percent agreement among these texts. What's more, in the less than 1 percent of variation that remains, not one essential belief is affected. How did this exercise increase your appreciation for how well the New Testament has been preserved?

CLUES TO CRACK THE COPYIST CONSPIRACY

Ehrman's claims have certainly had an effect on how people view the Bible. After I wrote a response to Ehrman's *Misquoting Jesus*, dozens of e-mails glutted my inbox, testifying to the breadth of Ehrman's influence. Here's one of many examples:

> I was once a very dedicated Christian who felt called to seminary. In my first course, Church History, I read something that made me realize I did not know the history of the formation of the New Testament. I read books by [Bruce] Metzger and [F. F.] Bruce, but found myself very concerned about the transmission of the gospel in the first century....I came across Bart Ehrman's works, and these threw me over the edge.

"Once a very dedicated Christian...Ehrman's works...threw me over the edge." I'd like to claim that this is the only e-mail I received that described this progression.

It isn't.

There are many, many more, yet the primary fault is not Dr. Ehrman's; he is simply writing what he perceives to be the truth about the texts.

The fault lies with the fact that Christians have not been trained to offer reasonable responses to the claims of such critics. Ehrman's claims shake some Christians' faith because he introduces ideas about the Bible that no one has equipped these believers to consider.

Can Christians offer any reasonable response to Ehrman's claims? Has the New Testament really been copied so poorly and edited so thoroughly that the message of the original authors has been lost? Is it true that copyist errors created some of the doctrines that Christians hold dear? Was Jesus really misquoted?

Or is there, perhaps, more to the story than Ehrman and others have told us?

KNOW MORE

The Gospels as we know them today...have been edited by Church fathers, centuries after the original words were spoken, to conform to their subsequent vision of orthodoxy.[11]
—JAMES CAMERON, producer of *Titanic* (1997) and
The Jesus Family Tomb (2007)

CLUE NUMBER 1: The overwhelming majority of the textual variants are so insignificant that they aren't even noticeable in translations.

In the first place, *Misquoting Jesus* grossly overestimates the significance of the differences between the manuscripts. Ehrman's estimate of four hundred thousand variants among the New Testament manuscripts may be numerically correct, but what Ehrman doesn't clearly communicate to his readers is *the insignificance of the vast majority of these variants.*

The overwhelming majority of these four hundred thousand supposed variations stem from differences in spelling, word order, or the relationships between nouns and definite articles. In other words, a copyist simply switched a couple of letters, misheard a word, or skipped a line of text. Such variants are readily recognizable and, in most cases, utterly unnoticeable in translations!

Here's example of this sort of variant: A text literally translated from Greek might have a definite article—the equivalent of the English word *the*—before the noun. In some Greek manuscripts of John 3:3, for example, the verse—translated very literally—begins, "Answered, the Jesus and said to him." In other Greek manuscripts of the same verse, the Greek definite article (translated "the" in English) is missing, so the opening line of the verse reads, "Answered, Jesus and said to him." Since English never places *the* in front of a proper name, anyway, this difference isn't even observable in any English translation! Regardless of the presence or absence of the article, the clause comes into English as, "Jesus answered and said to him" or some similar wording. In the end, more than 99 percent of the four hundred thousand or so differences fall into this category of variants that can't even be seen in translations![12]

Even when variants *are* noticeable in translations, they still don't affect any essential truth that's believed about Jesus. To be sure, a few variants might reorient the way that Christians perceive the nuances of a particular text. For example, early in the Gospel according to Mark, Jesus is described as healing a man with a skin disease. In some Greek manuscripts, here's how the incident is described: "Feeling compassion and stretching out His hand, he touched him and said, 'I want to.' Immediately, the skin disease fled from the man, and he was cleansed" (Mark 1:41–42). In a few manuscripts, though, the opening words of the text could be translated, "Becoming angry and stretching out His hand."

Could this difference change some of the questions that a Christian explores as he or she reads this text? Perhaps.

Yet with or without "becoming angry" in Mark 1:41, the Gospel according to Mark depicts Jesus as a passionate prophet,[13] rapidly crisscrossing Galilee and Judea as He moves toward His impending encounter with a Roman cross. By the third chapter, Jesus has already upset so many religious leaders that they're making plans to murder Him (Mark 3:6). He becomes annoyed when people don't trust Him, and so, perhaps, as He sees the unbelief around Him or as He notices the skin-diseased man's defiance of the Law of Moses, Jesus *was* angry (3:5; 9:23). At the same time, Mark makes it clear that Jesus constantly feels compassion for downtrodden people (6:34; 8:2; 9:22–23). As such, either reading of the text would fit Mark's presentation of Jesus. Nothing about this textual variant changes or challenges the believer's understanding of Jesus Christ.

The same can be said about most other supposed changes. John 1:18, for example, may have originally described Jesus as "the one and only Son" or "only begotten Son." Or the text could have read "the one and only God" or "only begotten God"—the manuscript witnesses to these two readings are, from my perspective, evenly divided. Here's what is most important, though: *both wordings affirm truths that are clearly expressed throughout John's Gospel.*

In support of "one and only God," John 20:28 unambiguously identifies Jesus as God, and the opening verses of John's Gospel also imply that Jesus was uniquely divine.[14] In support of "one and only Son," the familiar words of John 3:16 already refer to Jesus as "the only begotten Son" or "the one and only Son." As such, *both* possible readings of John 1:18 fit the larger context of the Gospel according to John. Even though authentic differences *do* exist among the manuscripts of John's Gospel, neither possibility contradicts anything in this Gospel or in the remainder of the New Testament. If some scribe *did* change "one and only Son" to "one and only God" or vice versa, the scribe simply emphasized a truth that was already present in John's Gospel.

Another example of this type of change can be found in the first letter of John. Here's an English translation of what you would find in 1 John 5:7–8 in *Textus Receptus*, a Greek New Testament created by a scholar named Erasmus in the 1500s:

> For there are three that bear witness in heaven: the Father, the Word, and the Holy Spirit; and these three are one. And there are three that bear witness on earth: the Spirit, the water, and the blood; and these three agree as one.

The problem is that the middle portion of this text appears in a Greek manuscript for the *first time* in the *early 1500s*, and there's every reason to think that it was a forged addition even in that text![15] When Erasmus put together the *Textus Receptus* in the 1500s, he himself questioned the authenticity of the middle clause.

In the overwhelming majority of Greek manuscripts, 1 John 5:7–8 reads more like this: "For there are three that testify: the Spirit, the water, and the blood; and these three are one." Bart Ehrman—along with every other competent biblical scholar who has looked at this text in the past hundred years—believes that someone expanded this text more than a thousand years after John's letter was written.[16] That's why the only translations that have included the longer version of these verses are renderings that are somehow bound to the *Textus Receptus*. By the time this phrase was added to John's first letter, Christians had embraced the doctrine of the Trinity for more than a millennium. Yet based largely on the variants in verses such as this one, the cover copy of *Misquoting Jesus* promotes the idea that "widely held beliefs concerning...the Trinity...stem from both intentional and accidental alterations by scribes"—a claim that the available evidences simply cannot substantiate. Despite what the cover of *Misquoting Jesus* suggests, the Christian doctrine of the Trinity has never depended on the longer version of 1 John 5:7–8. Matthew 28:19–20 and other New Testament texts state the concept of one God ("in the *name*," singular) expressed in three persons ("of the Father and of the Son and of the Holy Spirit") just as clearly as these words that some well-intended scribe added to 1 John.

Here's what I find as I carefully examine the differences between the ancient New Testament manuscripts: *no* textual variant affects any central element of the Christian faith, yet Dr. Ehrman continues to declare in *Misquoting Jesus* and in radio and television interviews, "There are lots of significant changes"[17]—a claim that the manuscript evidence simply does not support.

KNOW MORE

As textual critics examined the New Testament texts, they noticed certain similarities that allowed them to group the manuscripts into three "families." Each family represents a certain pattern of preservation and changes in the New Testament manuscripts. By comparing the families, textual critics are often able to determine *when* and *where* certain changes occurred:

1. The *Western* family of texts emerged and circulated primarily in Italy, Gaul (modern France), and North Africa. Some important Western witnesses are the papyri P48 and P38, as well as Codex Bezae (D). Copyists of the Western texts seem to have paraphrased frequently.

2. Texts from the *Alexandrian* family came from the area around Alexandria, Egypt. Because of the dryness of this area, many of the most ancient and most important texts—including P66, P75, Codex Sinaiticus, and Codex Vaticanus—come from the Alexandrian family.

3. The *Byzantine* family was the dominant text in the eastern part of the Roman Empire. Most Greek manuscripts of the New Testament are Byzantine texts, so the Byzantine text is also known as the Majority Text. Most scholars consider Byzantine manuscripts to be later and less reliable than Alexandrian manuscripts. When Erasmus collated the *Textus Receptus*, from which the King James Version was translated, the only texts available to him were Byzantine manuscripts.

KNOW MORE

critical scholar: term for a researcher who has been trained in disciplines such as:

textual criticism—comparison of biblical manuscripts with the goal of determining the original wording of biblical text

form criticism—analysis of the rhetorical structure of biblical texts

source criticism—analysis of possible sources that may have influenced the formation of biblical texts

redaction criticism—analysis of the ways in which biblical authors merged—or "redacted"—various sources

"Critical" and "criticism" refer to close analysis of the text, not to a negative approach to Scripture. Unfortunately, some scholars have used the term *critical scholar* to refer to scholars who approach Scripture with an attitude of suspicion, assuming some measure of falsehood in the text. An example of this would be this false claim from one Jesus Seminar fellow: "Critical scholars no longer think that any of these texts were written by authors who knew any of the disciples, or 'apostles' of Jesus....No critical scholar thinks about a historical Matthew when referring to the Gospel of Matthew or when using the name *Matthew*."[18] In truth, some of the most skilled critical scholars in the world identify the apostle Matthew as the author of the Gospel that bears his name.[19]

CLUE NUMBER 2: The science of textual criticism can almost always recover the original reading of a text.

The science of textual criticism is not—despite the way the name strikes our ears—concerned with criticizing the biblical text. In this context, *criticism* means "analysis" or "close investigation." The task of the textual critic is to look closely at copies of ancient documents and to determine which copy is closest to the original document.

Here's what textual criticism assumes: *it's impossible for all the copyists to have made the same mistake at the same time.* In other words, since changes creep into the manuscripts at different times and in different places, it is possible to compare several manuscripts to discover *when* and *where* the error occurred. The textual critic can then, in most cases, figure out the original wording of the text.

Let's look at a simple example of this process. In most Greek manuscripts of the Gospel of John, chapter 1, verse 6, reads something like this: "There was a man, having been sent from God, whose name was John." However, in a manuscript known as Codex Bezae or simply as "D," the text reads, "There was a man, having been sent from the Lord, whose name was John."

Like most differences between manuscripts, this variant doesn't affect the meaning of the text. Still, it's important for scholars and translators to determine which words appeared in the original text of the Gospel of John. How do they know which reading is closest to the original? Let's look at the evidence together and see what we find!

Codex Bezae includes not only Greek text but also Latin. Together, the style of writing in Codex Bezae, the use of vellum instead of papyrus, and the presence of Greek *and* Latin in the text suggest that this manuscript—the one that reads "from *the Lord*"—was copied around A.D. 500. Codex Bezae also seems to have originated in Western Europe.

The two primary manuscripts that agree on the other reading—"sent from *God*" instead of "sent from *the Lord*"—are known as Codex Sinaiticus and P66. Codex Sinaiticus was copied around A.D. 330. P66 probably dates from the late second century A.D., less than a century from the time when most scholars believe the Gospel of John was originally written! Codex Sinaiticus and P66 seem to have been copied in two different areas of Egypt.

From what you've learned in the previous paragraphs, which words do you think John originally wrote? "Sent from *God*" or "sent from *the Lord*"?

Given the agreement between Codex Sinaiticus and P66—manuscripts that were copied in two different places more than a century apart—and the fact that these two codices are centuries older than Codex Bezae, nearly every textual critic has concluded that John 1:6 originally read "sent from God." At some point, probably somewhere in Europe in the fifth century, a tired or careless scribe wrote "Lord" (Greek, *kyriou*) when he should have written "God" (Greek, *theou*).

I must admit to you that many textual issues are more complicated than the scenario I've presented here. Still, there are certain principles that, with rare exceptions, allow textual critics to determine the original form of the text. Bart Ehrman is fully aware of this fact. At one point in *Misquoting Jesus*, Ehrman even acknowledges, "I continue to think that even if we cannot be 100 percent certain about what we can attain to...that it is at least possible to get back to the *oldest* and *earliest* stage of the manuscript tradition for each of the books of the New Testament."[20]

Yet it seems that Ehrman wants—in the words of one reviewer—"to have his text-critical cake and eat it, too."[21] Despite admitting that it is possible to recover the "*oldest* and *earliest*" manuscript traditions, Ehrman finds space before the closing paragraphs of *Misquoting Jesus* to repeat his charge that "given the circumstance that [God] didn't preserve the words, the conclusion seemed inescapable to me that he hadn't gone to the trouble of inspiring them."[22]

KNOW MORE

uncial (from Latin term for the width of a printed character that occupies one-twelfth of a line): style of writing popular from the third until the eighth century A.D. Many important New Testament manuscripts, including Codex Sinaiticus and Codex Vaticanus, were written in uncial letters.

Codices of New Testament manuscripts are often named to connect them to their place of discovery (Codex Sinaiticus was discovered near Mt. Sinai) or to their source (Codex Bezae was once the property of Theodore Beza). These codices may also be given a letter designation. Codex Bezae, for example, is also known as "D."

Papyrus codices are usually designated with a "P" followed by a number, such as P52 or P66. Sometimes other letters are added to show where a piece of papyrus came from. For example, POxy refers to papyrus fragments discovered near Oxyrhynchus in Egypt.

CLUE NUMBER 3: **Early Christians were deeply concerned with preserving the original text of the New Testament.**

It is important to remember that the copyists were more concerned with preserving the words of Scripture than with promoting their own theological agendas. Despite his reservations about the earliest Christian scribes, Dr. Ehrman acknowledges this fact in *Misquoting Jesus*:

It is probably safe to say that the copying of early Christian texts was by and large a "conservative" process. The scribes...were intent on "conserving" the textual tradition they were passing on. Their ultimate concern was not to modify the tradition, but to preserve it for themselves and for those who would follow them. Most scribes, no doubt, tried to do a faithful job in making sure that the text they reproduced was the same text they inherited.[23]

In other words, early Christians wanted future generations to find the same truth in the New Testament documents that the first generations of believers had experienced, so their intent was to hand on to their successors the same text that they received.

This is evident in a complaint from a third-century church leader named Origen of Alexandria: "The differences between the manuscripts have become great," he fumed, "either through the negligence of some copyists or through the perverse audacity of others; they either neglect to check over what they have transcribed, or, in the process of checking, they make additions or deletions as they please."[24] Even though variants constituted less than a percent of Origen's copies of the Gospels, Origen of Alexandria referred to the differences that he saw as "great." Why? He earnestly desired to see the oldest readings preserved. As a result, even small changes in the text troubled him.

Most copyists seem to have regarded the text with the same reverence as Origen. When one copyist changed the wording of a text in a fourth-century manuscript known as Codex Vaticanus, a later copyist rewrote the original word and added this marginal note: "Fool and knave! Leave the old reading, don't change it!"[25] Certainly, copyists did alter the text from time to time, but the consistency of the available manuscripts of the New Testament demonstrates that these alterations were *exceptions*, not the rule.

KNOW MORE

Here are basic principles that most textual critics follow as they work to determine which manuscript preserves the original reading:

1. Compare the evidences *outside* and *around* the manuscript, such as (a) which reading is *oldest*, (b) which reading is supported by texts that were separated by the *farthest distance*, and (c) to which *textual family* the manuscript belongs.

2. Search *inside* the manuscript for which reading is more probable based on (a) what a copyist would be most likely to change, (b) which possible reading is shortest, (c) which reading might have been an attempt to harmonize one

text with another, and (d) what difficult words a copyist might have replaced with simpler ones.

3. Look at *other writings* by the same original author to see which reading is most similar to the author's other writings.

QUICK GUIDE

TOP TEN VERSES THAT WERE NOT ORIGINALLY IN THE NEW TESTAMENT... AND WHY NONE OF THESE CHANGES ARE ULTIMATELY SIGNIFICANT

At the end of the paperback edition of *Misquoting Jesus*, Bart Ehrman provides a list of the "Top Ten Verses That Were Not Originally in the New Testament." Let's take a close look at each one to see whether the changes are actually significant.

What's missing?	What do the critics claim?	Does it change anything that Christians believe about Jesus?
First John 5:7: "For there are three that bear witness in heaven: the Father, the Word, and the Holy Spirit; and these three are one."	"It is the only passage in the entire Bible that explicitly delineates the doctrine of the Trinity."[26]	No. In fact, the doctrine of the Trinity is also explicitly delineated in Matthew 28:19–20, where Christians are commanded to baptize in the "name" (singular) of the Father, Son, and Spirit.
John 8:7: "Let the one who is without sin cast the first stone." John 8:11: "Go and sin no more."	"Most scholars think that [John 7:53—8:11] was probably a well-known story, circulating in the oral tradition about Jesus, which at some point was added in the margin of a manuscript. From there, some scribe or another thought that the marginal note was meant to be part of the text."[27]	No vital beliefs about Jesus or about Scripture appear in this text. If, as even Ehrman admits, the story was part of an early oral tradition, it is very possible that the story was authentic, even if it didn't appear in the earliest manuscripts of John's Gospel.

What's missing?	What do the critics claim?	Does it change anything that Christians believe about Jesus?
Luke 22:44: "His sweat became like drops of blood."	"Rather than entering his passion with fear and trembling, in anguish over his coming fate, the Jesus of Luke goes to his death calm and in control.... It is clear that Luke does not share Mark's understanding that Jesus was in anguish, bordering on despair."[28]	No. Simply because Luke emphasized one aspect of Jesus's death—the willing submission of a righteous man to the cross—doesn't mean that he understood the death of Jesus differently. It simply means that he emphasized an aspect that Mark did not.
Luke 22:20: "This cup, poured out for you, is the New Covenant, in my blood."	"Luke...has a different understanding of the way in which Jesus' death leads to salvation than does Mark (and Paul, and other early Christian writers).... Jesus' death is...extremely important for Luke—but not as an atonement. Instead, Jesus' death is what makes people realize their guilt before God."[29]	No. In the first place, this text appears in the writings of Paul (1 Corinthians 11:23–25; see also Matthew 26:27–28; Mark 14:22–25). So, it's not a case of "misquoting Jesus." Furthermore, simply because Luke focused on one aspect of the death of Jesus does not imply that he didn't understand Jesus's death as an atonement too. Different emphases do not amount to contradictory understandings of the same event.

What's missing?	What do the critics claim?	Does it change anything that Christians believe about Jesus?
Mark 16:17–18: "In my name, they will cast out demons and speak with new tongues. They will take snakes in their hands; they will drink poison, and it will not harm them."	"Scribes thought the ending [of Mark's Gospel] was too abrupt....To resolve the problem, scribes added an ending [Mark 16:9–20]."[30]	No. It's true that the original version of the Gospel according to Mark may have ended at Mark 16:8; however, the resurrection of Jesus and His subsequent appearances to His disciples are still implied throughout Mark's Gospel (Mark 9:9; 14:28). The references to new tongues, snakes, and poison—whatever their meaning may be—appear in other biblical texts, too (Psalm 69:21, 29; Isaiah 11:8; Luke 10:19; Acts 2:4). In truth, the added verses provide a fifth witness, beyond the four Gospels, to the resurrection of Jesus.[31]
John 5:4: "Whoever was the first to step in, when the waters were disturbed, was healed."	"In our oldest and best manuscripts there is no explanation for why this man would want to enter the pool...but the oral tradition supplied the lack."[32]	No vital beliefs about Jesus are contained in this passage. Similar to John 7:53–8:11, this addition could represent an authentic oral tradition—in this case, an explanation of the people's perceptions of what happened at the Pool of Bethzatha.

What's missing?	What do the critics claim?	Does it change anything that Christians believe about Jesus?
Luke 24:12: "Peter...saw the linen clothes by themselves." Luke 24:51: "He was taken up into the heavens."	"It supports so well the...position that Jesus...had a real, physical body.... It stresses the physicality of Jesus' departure... It may be that a scribe involved in these controversies modified his text in order to stress the point."[33]	No, the physicality of Jesus's resurrection is already stressed elsewhere in Luke's Gospel. Jesus broke bread and ate fish after His resurrection— clearly physical actions (Luke 24:30, 42).

CRACKING THE COPYIST CONSPIRACY

As I examine *Misquoting Jesus,* I find nothing that measures up to the promotional copy. What I find is a great deal of discussion about a handful of textual variants, none of which ultimately change any essential belief that's presented in the New Testament. What's more, despite the sensational title of *Misquoting Jesus,* I find only a half-dozen times when Jesus *might* have been misquoted, and most of these supposed changes simply echo statements that are found elsewhere in Scripture.

And what about Dan Brown's contention that Constantine commanded the editing and embellishment of the Gospels to make Jesus appear "godlike"?[34] Such claims are clearly false. Emperor Constantine *did,* in A.D. 330, finance the copying and binding of fifty copies of the Christian Scriptures. This was not, however, "a new Bible," nor did it omit or embellish any aspect of the Gospels; Constantine's project was little more than a compilation of scriptures that Christians were already using.[35] How can we be certain of this fact? If such editing had occurred, Gospel manuscripts copied *before* A.D. 330 ought to differ from the manuscripts copied *after* this time. Yet when textual critics compare New Testament manuscripts that were copied *before* Constantine's fifty Bibles with manuscripts copied *after* the time of Constantine, there are no significant differences.

Have the New Testament manuscripts changed over the centuries? Without a doubt! But are the changes in the manuscripts "highly significant"?[36] Do any of them "affect the interpretation of an entire book of the New Testament," as Ehrman and others claim? Not that I can tell.

HOW TO PREPARE FOR FUTURE CHRIST CONSPIRACIES

Purchase a Bible that includes extensive textual notes. Such a Bible will have footnotes that say, for example, "The oldest manuscripts omit this verse," or "Other Greek manuscripts include this reading." As you read the New Testament, notice that *no essential truth in Scripture depends on a disputed verse.* In every case in which two or more options remain possible in the various manuscripts, every possible option simply reinforces truths that are already clearly present in the writings of that particular author and in the New Testament as a whole. There is no point at which any of the possible options would require readers to rethink an essential belief about Jesus or to doubt the historical integrity of the New Testament.

Conspiracy Number Five

GOSPEL TRUTH
OR GOSPEL FICTION?

WHAT'S the CONSPIRACY?

THE ACTS AND SAYINGS IN THE NEW TESTAMENT GOSPELS DO NOT necessarily represent actual, historical happenings. Decades after the death of Jesus, believers fabricated these words and deeds to fit the needs of their communities.

WHO SAYS SO?

- The Jesus Seminar

- John Dominic Crossan, *The Historical Jesus*

- Burton Mack, *Who Wrote the New Testament? The Making of the Christian Myth*

Warning! If you still believe in Santa Claus, please skip this introduction. It could ruin your next Christmas celebration.

"Daddy, is Santa Claus real or not?"

I should have anticipated my daughter's question. As Christmas approached, Hannah's fellow first-graders chattered constantly about Santa Claus, but our family didn't talk about the red-suited saint. I'd like to claim that the primary reason I ignored Santa had to do with some high and noble ethic, perhaps even something rooted in a profound theological truth or two. Truth be told, my main motive for refusing to refer to Santa as the great gift giver had little to do with ethics or theology. The reason that I wrote *my* name on the gift tags was because, if I'm going to spend that much money on presents for my child, I want her to know that *I* wrote the check, not Mrs. Claus.

That is probably why my child was a bit skeptical when her friends claimed that a chubby old coot would slide down our chimney on Christmas Eve and drop some presents beneath the tree. Being a bit historically inclined, I decided to provide more of an answer than Hannah probably needed.

"Is Santa Claus real?" I mused. "Well, sort of. Long ago, a man named Nicholas of Myra was a pastor in the country that's now called Turkey." I told Hannah the true story of a benevolent bishop known as Saint Nicholas—the

87

story of a kindly pastor who provided dowries for girls whose poverty-stricken families couldn't afford to find husbands for their daughters. When I finished the tale, Hannah's eyes looked a little glazed, but she seemed to have gotten the message.

"So where is Saint Nicholas now?" she asked.

"Well, he's in heaven, I suppose. He died in the fourth century. A few years before he died, the Roman emperor locked him up in a dungeon. Nicholas would probably have been killed because of his faith in Jesus, but the emperor died before Nicholas was executed."[1]

"OK, that makes sense." Hannah seemed satisfied as she skipped into the next room.

And me?

I felt pretty proud of myself, if you want to know the truth. Not only had I answered Hannah's question, but I had also provided a lesson in generosity and a lesson in history too! What amazing wisdom God had provided to my daughter through me—or so I thought until the next afternoon.

In case you weren't already aware of this fact, first-graders can really be blabbermouths sometimes. I mean, once they learn something new, they think they need to tell *everyone* about it, even when what they have learned can cause a lot of problems.

That explains why, on the day following my conversation with my daughter, several classmates ran crying to the teacher because Hannah's daddy, who knew *everything* about these sorts of facts, according to Hannah, had told Hannah that Santa Claus had been dead for more than a thousand years.

Not only was Santa Claus dead, but also an evil emperor had *tortured* him in a *dungeon*.

There are some first-graders who get way too worked up over Santa Claus, let me tell you. What's worse is that when first-graders get worked up, their parents and teachers get worked up too. Somehow, I had lived several years under the peaceful delusion that once you graduated from high school, you couldn't get into trouble at school anymore.

I was wrong.

Frankly, I don't think I'd gotten into that much trouble at school since the fourth grade when I dropped a headless snake down the back of a girl's jumper.[2] I must confess something, though: despite the difficulties that resulted from Hannah's lack of tact, I was glad that she didn't back down. Once she discovered that the familiar, red-suited Santa Claus was a legend, she wasn't afraid to say so.

Sadly, some people feel the same way about Jesus.

They are fairly certain that Jesus, like Santa Claus, may have been real, but so much folklore has emerged about Him that it's now nearly impossible to unearth the truth about Him.

What if they're right?

I mean, haven't *you* ever wondered if Jesus might fit in the same category as Santa Claus? Even if a popular prophet named Jesus *did* once walk the roads of Galilee, what if so many legends have arisen about Him that His true identity has been hidden? What if the Jesus that Christians worship today is more fiction than fact? What if the miraculous elements of Jesus's life—virgin conception, exorcisms, healings, and His resurrection from the dead—are legendary additions to the real story, just like Rudolph and the red suit, the chimney and the sleigh?

THE GOSPEL FICTION CONSPIRACY

This much is true: The earliest surviving records about Jesus were penned a couple of decades after the death of Jesus, and the Gospels didn't begin to circulate until the A.D. 60s or 70s. So, is it possible that during this time Gospel truth turned into legend before the Gospels were even written?

Several popular scholars think so.

Here's how John Dominic Crossan, a prominent fellow from the Jesus Seminar, has described what he sees when he reads the Gospel according to Matthew, Mark, Luke, and John: "[The Gospel writers] are unnervingly free about...change, correction, or creation in their own individual accounts."[3] According to another fellow from the Jesus Seminar, the earliest believers didn't even care if they preserved eyewitness truth about Jesus. Different groups of believers freely spun specious stories about Jesus to fit their own circumstances:

> The first followers of Jesus were not interested in preserving accurate memories of the historical person....Each group created Jesus...in the image appropriate for the founder of the school it had become or wanted to become.[4]

If these scholars are correct, the stories that you find between the covers of your New Testament may never have been intended to represent historical truth in the first place. At best, they were intended to communicate spiritual truths through a series of fictive fantasies, and *none* of these texts came from eyewitness testimony.

What was the content of Jesus's original message? And who did His earliest hearers understand Him to be? According to many scholars of the more skeptical sort, Jesus was a powerful human teacher. Others point to Jesus as an apocalyptic prophet who proclaimed the impending end of the world. There is one point on which nearly all of them agree, though: the stories of Jesus emerged over many years, and the primary sources behind the stories that we possess today were the circumstances of certain Christian communities, *not* actual events from the life of the historical character known as Jesus. "Stories were changed with what would strike us today as reckless abandon," one such critic claims. "They were modified, amplified, and embellished. And sometimes they were made up."[5] Through this process of modification and fabrication, early believers moved Jesus Christ from man to legend. At the pinnacle of this process, the human rabbi known as Jesus of Nazareth was, in the words of Elaine Pagels, "promoted" to the level of God.[6]

If these writers happen to be right, Jesus was, at best, a historical teacher or prophet around whom later believers wove legends that led Christians to view Him as divine.[7] If this supposition is true, the stories of Jesus belong in the same category as the legends of a red-nosed reindeer, Buddha's enlightenment beneath the bo tree, and George Washington's honesty beside the stump of his father's cherry tree. It's a tale that tells us more about our own hopes and desires than about any historical events that actually happened.

Hmm.

Documents originally written as novels that church leaders twisted into "Gospel truth"?

Billions of people throughout history deceived into thinking Jesus was more than human, when, in fact, He was mortal man or fantastic fiction?

The truth about Jesus lost or suppressed nearly two thousand years ago, only to be recognized anew in the past couple of centuries?

Sounds like another Christ conspiracy to me.

So is it possible to respond reasonably to such claims as these? I think so. Even if you don't quite agree with my assessment, take a look with me at the proofs that have been proposed to support each claim. Then, let's compare these proposals with historical data and see what we find!

> We have been betrayed by the Bible. In the half-century just ending, there is belated recognition that biblically based Christianity has espoused causes that no thinking or caring person is any longer willing to endorse.... Jesus needs a demotion.[8]
> —Robert Funk, founder of the Jesus Seminar (2000)

QUICK GUIDE

NEW TESTAMENT GOSPELS

Document	Source	Approximate Date of Composition
Gospel according to Mark	John Mark, translator for Simon Peter, based on his recollections of Peter's messages	A.D. 65–70
Gospel according to Matthew	Matthew, eyewitness of Jesus's life; perhaps written first in Aramaic and translated later into Greek	A.D. 65–85
Gospel according to Luke	Luke, physician of the apostle Paul, based on his investigation of eyewitness testimonies (Luke 1:1–3)	A.D. 65–90
Gospel according to John	John, follower of Jesus	A.D. 65–95

NOTHING NEW UNDER THE SUN

In the first place, it's important to be aware that *none of these proofs or proposals are new.* The American founding father Thomas Jefferson treated Jesus as a wise teacher, but he rejected anything that smacked of the supernatural as fiction. He referred to the teachings of Jesus in the New Testament Gospels as "diamonds in dunghills." The "dunghills" were, from the perspective of this founding father, the miracles attributed to Jesus. Thomas Jefferson even created his own version of the Gospels, stripping out every supernatural element![9] In the 1830s, the work of German theologian David Friedrich Strauss revolutionized New Testament studies by suggesting that the miraculous events in the New Testament didn't actually occur; they were fictional parables told to make symbolic points about spiritual living.[10] Theologically liberal scholars—including Rudolf Bultmann—throughout the nineteenth and twentieth centuries followed Strauss's lead in one way or another. According to Bultmann, the earliest Christians regarded Jesus as "a mythological figure."[11]

Still, the real question isn't whether these proposals are old or new. The crucial question is, where's the proof? What evidence do the skeptics offer to defend their campaign to consign the New Testament to the fiction section of your local library? In most cases, it comes down to a *matter of time.*

CONSPIRACY NUMBER FIVE

With few exceptions, the acts and sayings in the New Testament Gospels do not represent actual, historical happenings. Decades after the death of Jesus, believers fabricated words and deeds—including the story of the Resurrection—to fit the needs of their communities.

The TRUTH BEHIND the CONSPIRACY

In the decades between the time that Jesus walked the earth and the writing of the New Testament, the truth about Jesus was reliably preserved in oral traditions.

CLUES TO CRACK THE GOSPEL FICTION CONSPIRACY

Twenty years passed between the time when Jesus would have taught along the shores of Lake Galilee and the time when the apostle Paul penned the first New Testament documents. Another fifteen or more years passed before Matthew, Mark, Luke, and John penned the Gospels that bear their names. The skeptics claim that in the decades between the time of Jesus and the earliest written records about His life, any historical truth about Jesus that *may* have existed was distorted, embellished, and exaggerated. Here's how one critic describes the process:

> [The New Testament Gospels] were written thirty-five to sixty-five years after Jesus' death…not by people who were eyewitnesses, but by people living later.…Where did these people get their information from?…After the days of Jesus, people started telling stories about him in order to convert others to the faith.[12]…The Gospels of the New Testament contain…stories that may convey truths, at least in the minds of those who told them, but that are not historically accurate.[13] Stories based on eyewitness accounts are not necessarily reliable, and the same is true a hundredfold for accounts that—even if stemming from reports of eyewitnesses—have been in oral circulation long after the fact.[14]

Film producer James Cameron has even leaped onto this bandwagon, declaring, "There is no historical evidence that any of the authors [of the New Testament Gospels], if in fact they are individuals, actually heard the words of Jesus from his own lips."[15] (Of course, when someone produces a blockbuster such as *Titanic*, that automatically makes him an expert on historical records from the first century A.D.)

So what about the matter of time? Does the gap between the earthly history of Jesus and the written stories about Him really make it reasonable to regard the Gospels as fiction? Is the history found in the Gospels "a myth" or "a consensus hallucination," as James Cameron claims? Or is it possible that the New Testament Gospels have preserved more truth than the skeptics want to admit?

In the first place, it's crucial to be aware that even though written records about Jesus haven't *survived* from the A.D. 30s and 40s, it's still possible that written records existed. When the writers of the New Testament Gospels wrote about Jesus, they may have used such records.[16] Remember what Luke wrote in the mid to late first century? *"Many have put their hands to arrange a guided presentation about the deeds that have been fully carried out among us"* (Luke 1:1–2, emphasis added). This preamble suggests that Luke's Gospel may have incorporated reliable records about Jesus's life that have since been lost.

Still, even if the "many" testimonies that Luke described were merely the recollections of Mark, Matthew, Paul, and perhaps John, there is every reason to believe that the stories of Jesus recorded in the Gospels represent eyewitness testimony about the risen Lord.

 **Oral histories—the matter of time doesn't matter nearly as much as the critics claim.**

Have you ever played the game known as "Telephone"? The rules are simple: Everybody sits in a circle, and the leader whispers a sentence to one participant. That player whispers the sentence to the next player and so on until the sentence makes it all the way around the circle. Then, the final person tells the group what he or she heard, which typically isn't even close to how the original sentence sounded.

Personally, I think Telephone is a stupid game. In another context, I've explored some creative alternatives for playing this game:

> I last remember playing this game in the fourth grade when my teacher was trying to occupy an unruly class on a rainy day. I did not want to play Telephone; I wanted to do something constructive, such as painting my ruler like a lightsaber and smacking fellow students with it—a pastime for which Mrs. Redwing did not share my passion. So, each time a sentence reached me, I changed it completely. The student beside me might say, "The sky is dark and gray today"—but what I would whisper to the next student was something like, "Mrs. Redwing's hair looks like a mangy Wookiee's armpit." For some reason, I found

this to be considerably more amusing than my teacher did; I think she was just jealous because *her* ruler wasn't painted like a lightsaber.[17]

Despite my distaste for the game, Telephone does make one truth crystal clear: Messages can change considerably as they move from one person to another. Words can be misheard, misunderstood, or misconstrued. As they pass to more persons, the message becomes more mangled until, in some cases, the original message is irrecoverable.

Is that perhaps what happened in the decades between the death of Jesus and the earliest surviving documents about Jesus? What if, as the message of Jesus spread across the Roman Empire, His original message became radically altered? What if the events of His life were exaggerated for dramatic effect? What if the teachings and narratives found in the Gospels are simply the befuddled result of these embellishments?

That's precisely what some scholars have suggested.

After all, if a circle of schoolchildren can't maintain a single sentence in the center of a classroom on a rainy day, how could thousands of people have accurately preserved the story of Jesus across the vast expanse known as the Roman Empire? According to Jesus Seminar fellow John Dominic Crossan, "The oral memory of his first audiences could have retained, at best, only the striking image, the startling analogy, the forceful conjunction, and, for example, the plot summary of a parable that might have taken an hour or more to tell and perform."[18] Crossan goes so far as to claim that the first followers of Jesus misremembered the key events of their Master's life as they proclaimed His message throughout the Roman Empire.[19] "Much of the lore recorded in the gospels," one founding fellow of the Jesus Seminar has declared, "is wrapped in memories that have been edited, deleted, augmented, and combined many times over many years."[20]

If this is true, any trust that you might place in the biblical personage known as "Jesus Christ" is rooted in the misconstrued memories of His first followers. All that may remain of His authentic teachings are occasional striking images, scattered in disconnected fragments throughout a handful of ancient documents. All that remains of Jesus Himself is wishful thinking about what sort of person this mortal rabbi might have been.

So, what *did* persist from the original teachings of Jesus when the Gospels and epistles were written? Is it possible that some substantive truth about Jesus somehow survived? And if certain truths about Jesus *did* persist beyond the publication of the first Gospels, where precisely have the critics gone wrong?

Here's the primary problem that I find in the critics' claims: *they forget what people in oral cultures could remember.*

You and I live in a *written culture.* That is to say that if we need to remember a certain truth or task, we write it down. High levels of literacy and easy access to writing materials turn all sorts of items—napkins and notepads, tabletops and palms, maybe even the margins of this book—into targets for our thoughts. The results of this cultural shift go beyond the marked-up margins of this book, however. It has resulted in what one historian has called "the dethronement of memory."[21] To recall crucial truths, we no longer rely primarily on our capacity to remember; we depend on written words supplemented by pictures.

In the first century A.D., that wasn't the case at all. More than three-fourths of the population probably could not read. Even among people who *could* read, writing was typically a task reserved for professional scribes.[22] So, their culture remained an *oral culture*—a culture where persons received and passed on truths in oral form. Teachers used rhythm, rhyme, repetition, and alliteration to imprint instructions on their students' minds, telling and retelling truths until the vital content could be recalled at a moment's notice. When especially significant events occurred, communities rapidly preserved the essential content in pithy oral histories.[23]

Whenever discussions of teaching methods emerged among the Jewish rabbis, it is clear how highly they valued the capacity to pass on oral traditions and histories. Here's how one first-century Jewish author described the process: "Instruction proceeds in a leisurely manner; he lingers over it and spins it out with repetitions, thus permanently imprinting the thoughts in the souls of the hearers."[24] A rabbi named Perida was said to have repeated every teaching four hundred times. If a pupil still failed to comprehend the teaching or to remember the essential content, Rabbi Perida reiterated the teaching *another* four hundred times.[25] As a Jewish teacher with a band of disciples, Jesus would have been expected to train His followers to preserve His teachings.

In such a context, John Dominic Crossan's claim about the collective recollections of early Christians—"the oral memory of his first audiences could have retained, at best, only the striking image, the startling analogy, the forceful conjunction...the plot summary of a parable"—is simply false. Jesus was a first-century Jewish teacher; as such, His first followers would have learned and preserved His teachings with a high degree of accuracy.

> **KNOW MORE**
>
> At the end of the first century A.D., some Christian leaders
> still relied on oral accounts of Jesus's life alongside the
> written Gospels and apostolic epistles. Papias of Hierapolis
> put it this way: "If anyone who had served the elders came,
> I asked about their sayings in detail—what, according to
> the elders, Andrew or Peter said, or what was said by Philip
> or Thomas or James or John or Matthew or any other of
> the Lord's followers.... For I perceived that what was to be
> obtained from books would not profit me as much as what
> came from the living and surviving voice."[26]

CLUE NUMBER 2: Even before the Gospels were written, reliable oral histories about Jesus circulated among Christians.

It wasn't only what Jesus *taught* that was preserved in oral histories but also what Jesus *did*. How do we know this? At least two snippets of oral history clearly appear in Paul's first letter to the Corinthians. In both cases, Paul introduced his words with the Greek words *paralambano* ("I received" in most English translations) and *paradidomi* ("I passed on")—terms that, when placed together, signaled readers in the ancient world that the writer was preparing to cite oral history (1 Corinthians 11:23–25; 15:3–7).[27]

In one of these instances, Paul repeated the words of Jesus that were spoken at the Last Supper; in the other, Paul summarized his essential proclamation about the death and resurrection of Jesus. Both times, Paul also reminded his readers that they had already heard these traditions during his first visit to Corinth. Five years had passed since Paul founded the church in Corinth, yet Paul was very clear that these were the same truths that he had taught the Corinthian Christians when he first gathered them together. From this, it's apparent that Paul did *not* recklessly revise oral histories to fit each context; he certainly didn't embellish vital facts about the life of Jesus. Paul proclaimed the same essential message about Jesus in each place.

So when would Paul have received these traditions?

In the case of Paul's proclamation about the Resurrection, this tidbit of oral history had already circulated in Judea in the Aramaic language for at least a couple of years when Paul visited Jerusalem around A.D. 35.[28] It was, in fact, while Paul was visiting Jerusalem that he probably learned the tradition. That places the emergence of this tradition within months of the time when Jesus was believed to have died! What's more, it points to an origin in the precise place where eyewitnesses—people who could have verified the accuracy of the tradition—would have lived. It's very possible that Paul received other oral histories about Jesus at that time, too.[29] So what do we learn from these traditions? In the decades that followed the death of Jesus, consistent summaries of key events from the life of Jesus circulated among the people who would actually have known Him.

> I passed on to you...
>
> That the Lord Jesus, in the night in which He was betrayed, took bread, and when He had given thanks, broke it and said, "This is My body, which is for you; do this in remembrance of Me."
>
> Likewise He took the cup also after supper, saying, "This cup is the new covenant in My blood; do this, as often as you drink, in remembrance of Me."
>
> —Oral history about Jesus (originated in the A.D. 30s)

> I passed on to you...
> That the Messiah died on behalf of our sins according to the
>   Scriptures
> and that he was buried,
> and that he rose on the third day according to the Scriptures,
> and that he was seen by Cephas,
>   then the Twelve,
>   then he was seen by more than five hundred brothers at once...
>   then he was seen by James,
>   then by all the apostles.
>
> —Oral history about Jesus (originated in the A.D. 30s)

QUICK GUIDE

IMPORTANT DATES IN THE DEVELOPMENT OF EARLY CHRISTIANITY

28–30: Approximate dates of Jesus's earthly ministry, beginning in the fifteenth year of Caesar Tiberius (Luke 3:1).

33: Approximate date when Paul saw Jesus on the road to Damascus (Acts 9).

33–35: Probable dates for Paul's time in Arabia (Galatians 1:17).

35–47: Paul travels to Damascus, Jerusalem, and Tarsus (Acts 9–12).

47–49: Paul goes to Asia Minor on his first missionary journey. In A.D. 49, Caesar Claudius expels all Jews from Rome because of riots that occurred—according to Roman historian Suetonius—"on account of a certain Chrestus," probably a reference to Jesus Christ (Acts 13–15).

49–53: Paul embarks on his second missionary journey, establishing a church in Corinth around A.D. 50 (Acts 16–18).

53–57: Paul travels to Ephesus on his third missionary journey (Acts 18–21). During this time, Claudius Caesar dies, and Jews return to Rome.

57–61: Paul is arrested in Jerusalem, spends two years in Roman custody before appealing to Caesar, then waits two years for Nero Caesar to hear his appeal (Acts 21–28).

61–66: Paul may have been released following his appeal, perhaps traveling to provinces west of Rome. Passing through Rome, Paul may have been arrested and executed—along with Simon Peter—in the aftermath of the A.D. 64 fire that destroyed much of Rome. It could have been during this time that 1 Timothy, 2 Timothy, and Titus were written.

66–73: After years of enduring antagonism from Roman governors, the Jews revolt. The rebellion culminates in seven years of extreme tribulation for Christians and Jews. In A.D. 70, the Romans destroyed the Jewish temple in Jerusalem, leaving it violated and desolated. The Gospel according to Mark—and perhaps Matthew's and Luke's Gospels too—may have emerged during this time.

CRACKING THE GOSPEL FICTION CONSPIRACY

So what about the claims that Gospel truth was turned into fiction before the Gospels were even written?

Highly unlikely, especially in the oral culture of the Jewish people in the first century A.D.[30]

The practices of first-century Judaism suggest that the earliest Christians probably preserved essential truths about Jesus in reliable segments of oral history. Paul's letters show how these oral histories remained relatively unchanged as they made their way across the Roman Empire. Less than two generations after the actual events,[31] the New Testament Gospels incorporated these oral histories into written accounts of Jesus's ministry. Since these writings emerged while eyewitnesses were still living, these eyewitnesses could have been consulted to confirm or deny the truth of each claim. Even after the first century, the Gospels were known to represent the testimony of apostolic eyewitnesses. Justin—a defender of the Christian faith, writing from Rome in the mid-second century—referred to a quotation from Mark 3:16–17 as coming from the "recollections of Peter."[32] Around A.D. 200, Tertullian of Carthage declared:

> We present as our first position, that the Gospel testimony has apostles for its authors, to whom the Lord himself assigned the position of propagating the Gospel. There are also some that, though not *apostles*, are *apostolic*—they do not stand alone; they appear with and after the apostles....So, John and Matthew, of the apostles, first instill faith into us while the apostolic writers Luke and Mark renew it afterwards....Never mind that there occurs some variation in the order of their narratives, as long as there is agreement in essential matters of faith.[33]

Within mere months of the moment that Jesus died, a consistent strand of Christian tradition had emerged that tied the truths now found in the New Testament Gospels to eyewitnesses of the risen Lord.[34] Especially when it comes to the reports of the resurrection of Jesus Christ, the oral histories emerged early, they emerged in the context of eyewitnesses, and they remained relatively unchanged as they spread across the Roman Empire. Eventually, these oral histories made their way into the documents that we know as the Gospels. Perhaps most important of all, this movement from oral history to written history occurred before the end of the first century, while eyewitnesses of the original events were still living.

HOW to PREPARE for FUTURE CHRIST CONSPIRACIES

Each time someone raises the question of whether the New Testament Gospels are history or fiction, consider this: The earliest references to Jesus—and the only ones that were likely to have been written while eyewitnesses were still alive—are the ones found in your New Testament. What's more, the most essential information in these Gospels circulated in the form of fixed oral histories for several decades before the Gospels were written. If a fictionalized Jesus had been fabricated while people who knew Him were still alive, the eyewitnesses of His life could have protested.

Conspiracy Number Six

The MYSTERIOUS CASE of the MYTHICAL MESSIAH

WHAT'S the CONSPIRACY?

J ESUS MAY HAVE NEVER EXISTED AT ALL. DECADES AFTER THE DEATH OF Jesus, believers fabricated the Gospel stories from pagan myths.

WHO SAYS SO?

- *The God Who Wasn't There* film

- Timothy Freke and Peter Gandy, *The Laughing Jesus* and *The Jesus Mysteries*

- Tom Harpur, *The Pagan Christ*

- Robert Price, *Deconstructing Jesus* and *The Incredible Shrinking Son of Man*

A few weeks ago, I was seated at Starbucks, writing this book. A fellow customer eyed my notebook computer and the stack of books that teetered on one corner of my table. Since I spend more time at Starbucks than most of the managers, I recognized the man as a consistent and likable customer whose comments tended to be pretty perceptive.

"Writing a term paper?" he asked.

"A book," I replied with a smile.

As he lifted an iced mocha from the bar, he pressed, "What about?"

"Jesus," I replied.

"Really?" he sipped his drink. "I just read some books about Jesus and mythology. I used to be a Christian, you know. Now I can't find enough evidence to make me believe. Sometimes I'm not sure the guy even existed. I mean, the earliest records about Jesus came twenty years after He died, didn't they? And only a couple of Roman historians mentioned Him. Even if Jesus *did* exist, all we can know about Him is what people said later—a *lot* later. It seems more likely to me that Jesus never even existed."

More likely that Jesus never even existed.

The earliest records came twenty years after He died.

100

Only a couple of Roman historians mention Him.

The man was partly correct. The earliest surviving sources that describe Jesus *did* come twenty or more years after His supposed death. His name only shows up in a couple of Roman histories, and these appearances are disputed. Could it be that the man was right about Jesus? How much evidence exists to support the idea that someone such as Jesus even existed? Is it possible that what we worship as "Jesus" is actually a myth that emerged in the decades after His death?

CONSPIRACY NUMBER SIX

Jesus never existed at all. Decades after His supposed death, believers fabricated the Gospel stories from myths.

The TRUTH BEHIND the CONSPIRACY

The parallels between Christianity and paganism aren't nearly as parallel as the critics suppose. The sparseness of references to Jesus in historical literature has more to do with the dismissive attitude of cultured writers toward Christian faith than with the question of whether Jesus existed.

The MYTHICAL MESSIAH CONSPIRACY

That's precisely what some proponents of the "Christ Myth" hypothesis want people to believe. From the perspective of these critics, not only *the stories of Jesus* but also *Jesus Himself* are complete fiction. Jesus never lived, and Jesus never died, because Jesus never even existed.

This isn't a new idea: In the late 1700s, the French philosophers Voltaire and Dupuis tried to trace the origins of Christian faith to ancient astrological myths.[1] A few years later, a German theologian named Bruno Bauer introduced his theory that Jesus never existed[2]—an idea that had a profound effect on Bauer's most famous student, Karl Marx.[3] Few people followed Bauer's lead throughout most of the twentieth century, but in the closing decades of the twentieth century, Bruno Bauer's theory experienced a resurrection of sorts.

In a book titled *The Christ Conspiracy*, a self-proclaimed expert in the world's religions who calls herself "Acharya S." makes the case that everything in the New Testament can be traced to pagan sources. In *The Jesus Legend* and *The Jesus Myth*, a professor named G. A. Wells claimed that the apostle Paul and the earliest Christians viewed Jesus as a mythical symbol, not as an actual, historical person.[4] In 2005, Brian Flemming—host of a radio program known as *The Rational Response Squad*—even produced a movie titled *The God Who Wasn't*

There to promote the idea that Jesus never existed. Here's how the promotional materials for *The God Who Wasn't There* put Flemming's point of view:

> *The God Who Wasn't There*...asks the questions few dare to ask. And when it finds out how crazy the answers are, it dares to call them crazy....In this provocative, critically acclaimed documentary you will discover: The early founders of Christianity seem wholly unaware of the idea of a human Jesus, the Jesus of the Gospels bears a striking resemblance to other ancient heroes and the figureheads of pagan savior cults...and God simply isn't there.[5]

In the best sellers *The Laughing Jesus* and *The Jesus Mysteries*, Timothy Freke and Peter Gandy—two proponents of the hypothesis that Jesus was purely fictional—claim that *no one* treated Jesus as a real, historical person until the mid-100s A.D.

That's right: for more than a century after the time when Jesus supposedly walked and talked on Planet Earth, no one—not even Christians—believed that Jesus was a real person. "The original Christians didn't see Jesus as an historical man," Freke and Gandy claim. "[The Gospels] tell us nothing at all about an historical Jesus because no such man ever existed."[6] In the mid-100s, according to Freke and Gandy, a Christian writer named Justin began to take the Gospels to be truthful descriptions of actual events—something that, from Freke and Gandy's perspective, no previous Christian had even considered:

> In the early first century Paul has a simple myth of Jesus....By the middle of the second century, the story had developed into a profound and complex allegorical novel set in Palestine. But once the symbolical story of Jesus had become a quasi-historical narrative, it was only a matter of time before people started taking it literally as a record of actual events....Justin is the first of the Literalist Christians.[7]

A "literalist Christian" is, from the perspective of Freke and Gandy, anyone who believes that the events described in the New Testament Gospels actually occurred. In their reconstruction, no one was a literalist Christian until the middle of the second century! Until that time, Christians saw Jesus as myth and nothing more.

Jesus never existed.

It's a fairly bold claim that the Christ-myth crowd is making.

If they're correct, there's no point in discussing the historical truth about Jesus, because Jesus wasn't even a historical person. For that matter, there's no point in seeking any truth about Jesus, because there was no Jesus. Simply put, if the critics are correct, Christianity is the ultimate hoax of human history.

KNOW MORE

Justin the Martyr (Christian writer and apologist, lived A.D. 100–165): a pagan philosopher who became a follower of Jesus Christ. Invested the remainder of his life articulating and defending Christianity in the face of pagan and Jewish criticisms. Executed for his faith in A.D. 165.

Why should we consider the stories of Osiris, Dionysius, Adonis, Attis, Mithras, and other Pagan Mystery saviors as fables, yet come across essentially the same story told in a Jewish context and believe it to be the biography of a carpenter from Bethlehem?[8]
—TIMOTHY FREKE and PETER GANDY, *The Jesus Mysteries* (1999)

CLUES TO CRACK THE MYTHICAL MESSIAH CONSPIRACY

So how could anyone come to such a conclusion? How can someone claim that Jesus never existed? What's the proof for a mythical Messiah?

Nearly every proponent of this hypothesis appeals to three primary proofs: First, there's the *problem of the pagan parallels*. Some aspects of Christian faith can be found in religions that predate Christianity. According to the critics, this proves that Christianity borrowed these ideas from the pagan faiths. "The Jesus story has all the hallmarks of a myth," Timothy Freke and Peter Gandy claim. "And the reason for this is quite simple. It is a myth. Indeed not only is it a myth, it is a Jewish version of a Pagan myth!"[9]

There's also the *silence of the historical texts*. Jesus isn't mentioned in surviving historical sources that were written during the time that He supposedly walked and talked on this planet. If He had truly been a miracle worker who died and rose from the dead, historians in His own day would have mentioned Him—or at least that's what some critics claim. So, Jesus must never have existed at all.

Finally, there's the claim that *the earliest Christians weren't concerned with an earthly Jesus*. The earliest Christians, including Paul, knew that Jesus was a myth, according to these critics. It wasn't until later that "literalist Christians" emerged—Christians who understood Jesus to be a real, historical person.

How strong is the case for a mythical Messiah? Let's take a careful look at the pagan parallels and at what the historical texts have to say about Jesus! Let's see if the proofs can bear the weight of the critics' claim that Jesus never existed.

 **Justin was *not* the first "literalist Christian."**

According to Freke and Gandy, the apostle Paul understood Jesus as a vague, mythical Messiah, not as a historical person in a particular time and place. "Paul has a simple myth of Jesus,"[10] they claim, and it wasn't until Justin began to write about Jesus in the mid-second century that Christians treated Jesus as a real person. Freke and Gandy even claim that Paul's letters prove their hypothesis. Despite such claims from the Christ-myth crowd, a careful reading of Paul's letters proves the precise opposite.

Simply put, Paul was a "literalist Christian" long before Justin the Martyr was even born.

Even in his earliest letters, Paul connected Jesus with particular followers and family members who still lived in specific places. "In *Jerusalem*," Paul informed the Galatians, "I saw...James *the Lord's brother*" (Galatians 1:17–19). Paul knew that Jesus had been physically born in a Jewish context. "God sent His Son, *born of a woman, born under the Law*," he wrote to Christians in Asia Minor (Galatians 4:4). Paul recognized a physical resurrection at a particular point in time ("on the third day")[11] that particular people witnessed (1 Corinthians 15:3–7). If Jesus *was* a nonhistorical myth, Paul didn't know it. As far as Paul knew, what he proclaimed about Jesus— even in churches in provinces far from Jerusalem—was rooted not only in Paul's personal experiences but also in relatively recent historical events in the region of Judea.

CLUE NUMBER 2: **Pagan parallels neither prove nor disprove the truth of the New Testament writings.**

So what about *the problem of the pagan parallels*? Even in ancient times, critics of Christianity noticed parallels between Christian beliefs and pre-Christian myths. In the late second century, a pagan philosopher named Celsus charged, "The Christians have used the myths of Danae and the Melanippe, of the Auge and Antiope in fabricating this story of virgin birth!"[12] In the simplest possible terms, here's what the critics contend: The most marvelous claims in the Gospels—a miraculous birth, for example, as well as the idea of a deity who dies and rises again—are paralleled in pagan religions that predate Christianity. So, it is claimed, Christians must have fabricated these miracles based on their knowledge of pre-Christian religions.

To be sure, there *are* similarities between certain events in the Gospels and the ancient myths of Egypt, Persia, and other nations. Long before the first century A.D., Egyptians deities such as Osiris, Adonis, Attis, and Horus were believed to have risen from the dead. The Persians—previous to the time of Jesus— venerated Mithras, a deity whose birth may have been marked by visits from shepherds.[13] When was Mithras born? According to some sources, soon after the winter solstice, around December 25![14] These evidences have led one duo of writers to declare, "The traditional history of Christianity cannot convincingly explain why the Jesus story is so similar to ancient Pagan myths."[15]

Can we really be so certain? Do these pagan parallels mean that Christian concepts were borrowed from previous religions? Do such parallels disprove the presentation of Jesus's life that's found in the New Testament?

Not really.

In the first place, the supposed parallels are not nearly as parallel as the skeptics suppose. When the original sources of the pagan legends are closely examined, they typically have little in common with the New Testament narratives. For example, there *are* dying and rising gods in some earlier religions, but these deities died and arose each year, certainly not the same pattern as Jesus's once-for-all sacrifice for the sake of others![16] The pagan tales of miraculous birth are closer to divine impregnation—a mortal woman conceives a child as a result of sexual relations with a god—than to the virginal conception described in the Gospel according to Matthew and Luke.

What about the Mithras legend? The birth in a cave with shepherds in attendance? The birth of Mithras was, to say the least, *very* different from anything that's found in the New Testament. In the first place, Mithras was birthed from solid stone, and...well...he got stuck on the way through. (I guess you could say he got off to a rocky start.) So, some nearby folk who *may* have been shepherds intervened and pulled him from the stone.[17] Yet some writers continue to connect his birth in a cave, assisted by some people who might have been shepherds, to the birth of Jesus in a stable with shepherds arriving soon afterward. A few critics even continue to call this birth of Mithras a "virgin birth"![18] I must admit that this vexes me even more at a *biological* level than at a *historical* level. I guess that birth from a rock is *sort of* a virgin birth, but how can you tell if a rock is a virgin, anyway? And how, precisely, do rocks lose their virginity? Parallels of this sort are simply too vague to support the claim that Christians borrowed their beliefs from pagans of previous generations.

James Tabor, a professor at the University of North Carolina, doesn't believe in the virginal conception of Jesus, and he denies that Jesus could have risen from the dead. Yet even he sees how radically the stories of Jesus in the New Testament Gospels differ from any pagan parallels:

> When you read the accounts of Mary's unsuspected pregnancy, what is particularly notable...is an underlying tone of realism that runs through the narratives. These seem to be real people, living in real times

and places. In contrast the birth stories in Greco-Roman literature have a decidedly legendary flavor to them. For example, in Plutarch's account of the birth of Alexander the Great, mother Olympias got pregnant from a snake; it was announced by a bolt of lightning that sealed her womb so that her husband Philip could not have sex with her. Granted, both Matthew and Luke include dreams and visions of angels but the core story itself—that of a man who discovers that his bride-to-be is pregnant and knows he is not the father—has a realistic and thoroughly human quality to it. The narrative, despite its miraculous elements, "rings true."[19]

The New Testament narrative—unlike the supposed pagan parallels—"rings true" from a historical perspective. Despite the claims of pagan parallels, the parallels simply aren't very parallel.

What's more, proponents of the mythical Messiah conspiracy consistently confuse later Christian traditions with what's found in the Gospels. It's true, for example, that pagan practices influenced the celebration of Christmas near the winter solstice, but the New Testament documents never suggest a date for the birth of Jesus in the first place! The selection of a date to celebrate Christmas occurred centuries after the time of Jesus. As such, the celebration of Christmas has no relevance whatsoever when it comes to a discussion of the authenticity of the story of Jesus. The same holds true when it comes to connections between pagan fertility festivals and later Easter celebrations. Similarly, later Christian art incorporated both Egyptian and Mithraic motifs, especially when depicting Jesus and His mother. Yet later imitations of pagan themes have *nothing* to do with whether the events in the New Testament actually occurred. It simply means that ancient Christian artists should have been a bit more creative![20]

Let's suppose for a moment, though, that some patterns that were present in the life of Jesus *could* be pinpointed in previous religions. Would this disprove Christian faith, as critics claim?

Not really.

The real question isn't, Are there similarities between the New Testament's descriptions of Jesus and some previous religious practices? Perhaps there *are*, although I must admit that every parallel I've examined has turned out to be vague and weak once it's examined in its context. The crucial question is, Did the events described in the New Testament actually occur? The answer to this question simply doesn't depend on parallels in pagan practices.

Even if clear parallels *did* exist between the story of Jesus and previous religious expectations, this wouldn't warrant the belief that Christians "borrowed" these tenets from other faiths. It would mean that when God dropped in on the human race, He chose to reveal Himself in ways that the people in that particular culture could most readily comprehend. If that's indeed the case, perhaps the myths of dying gods and miraculous births are rooted in longings that run deeper than mere human imagination. Maybe these "myths" stem from longings that God Himself placed in humanity. C. S. Lewis addressed this possibility with these words:

> In the New Testament, the *thing really happens.* The Dying God really appears—as a historical Person, living in a definite place and time....The old myth of the Dying God...comes down from the heaven of legend and imagination to the earth of history. It *happens*— at a particular date, in a particular place, followed by definable historical consequences. We must not be nervous about "parallels" [in other religions]...they *ought* to be there—it would be a stumbling block if they weren't.[21]

When it comes to parallels between the New Testament story of Jesus and the myths of pagan gods, the supposed connections are simply too vague to make any definitive claims. Even if some parallels *were* indisputable, the parallels still wouldn't call the New Testament into question. It would simply mean that God worked out His plans in ways that matched the context within which "the Word became flesh and pitched His tent among us" (John 1:18).

QUICK GUIDE
PARALLELS AND PROBLEMS BETWEEN JESUS AND MITHRAS

Parallel	Problem
Mithras was born of a virgin in a cave.	Mithras was born from stone and left a cave behind him in a cliff. Anahita is sometimes identified as the mother of Mithras, but Anahita was actually the consort of Mithras.
Mithras was born on December 25, with shepherds in attendance.	It's uncertain whether the attendants of the birth of Mithras were shepherds. The date of the winter solstice has no relevance for the authenticity of the Gospels; this date was connected with the birth of Jesus hundreds of years after the Gospels were written. The Gospels make no claims about when Jesus was born.

Parallel	Problem
Mithras had twelve followers.	One piece of artwork depicts Mithras surrounded by twelve faces, but there is no evidence that these were "disciples" of Mithras. In fact, Mithras had only two companions, Albederan and Antares.[22]
Mithras was identified as a lion and a lamb.	There is no surviving evidence for the connection of Mithras to a lamb. He was identified as a lion, but that imagery existed among the Jewish people (Genesis 49:9) several centuries prior to the emergence of Mithraic myths.[23]
Mithras initiated a meal in which the terminology of "body and blood" was used.	The earliest evidence of such terminology is from the mid-second century—nearly one hundred years after the Gospels were written.[24] In this instance, it is more likely that Mithraism borrowed from Christian practice.
Mithras sacrificed himself for the sake of others.	Mithras is frequently depicted in the act of sacrificing a bull, but Mithras himself never becomes the sacrifice.
Mithras rose from the dead on the third day; his followers celebrated his resurrection each year.	There is no surviving evidence from the pre-Christian era for a resurrection of Mithras on the third day.[25] Because of his association with the sun, it is possible that followers of Mithras celebrated his renewal or rebirth each year.[26]
The resurrection of Mithras was celebrated on Sunday.	There is no evidence from the pre-Christian era for a celebration of the resurrection of Mithras on the first day of the week, though the followers of Mithras—and of other sun-related deities—did worship their gods on Sunday. The reason for the emphasis on "the first day of the week" in the New Testament Gospels was, however, more closely tied to the fact that, in Genesis 1, God's work of creation began on the first day. The implication was that, through the resurrection of Jesus, God was initiating a new beginning, a re-creation of His world.

The writers who should have mentioned Jesus *did* mention Him—the ones who didn't had a good reason.

It seems like a convincing argument at first. If Jesus had truly been a miracle worker who died and rose from the dead, historians in His own day would have mentioned Him. So, since Jesus *doesn't* play a decisive role in any first-century Jewish or Roman sources, Jesus must have been a mere mortal— or maybe He never existed at all. Here's how a couple of proponents of the "Christ myth" describe the situation:

> The Romans kept detailed legal records, but no record of the trial or crucifixion of Jesus has ever been found....From all the Roman authors, there are three small passages in Pliny, Suetonius, and Tacitus....But these authors were writing in the second century, long after the supposed life of Jesus, and all they actually tell us is that a few Christians existed in the Roman world at this time, which has never been in doubt.[27]

A few of these facts are correct, and a few are false, but the entire presentation represents a profound misconception of first-century history and culture.

In the first place, while it's true that Romans kept detailed legal records, only a tiny percentage of these records have survived, especially from the regions where Jesus lived and taught. Why? Nearly all of these documents were recorded on papyrus, and, outside of an arid desert, papyrus documents decay rapidly. That's why so few Roman imperial documents have survived outside Egypt and North Africa.

There's another factor that also would have prevented the survival of Judean and Galilean documentation: In the Jewish-Roman conflict that culminated in the destruction of the temple in A.D. 70, the Jewish troops overwhelmed the imperial repositories and residences where Roman officials would have retained such records. When the Romans reconquered these regions, imperial buildings and the records in them were destroyed.[28] So, the absence of official Roman records provides no proof about the existence or nonexistence of Jesus. The truth is that no one can know what sorts of records the Romans might have maintained regarding Jesus. The ravages of time and the violence of the Jewish-Roman wars have obliterated these records.

What about Roman histories? Why don't Roman historical writings from the time of Jesus mention His name? In the first place, the only surviving Roman history that was penned around the time of Jesus came from an army general named Velleius Paterculus. Paterculus completed his text in the early

A.D. 30s[29]—several years before any information about Jesus would have reached a retired general in the city of Rome. It's no surprise that Paterculus never mentions Jesus.

What's important to recognize in this context is how insignificant Jesus would have seemed to Roman writers. Since Jews refused to worship the gods and goddesses of Rome, Jewish people weren't particularly popular among the Romans to begin with. Would-be messiahs would have been even *less* popular. In fact, such persons rarely made it into Roman texts unless they incited military revolts, something that Jesus specifically forbade His followers to do (Matthew 5:39; 26:52). As such, even if first-century Roman historians *had* heard of Jesus, it's doubtful that they would have included His name in their writings.

So when *would* a Roman text have mentioned Jesus?

Only when so many people identified themselves with Jesus that their loyalty to Jesus became a problem for the Roman Empire.

As it turns out, this is precisely what we find in the historical texts. By the late first or early second century, Christians could probably be found in every major city of the Roman Empire. When it came to religion, Christians were even more troublesome than the Jews had been—or, at least, that's how they would have seemed to the Romans. Jews had at least been willing to offer sacrifices to their own God on Caesar's behalf. Christians refused even to sacrifice a pinch of salt in Caesar's name to call for divine goodwill toward Caesar! In the early second century, when Christian practices began to be perceived as an imperial problem, it would be reasonable to expect references to Christianity to appear in Roman histories.

Guess what?

When we look at Roman history, that's precisely what we find.

Two popular histories of Rome emerged in the early second century, and both of them seem to make some reference to Christians. As they researched the recent century of the Roman Empire, here's what the historians Suetonius Tranquillus and Cornelius Tacitus mentioned about the Christian movement:

> *From Suetonius*: Since the Jews were causing disturbances due to a certain *Chrestus*, he [Emperor Claudius] expelled them from Rome.[30]

> *From Tacitus*: Nero fastened the blame [for the fire in Rome] and inflicted the most fastidious tortures on a class despised for their sacrileges, the ones called "Christians" among the people. *Christus*—from whom they derive their name—suffered the extreme penalty during the reign of Tiberius at the hand of one of our procurators, Pontius Pilate, and—though the malicious superstition was stopped for a moment in this way—it again broke out not only in Judea (the primary source of

the evil) but also in Rome (where all things hideous and shameful from every part of the world find their center and turn popular).[31]

There is little doubt that both of these references are genuine. The expulsion of the Jews from Rome is mentioned not only by Suetonius but also in the Acts of the Apostles. Luke doesn't tell us *why*, perhaps because he was embarrassed by the fact that Christians had contributed to social upheaval in Rome (Acts 18:2). The fact that the title of Jesus is spelled "*Chrestus*" instead of the usual "*Christus*" in the citation from Suetonius has caused some persons to wonder if the text actually referred to followers of Christ in the first place. A Roman writer such as Suetonius would have been unfamiliar with Jewish expectations of a "Christ" or "Messiah." Furthermore, *Chrestus*—which means "useful"—was a common name, especially among slaves. In his context, Suetonius's misspelling of the title is completely understandable.

A small handful of scholars have also questioned the quotation from Tacitus, claiming that a Christian copyist added these words later.[32] Yet it seems almost impossible that Christian copyists would have described their own faith in such harsh and negative terms.

So what do we learn about Jesus from these texts?

From Suetonius, we learn very little, except that the message of Jesus Christ caused conflict between Christians and Jews in the mid-first century. Tacitus is far more helpful. From this historian, we learn that Christ was known even among the Romans to have been a human being, crucified under Pontius Pilate in a particular time and place. Tacitus also lets us know why Jesus's followers were known as "Christians." What's more, the etymology that Tacitus reported for the word *Christian* meshes perfectly with the connection that's clear throughout the Christian Scriptures, especially in Luke's writings. (See Acts 11:26.)

There's another Roman reference to the Christian movement found in an early second-century imperial letter. In A.D. 112, a governor named Pliny the Younger wrote to the Roman emperor Trajan, wondering how to handle Christians. From this letter, we learn little about Jesus Himself, but we *do* learn that second-century believers worshiped "Christ as...a deity."

> They meet on a fixed day before dawn and sing responsively a hymn to Christ as to a deity. They bind themselves by oath...not to commit fraud, theft, or adultery, nor to falsify their trust, nor to refuse to return a trust when called upon to do so. When this is finished, it is their custom to dismiss and to assemble again to partake of food—ordinary and innocent food.[33]
>
> —PLINY THE YOUNGER, Roman governor (A.D. 112)

What about the Jewish writers? What did they have to say about Jesus? According to Freke and Gandy:

> Jewish writers...should be more interested in such a famous Jew as Jesus, but here the situation is even worse. Philo should mention him, as he lived at exactly the same time that Jesus is claimed to have been stirring up trouble in Jerusalem. And yet in his numerous books he makes no mention of Jesus or any of the events described in the New Testament. The one Jewish historian who does mention Jesus is Josephus....The passage was not to be found in Josephus at the beginning of the third century and must have been inserted into the text in the early fourth century, after Christianity had been made the religion of the Roman Empire.[34]

Despite the claims of Freke and Gandy that Philo of Alexandria should have mentioned Jesus, Philo would have had *no* reason to do so. First off, Philo—a Jewish philosopher who lived in Egypt—probably died around A.D. 47, before the Christian movement had made a worldwide impact.[35] As far as we know from his writings, Philo never set foot in Galilee. He went to Judea once, but it's uncertain *when* he made this trip.[36] He appeared before Emperor Caligula in A.D. 40, but there would have been little likelihood of running into many Christians in Rome during that time.

My question for those who think Philo ought to have mentioned Jesus is this: Why would a Jewish philosopher who died in Egypt in the 40s have written about a supposed Messiah whose movement originated in Judea and Galilee? Why would Philo have focused on a movement that would have seemed—to this Jewish philosopher—like a foolish, fleeting offshoot from mainstream Judaism? The answer is simple: *he wouldn't have.* Philo may never even have heard about Jesus. Even if he had heard about Jesus of Nazareth, he would have had no reason to mention this carpenter-turned-Messiah.

The Jewish historian Flavius Josephus wrote his history of the Jewish people around A.D. 93. His histories of the Jewish wars and of the Jewish people do focus on Judea and Galilee during the years of Jesus's ministry. Plus, Josephus served at one point as governor of Galilee. As such, Josephus might be expected to have mentioned Jesus—and he did! Unfortunately for contemporary historians, a third-century Christian copyist expanded one of Josephus's references to Jesus to the point that it's nearly impossible to discover what Josephus originally wrote. Here's how the embellished reference to Jesus reads:

> About this time there lived Jesus, a wise man—if one should even call him a man. He worked amazing miracles, and he taught in such a way that people gladly received the truth. He won over many Jews

and Greeks. He was the Messiah. When Pilate, having heard him accused by men of the highest standing among us, condemned him to be crucified, those who had in the first place come to love him did not stop. On the third day he appeared to them restored to life. The prophets of God had prophesied these things and many other amazing things about him. The tribe of the Christians, so called after him, has to this day not disappeared.[37]

Clearly, Josephus—a Jewish supporter of the Roman emperor Titus, with little positive to say about messianic expectations—would never have accepted Jesus as "the Messiah" or affirmed the truth of His resurrection. There *does* seem to have been some reference to Jesus in the words that Josephus originally wrote. The precise content has, however, been mangled beyond positive recovery. What's important about this portion of Josephus, though, is simply the fact that he did mention Jesus as an actual, historical person. What's more, this isn't the only place that Josephus mentioned Jesus. Later in his history, Josephus recorded these words:

[The high priest] gathered the legal experts of the Sanhedrin and brought them, with certain others, a man called James, the brother of Jesus who was called the Messiah. Accusing them of having transgressed the law, he delivered them up to be stoned to death.[38]

At the very least, Josephus knew, in the first century A.D., that Jesus existed and that some persons had ascribed to Him the title "Christ" or "Messiah." Josephus most likely didn't accept Jesus as his Messiah, but he never questioned Jesus's existence.[39]

A similar pattern can be found in later Jewish rabbinic writers, and many of these writers depended on first-century traditions for their data.[40] Later, rabbis called Jesus a magician, disparaged Him as a heretic, referred to Him as the illegitimate child of Mary and a Roman soldier, and mentioned His crucifixion, but they never questioned His existence. If the nonexistence of Jesus had been a real possibility, the rabbis would certainly have mentioned it in these contexts, yet they never did.[41] They assumed the historical existence of Jesus.

So what of the claim that Jesus never existed, simply because He wasn't mentioned in first-century Jewish and Roman writings? It's a ridiculous claim rooted in ignorance of the cultural and literary context of the earliest Christians. Until Christianity became an empire-wide movement, it seemed like a deviant form of Judaism; Romans and Jews alike most likely expected Christian faith to fade in a few years. The sparseness of references to Jesus had more to do with the dismissive attitude of cultured writers toward Christian faith than with the question of whether Jesus existed.

CRACKING THE MYTHICAL MESSIAH CONSPIRACY

I moved my computer to the side and said to the man with the iced mocha, "You're right that the Gospels and Paul's letters weren't written until twenty years or more after the time of Jesus, but I still think there's good reason to believe that Jesus existed. I would even say that the Gospels represent reliable information about Jesus."

"After twenty *years*? That's ridiculous! Even if they *started* with a true story, how can a story stay reliable after it's floated from person to person for twenty years? Every person would change it just a little. After two decades, there wouldn't be any truth left!"

"That might be true," I admitted, "except for the fact that fixed oral histories developed a *lot* earlier than the Gospels were written—most likely, within a few months after Jesus was crucified. That's how the first followers of Jesus kept the facts that really mattered from getting changed."

"OK; if all that's true, why don't the Romans mention Jesus? Or Philo, for that matter?"

And so we talked for an hour or so about Roman history, ancient mythology, and the traditions that Paul passed to the church in Corinth. When he left, he still wasn't convinced that Jesus was alive, but he did believe that once upon a time Jesus existed. Such faith may not be enough to move him into God's kingdom, but it's a great place to start.

HOW TO PREPARE FOR FUTURE CHRIST CONSPIRACIES

Whenever you're confronted with a supposed parallel between a New Testament text and a pagan practice, track down every original reference. Look carefully at *when* the pagan practice emerged and *whether* the pagan practice really parallels the New Testament. When it comes to the absence of Jesus from many first- and second-century historical sources, ask yourself this question: Which option makes more sense: (1) to trust the *silence* of Roman and Jewish texts that were written in the century following the supposed time that Jesus lived, or (2) to trust the explicit *statements* of New Testament texts that were written while eyewitnesses would still have been alive? To explore the mythical Messiah conspiracy in more detail, equip yourself with *The Jesus Legend* by Paul Eddy and Greg Boyd—an outstanding and thorough response to skeptics who wish to treat the New Testament Gospels as fictional works.

Conspiracy Number Seven

CODES IN THE GOSPELS, SECRETS IN THE SCROLLS

WHAT'S the CONSPIRACY?

HE DEAD SEA SCROLLS AND PERHAPS EVEN THE NEW TESTAMENT books include encoded secrets about Jesus—information that, if decoded, could completely change everything that Christians believe.

WHO SAYS SO?

- Michael Baigent and Richard Leigh, *The Dead Sea Scrolls Deception*

- Robert Eisenman, *The New Testament Code* and *James the Brother of Jesus*

- Barbara Thiering, *Jesus the Man, Jesus and the Riddle of the Dead Sea Scrolls*, and *The Book That Jesus Wrote*

Muhammad edh-Dhib lost his sheep, and he didn't know where to find them. In the process of looking for his sheep, the young shepherd made a discovery that would impact the world long after the wayward flock was forgotten. He tossed a rock into a cave, probably to determine whether some of his animals had found shelter in the shadowed interior. What he hoped to hear was the bleating of a stone-struck sheep, but that wasn't what he heard at all. What the shepherd heard instead was the shattering of pottery.

Amid the shards of a broken pottery jar, there were treasures more valuable than any sheep in Muhammad's flock. What Muhammad glimpsed when he scrambled up that stony slope in 1947 were the first of the documents that would become known as "the Dead Sea Scrolls."[1] Each scroll had been wrapped in linen and brushed with malodorous pitch. For nearly two millennia, pottery, linen, and pitch had preserved these ancient rolls of parchment.

As more scrolls were discovered, a panel of experts was assembled to translate the scrolls and to reconstruct their origins. Some persons on the panel quickly released information about their assigned documents. The rest of the experts weren't so prompt. As a result, scholars and students throughout the world found themselves waiting for a tiny clique of experts to publish the manuscripts.

115

And they waited.

And waited.

And still, they waited.

With a few exceptions,[2] the original panel of experts never got around to publishing *anything* about the scrolls, cutting off not only the public but also fellow scholars from the most significant archaeological discovery of their time! One researcher said that the committee's failure to share the contents of the scrolls could become "the academic scandal *par excellence* of the twentieth century,"[3] and indeed it was.

Finally, in 1991—fifty-four years after a rock from the hand of Muhammad edh-Dhib hurtled into a cave near an abandoned commune known as Qumran—the editor of the journal *Biblical Archaeology Review* and a handful of determined scholars forced the entire contents of the scrolls to be made public. The original panel of scholars cried foul, claiming that the contents of the scrolls had been "pirated" and "stolen."[4] But it was too late. The Dead Sea Scrolls were now available to the world. In the end, these documents provided additional copies of several texts from the Old Testament, as well as commentaries and community rules—important documents for scholarly research, to be sure, but nothing earthshaking.

Or so it seemed at first.

But what if that's not the whole story?

CONSPIRACY NUMBER SEVEN

The Dead Sea Scrolls and perhaps even the New Testament books include encoded secrets about Jesus—information that, if properly understood, could completely that Christians believe.

The TRUTH BEHIND the CONSPIRACY

The reason for the connections between New Testament documents and the Dead Sea Scrolls is because both texts were rooted in the Hebrew Scriptures and in Jewish culture, not because the biblical authors based their beliefs about Jesus on anything at Qumran and certainly not because of codes in the texts.

THE DEAD SEA SCROLLS CONSPIRACY

What if the *real* reason for the delays in the publication of the Dead Sea Scrolls had nothing to do with the selfishness of a few scholars and everything to do with the scrolls' scandalous content? Could it be that the scrolls were suppressed to protect people's faith? What if, when read alongside the New Testament and other ancient documents, the scrolls revealed sordid secrets that could destroy the entire Christian faith?

Suppose, for example, that nearly all of Jesus's teachings could be traced to the Dead Sea Scrolls. Suppose that Christian faith originated not with Jesus but with Paul. What if—sometime in the late A.D. 30s—Paul and James the brother of Jesus settled their theological differences in a bloody brawl that left James lying in front of the Jerusalem temple with a broken leg?

What if the Dead Sea Scrolls reveal codes in the Gospels that point not only to Jesus's marriage to Mary Magdalene but also to His subsequent separation from Mary, after which He hooked up with Lydia of Philippi? That's what a biblical lecturer named Barbara Thiering claims that she discovered! This union with Lydia occurred—according to Barbara Thiering—precisely at midnight on Tuesday, March 17, A.D. 50.[5] (If Dr. Thiering had searched a little longer, perhaps she could even have told us the exact second when Jesus kissed the bride.)

Where did Thiering find the inspiration for these reinterpretations of the New Testament texts? In the Dead Sea Scrolls, of course.

Believe it or not, these claims don't come from a bizarre suspense novel or even from a soap opera that's spent one too many seasons blundering into the supernatural realm. These are real claims made in best-selling books that claim to represent reliable historical research. The Dead Sea Scrolls were suppressed, two popular conspiracy theorists claim, because the scrolls contain "the spiritual and religious equivalent of dynamite—something that might just conceivably demolish the entire edifice of Christian teaching and belief."[6]

Oh, my.

Here we go again.

Hidden truths discovered in long-deserted caves?

Scrolls suppressed because they might "demolish the entire edifice of Christian teaching and belief"?

"The spiritual and religious equivalent of dynamite" within these documents?

Sounds like another conspiracy to me.

So what's the historical evidence for such claims? Are there *really* scandalous secrets in the Dead Sea Scrolls? What codes about Jesus and James and Paul might be concealed in the New Testament manuscripts? How could we possibly crack such codes? Let's take a look at the historical evidence to find out—but first, let's take a trip to the caves of Qumran to learn a little more about the Dead Sea Scrolls!

> One can only imagine the reaction of [the initial translators of the Dead Sea Scrolls] on first discovering the seemingly extraordinary parallels between the Qumran texts and what was known of "early Christianity." It had hitherto been believed that Jesus' teachings were unique.... It must have seemed as though they were handling the spiritual and religious equivalent of dynamite—something that might just conceivably demolish the entire edifice of Christian teaching and belief.[7]
>
> —MICHAEL BAIGENT and RICHARD LEIGH,
> *The Dead Sea Scrolls Deception* (1991)

A TRIP TO QUMRAN

Step out of the tour bus near the northwest corner of the Dead Sea, and feel the endless waves of heat. Wave away the vendors selling drinks at a cost of ten shekels per cup—unless, of course, you're so thirsty that a few ounces of watered-down lemonade are actually worth the equivalent of six dollars! Mere minutes from Jerusalem, you have moved from metropolitan chaos to sheer desolation. On one side, the Dead Sea stretches into the distance, the blue of the sea nearly blending into the hues of the eastern sky. As you meander westward, you notice circular orifices that geological cataclysms and centuries of gusting sand have gouged into the limestone cliffs. For nearly two thousand years, these caves concealed the Dead Sea Scrolls.

Standing near the southernmost cluster of caves, you glimpse the ruins of a long-deserted settlement. Here it appears that a discontented Jewish sect may have maintained a thriving religious community in the second century B.C. and again in the first century A.D. At some point, this community probably preserved more than a thousand sacred scrolls. Some scrolls contained copies of Old Testament texts. Others provided explanations and applications of the Hebrew Scriptures. Still others preserved rules for the Qumran community.

These community rules contain some of the more entertaining lines in the Dead Sea Scrolls—well, at least they entertain *me*. In the Qumran community, waving at someone with your left hand led to ten days of punishment. Spitting, snorting at something that wasn't supposed to be funny, or accidentally mooning someone warranted thirty days of penance. For streaking, the penance lasted six months.[8] Evidently, once you joined the Qumran community, you kept your jokes to yourself, your spit in your mouth, your left hand in your pocket, and your loincloth securely tied.

When the Roman army ravaged the province of Judea around A.D. 70, the community sealed their sacred texts in jars and hid them in nearby caves. After Muhammad edh-Dhib tossed his rock into a cave near the Qumran Valley, archaeologists and amateur treasure hunters unearthed hundreds of fragments and scrolls in eleven caves scattered along two miles of stony cliffs. Most likely, the community planned to return to the caves to recover their scrolls, but, as far as we know, none of them ever made it home.

Here's how the historian Josephus described the butchery that the Romans brought to Jerusalem and Judea in A.D. 70:

> The Romans went in numbers through the city streets, with swords drawn. They slaughtered everyone they caught, setting fire to the homes where Jews had fled…until corpses clogged the streets. The city ran with so much blood that it was the blood of the Jews that quenched the fires in the houses.…After the soldiers tired of killing…they slaughtered the old and the ill…as well as those that had been rebels and robbers…then, they chose the tallest and most beautiful young men for the triumph parade, and—as for the rest of those who were older than seventeen years—they were chained and sent to the Egyptian mines.[9]

This was most likely the fate not only of the citizens of Jerusalem but also of the Jews from Qumran, and so the keepers of the scrolls died, never knowing the fate of their precious rolls of papyrus and leather.

Seems simple enough, doesn't it? Some theorists remain unconvinced by this explanation, though.

According to the conspiracy theorists, there's far more to the story of the Dead Sea Scrolls than most scholars want to admit. So much more, in fact, that the scrolls could spell the end of Christianity as we know it.

KNOW MORE

Dead Sea Scrolls: Ancient scrolls and fragments, representing approximately 813 original documents, found in eleven caves scattered along a two-mile stretch of limestone cliffs, near the Dead Sea. Roughly one-third of the documents represent copies of the Hebrew Scriptures, and another one-third or so are commentaries on the Scriptures. The remaining documents describe the rules and expectations of the group that preserved the scrolls. The scrolls were copied between the second century B.C. and the Roman conquest of Judea in A.D. 70.

Most scholars place the scrolls at the beginning of this range, in the first and second centuries B.C., and understand the copyists to have been a Jewish sect known as the "Essenes." Others believe that some—if not all—of the scrolls fit most naturally in the decades leading up to the destruction of Jerusalem. If this is the case, Essenes may have preserved the texts, but it is also possible that refugees from Jerusalem hid the texts in the caves around Qumran in A.D. 70.

CHRISTIANS AT QUMRAN?

From the perspectives of several popular writers—*Holy Blood, Holy Grail* authors Michael Baigent and Richard Leigh, for example, and university professors Barbara Thiering and Robert Eisenman—belief in Jesus emerged at Qumran.[10] Yes, that's right; there was a time, according to these authors, when Christians and the keepers of the Dead Sea Scrolls constituted the same group. At first glance, this thesis almost makes sense. After all, there *are* quite a few parallels between the Qumran community and the earliest Christians. The Qumran community practiced ceremonial washings, for example, to signify repentance of sin.[11] The community's guidelines for these washings even commanded complete immersion in water.[12] The community regularly participated in a communion meal of bread and wine, and they anticipated a time when they would share this meal with the Messiah.[13]

The Qumran scrolls also described their leader as "the Righteous Teacher"—similar to the early church's description of the Messiah as "the Righteous One" (Acts 3:14; 7:52; 22:14). Baigent and Leigh describe such titles as "specifically and uniquely Qumranic in character."[14] Perhaps most significant, it has been claimed that the Dead Sea Scrolls describe a Messiah who suffers and dies[15] as well as someone known as "Son of God" and "Son of the Most High"—concepts quite familiar to readers of the New Testament (Mark 5:7; Luke 1:32–35; 8:28; 24:26, 46; Romans 5:6–8).[16]

According to Baigent and Leigh, the similarities between the practices of the Qumran community and the earliest Christians provide positive proof that Christian beliefs didn't come from eyewitness experiences with Jesus. Christian faith evolved from the tenets and texts of the Qumran community—and that's why church authorities suppressed the Dead Sea Scrolls.

These connections between Jesus and Qumran could—in the estimation of Baigent and Leigh—shatter everything that Christians believe about Jesus. Since terms such as "Son of God," "Son of the Most High," and "Righteous One" can be found in the Dead Sea Scrolls, it must have been the traditions of the Qumran community that caused such titles to be ascribed to Jesus, not eyewitness testimony about Jesus. Since baptism originated at Qumran, the baptism that John and the disciples of Jesus practiced must have come from Qumran too. Since the Messiah expected at Qumran wasn't explicitly divine, Jesus must not have been divine. These are the truths that, according to these authors, could "demolish the entire edifice of Christian teaching and belief." "It had been hitherto believed," Baigent and Leigh have written, "that Jesus' teachings were unique." The Dead Sea Scrolls demonstrate that His teachings may not have been so unique after all. The revelation that the New Testament Gospels echo the Dead Sea Scrolls could—Baigent and Leigh claim—"at a single stroke undermine the faith to which millions [cling] for solace and comfort."[17] And so, they claim, the scrolls were suppressed.

> ### KNOW MORE
>
> 1QpHab? 11QPsa? 4Q285? Aren't those the names of protocol droids in the *Star Wars* movies? No, they're designations for Dead Sea Scrolls! At first, the numbering system for the Dead Sea Scrolls looks confusing, but it really isn't. The first number tells *which cave* the scroll or fragment came from. Q stands for "Qumran," and the final letters or numbers either abbreviate the document's title or provide a numeric designation for the fragment. So, 1QpHab is a *pesher* (p) in the Book of Habakkuk (Hab) that was discovered in the first cave at Qumran (1Q). 11QPsa is a psalm found in cave 11, and 4Q285 was the two hundred eighty-fifth fragment identified from cave 4.

HOW PAUL CREATED CHRISTIANITY—OR DID HE?

The parallels between the New Testament and the Dead Sea Scrolls aren't the only scandals in the scrolls, though—at least that's what California State University professor Robert Eisenman, along with Michael Baigent and Richard Leigh, want us to believe. According to these authors, the first followers of Jesus held beliefs that differed radically from anything that contemporary Christians might practice or perceive about Jesus.

Here's what Eisenman claims: In the beginning—before apostles or epistles or New Testament Gospels—there was Jesus and His family. Jesus, as His family knew Him, was a popular prophet, proclaimed by many to be the Messiah. His teachings were profound, perhaps even divine. Jesus Himself, however, was a mere mortal. When Jesus died, leadership of His messianic movement moved to His brother James. The messianic movement led by James was thoroughly Jewish and excluded any possibility of embracing non-Jews.

However, there was another leader on the loose—someone outside the family who saw more in Jesus than a mere Messiah.

His name was Saul of Tarsus.

He is known to most of us as Paul.

According to the conspiracy theorists, Paul twisted the teachings of Jesus and invented "his own highly individual and idiosyncratic theology"—a theology that embraced non-Jews on the basis of their faith in Jesus. Paul falsely attributed this theology to Jesus and established, "for the first time, worship of Jesus."[18] So Paul, not Jesus or His original apostles, created the faith of the New Testament, a faith that promoted Jesus from a messianic teacher to the risen Lord. So successful were Paul's efforts that, according to one scholar, memories of James were "largely erased" and the original form of Christian faith was "marginalized and suppressed."[19]

This wasn't simply a clash of *ideas*, though. In the midthirties A.D., the clash turned violent. According to Robert Eisenman, Paul and James the brother of Jesus ended up in a free-for-all slugfest in front of the Jewish temple. Paul started the skirmish when he grabbed a blazing torch from the altar and took a swing at James and his friends. Before their aggressive negotiations ended, Paul landed a punch so solid that James somersaulted down the temple steps, breaking at least one of his legs when he landed.

Where do the conspiracy theorists find proof for such theories? In radical reconstructions that claim to decode the Dead Sea Scrolls, the New Testament, and a handful of other ancient documents. Eisenman even claims that his reconstructions have "*cracked the codes*' of some of the *'theological disinformation'* . . . involved in these documents."[20]

Eisenman's code cracking runs far beyond repainting perceptions of Paul, though. He also reworks what precipitated the production of many of the scrolls at Qumran. There's a "Righteous Teacher" who's mentioned in several Dead Sea Scrolls. According to Eisenman, that's a coded reference to James the brother of Jesus. And "the Spouter of Lies" or "Scoffer" who makes an appearance in some scrolls? Eisenman, Baigent, and Leigh concur that this must provide a cryptic reference to the apostle Paul.[21] And what about the clash that left James on crutches? Eisenman points to a document known as *Recognitions of Clement* for proof of the slugfest on the temple stairs.[22]

According to theorists such as Eisenman, here's what had happened by the time Christians began to write the texts that became the New Testament: Paul's fabricated version of Christian faith had already gained the upper hand, which isn't surprising if people who resisted the logic of Paul and his posse found themselves lying with a broken leg near the bottom of the stairs! So, the New Testament authors edited and encrypted the stories of their faith until only the tiniest traces of the original traditions remained. In the Acts of the Apostles, Luke turned stories of James inside out to drive home his point that Paul's version of Christian faith represented the winning side. As a result, Acts and other New Testament books contain encoded reflections of the real events of the first century A.D. These codes are so frequent in the New Testament that the clear historical meaning of a New Testament text "may represent a circumlocution or euphemism for something entirely different—sometimes, in fact, something just the opposite."[23] These patterns of "circumlocution" and "euphemism" are the codes that Eisenman claims to have cracked.[24] Whenever something doesn't fit Eisenman's model, he can simply claim that it's an encoded "circumlocution or euphemism" that has "the opposite" meaning of its clear historical intent—a convenient interpretative method, to be sure!

Here are a few examples of how Eisenman's methodology works: Remember the election of Matthias as a replacement for Judas in the first chapter of Acts (vv. 23–26)? According to Eisenman, that's actually Luke's retelling of how the earliest Christians elected James as their leader after the death of Jesus, but Luke reworked the account to remove James from the church's story.[25] And the recounting of how Judas fell "headlong" and "burst open" (Acts 1:18)? That's a veiled jab at James's tumble down the temple steps![26] And the argument between Greek-speaking and Hebrew believers over food distribution recorded in Acts 6? It never happened, Eisenman suggests; it's an encoded rewrite of conflicts between Paul's disciples and the earliest Christians.[27] "What one has in such instances is a species of 'shell-game,'"[28] Eisenman contends, where Luke switched one character or event with another to shroud the sordid origins of Christian faith. In this way, "James the Just has been systematically downplayed or written out of the tradition"[29]—or so Eisenman claims.

CRACKING THE PESHER CODE

Australian professor Barbara Thiering also finds hidden codes in the New Testament texts, and she too claims that she can decrypt them. Her decryptions rely on a literary tool—dubbed "the *pesher* method"—that she claims to have found in the scrolls from Qumran. Thiering's primary inspiration for the pesher method comes from commentaries on Old Testament books such as Habakkuk, found among the first Dead Sea Scrolls. The commentator from Qumran applied Habakkuk's prophecies to circumstances at Qumran; these applications were known as "interpretations" or, in Hebrew, "peshers." Here's an example of one of the Habakkuk peshers:

And the Lord answered and said to me, Write the vision! Make it plain
on the tablets so that it may be read speedily (Habakkuk 2:2)....

Interpreted [*pesher ha-davar*] this concerns the Righteous Teacher,
to whom God revealed all the mysteries of the words of his servants,
the prophets.[30]

So, the Qumran commentator takes a message that was first given to
Habakkuk and applies it to the mysterious "Righteous Teacher."

Occasionally, a certain word might carry a familiar, secondary meaning in
a pesher. For example, the word "Kittim" in Jewish literature often alluded to
a current ruling nation.[31] So, the peshers of Habakkuk referred to the ruling
Romans as "Kittim."

Thus far, there's nothing out of the ordinary in Thiering's theories, but
when she moves from the Dead Sea Scrolls to the New Testament Gospels,
everything suddenly turns very strange.

According to Thiering's pesher method, the New Testament Gospels are
reversed peshers. The Gospel writers—instead of beginning with an ancient
text and developing a pesher from that text—penned their peshers first. Then,
they expected enlightened readers to reconstruct certain original events from
these peshers. Oddly enough, no biblical scholar in the past two thousand
years noticed this process of pesher coding. In fact, *no one* seems to have caught
these pesher codes, which are, according to Thiering, the keys to finding the
true meaning of the New Testament Gospels, until Barbara Thiering unveiled
them a few years ago. Not only Thiering herself but also conspiracy theorists
such as Laurence Gardner, author of such best sellers as *The Magdalene Legacy*
and *Bloodline of the Holy Grail*, find proofs for their theories in the pesher
method.[32]

Here's a small sampling of what Thiering's pesher method has supposedly
revealed about the biblical texts:

■ The Greek word *mello* means "about to" throughout Greek
   literature but not in the pesher method. Interpreted using the
   pesher method, *mello* means "three." So, for example, Acts 12:6
   doesn't mean, "Herod was about to bring him out"; it means,
   "Herod would lead him out in three hours."

■ The Greek word *limos* means "famine" throughout Greek literature but not in the pesher method. Interpreted using the pesher
   method, *limos* means "three and one-half years between a north
   solar year and a south solar year,"[33] which completely changes
   the meaning of texts such as Matthew 24:7 and Acts 11:28.

- Jesus never went to Jerusalem or Galilee. These are coded peshers for other places. Interpreted using the pesher method, these place names refer to different areas or buildings in the Qumran settlement.[34]

- Interpreting the Gospels according to peshers of this sort, Thiering concludes that on Friday, March 20, A.D. 33, at 3:00 p.m., Jesus drank snake venom while hanging from a cross at Qumran.[35]

- Jesus recovered from the effects of the poison in a nearby tomb; Simon Magus rolled away the stone from the door of the tomb, sat on the stone, and declared it to be the throne of the pope—an interesting supposition, since the concept of a papal throne emerged many decades *after* the Gospels were written.

- While sitting on the stone, Simon dubbed himself "Pope Lightning." When Jesus emerged from the tomb, Pope Lightning claimed that he'd performed a miracle.[36]

- On Tuesday, March 17, A.D. 50, at midnight, Jesus married Lydia, who was a female bishop and a member of a group known as "the Thyatira Virgins."[37] No one knows how or where Jesus died, but He was sighted in A.D. 64 in Rome.[38] He was sitting in a booth at the Waffle House with Luke Skywalker and Elvis. (OK, OK. I *did* make up the part about Elvis, Luke Skywalker, and the Waffle House, but everything else comes straight from Dr. Thiering's peshers.)

According to Barbara Thiering, these claims are not conjecture; they come "from a reading of the text by the pesher method."[39] Each of these peshers should have been obvious to everyone, of course, but somehow millions of readers over the past twenty centuries completely missed them.

If the claims of the code breakers are correct, the New Testament does not contain a historical record of Jesus or the early church. What it contains are bizarre codes, rewritten histories, and the fragmented remnants of a theology that died with the defenders of Qumran. The roots of Christianity can be traced to the Dead Sea Scrolls and to the political machinations of a missionary named Paul[40]—not to eyewitness testimony about Jesus. For the few who can see through this haze of codes, it's clear that Jesus was a mere mortal and that the New Testament writings are little more than spin-doctored crypto-grams. If Barbara Thiering's pesher method possesses any validity at all, it's possible that centuries of Christians have completely missed the point of the New Testament texts.

CRACKING THE DEAD SEA SCROLLS CONSPIRACY

So what *do* the scrolls from Qumran tell us about the earliest Christians? Do the Dead Sea Scrolls really rock the foundations of Christian faith? Or are there some facts that the code breakers and conspiracy theorists have reworked to fit their own agendas?

In the first place, it's important to know that each of these speculations shares one common problem: for any of them to work, the Qumran texts must have been composed in the first century A.D., between the death of Jesus and the Roman conquest of Judea. While this is *possible*,[41] it is by no means certain. In fact, the vast majority of scholars places the scrolls in the first and second centuries B.C.—several decades *before* the time of Jesus! Scientific analyses of the Habakkuk pesher scroll have supported this hypothesis. In 1994, the results of carbon 14 testing at the University of Arizona suggested that the scroll originated between 120 B.C. and 5 B.C.[42] If the Dead Sea Scrolls *were* copied in the centuries before Christ, *none* of the most popular conspiracy theories are completely workable.

For the moment, though, let's suppose that the inhabitants of Qumran *did* copy their scrolls in the first century A.D.[43] Would that cause these conspiracy theories to become more believable?

Not really.

Even if the Dead Sea Scrolls *did* come from the first century A.D., serious historical difficulties still stand in the way of the conspiracy theorists. If you don't believe it, take a look with me at a few problems that plague several of the most popular conspiracies that have been concocted around the Qumran scrolls!

 **Parallels between the teachings of Jesus and the teachings at Qumran point to a common heritage, not to a borrowed faith.**

Remember the claims of Michael Baigent and Richard Leigh about the parallels between the New Testament and the Dead Sea Scrolls? If the teachings of Jesus aren't completely unique—Baigent and Leigh contend—"the entire edifice of Christian belief" could fall apart.[44]

The question that Baigent and Leigh fail to answer is *why*.

Why does "the entire edifice of Christian belief" depend on the complete uniqueness of every word that Jesus spoke? The Qumran community and the context into which Jesus was born shared a common heritage of Hebrew Scriptures and Jewish culture. Why would Christianity fall apart if Jesus employed ideas from this culture to drive home His point? Wouldn't it make sense for prophets such as John the Baptist and Jesus of Nazareth to use familiar words and practices to help people to understand their message?

In fact, that's precisely what John and Jesus did.

To communicate their teachings, not only Jesus and John but also the New Testament authors appealed to familiar patterns within their culture. Many parallels to the teachings of Jesus—clauses such as "Your will be done on earth as it is in heaven" (Matthew 6:10), for example, and, "With the measure with which you measure, it shall be measured to you" (Matthew 7:2)—can be found in the teachings of Jewish rabbis.[45] So, why should parallels between the practices of Jesus and the patterns of the Qumran community surprise anyone? The practices of Jesus and of the Qumran community emerged in the context of a shared heritage of Hebrew Scripture and Jewish culture. In such a context, parallels ought to be expected.

Remember the ceremonial washings that were mentioned in the Dead Sea Scrolls, the ones that seemed so similar to baptism? What the conspiracy theorists *don't* mention is how a shared Jewish background probably provided a basis for baptism in *both* groups, not only among the earliest Christians but also in the Qumran community. Believe it or not, the Qumran community didn't invent baptism, and, for that matter, neither did Jesus or John. In fact, the Jewish people probably practiced some form of baptism before Jesus and John were even born. If a non-Jew wanted to embrace the Jewish faith, he or she went through ritual washing as an outward sign of inward repentance and cleansing. This washing seems to have been based on the ritual baths—or *miqveh*—prescribed in the Jewish law (Leviticus 14–17).[46] When John arrived on the scene, he made a radical claim: Everyone, regardless of their racial or religious relationships, needed to repent. Because ritual washing was one of the most common outward signs of repentance in his culture, he called his hearers to express their repentance through baptism (Matthew 3:1–10).

So what about the communion meal that the Qumran community observed? The bread and wine of the Passover meal had been part of the Jewish tradition for more than one thousand years (Exodus 12:1–28). At least as early as the time of the Old Testament prophets, the Jews anticipated a time when they would enjoy a banquet with God's Messiah (Isaiah 25:6–8). Together, these two practices provided the background not only for the ritual meals at Qumran but also the communion meal that Jesus commanded His followers to keep.

What about the titles for the Messiah that appear in the New Testament and in the Dead Sea Scrolls—titles like "Son of the Most High" and "the Righteous One"? All of these can be traced to a common foundation in the Old Testament. The Hebrew Scriptures predicted the coming of a king who would be God's Son (2 Samuel 7:14; Psalm 2:7), and "Most High" had been one of God's titles for more than a millennium (Genesis 14:20–22; Numbers 24:16; Psalm 9:2; Daniel 7:14–18). So, it shouldn't surprise anyone that "Son of the Most High" appears as a messianic moniker in the Dead Sea Scrolls and in the New Testament.[47] In the same way, "Righteous One" appears in the Old Testament as a description of God (Proverbs 21:12; Isaiah 24:16) and of God's Messiah (Isaiah 53:11). So the term is hardly "specifically and uniquely Qumranic in character,"[48] as Baigent and Leigh claim. Although the identity of "the Righteous Teacher" in the Dead Sea Scrolls cannot be determined with absolute certainty,[49] the "Righteous" title in the Dead Sea Scrolls changes nothing that anyone believes about Jesus. Centuries before Jesus was born, "Righteous" was a common title for Israel's God and for the expected Messiah.

What about the claim of Baigent and Leigh that the Dead Sea Scrolls describe a Messiah who suffers and dies? According to these theorists, such a reference would mean that early Christians fabricated stories about a suffering Messiah to fit the Qumran community's expectations. When it comes to the supposed references to a dying Messiah in the Dead Sea Scrolls, the conspiracy theorists face some serious difficulties. What the scroll from Qumran most likely says is, "The Branch of David"—that's a reference to a messianic figure, based on prophecies in Isaiah 11:1 and Jeremiah 23:5—"will kill him with blows and with wounds."[50] The text is too badly fragmented to know precisely *whom* the Branch will kill. It is conceivable to reconstruct the text in such a way that the Branch of David is the one *being* killed. Yet in the context, the author of this fragment refers to Isaiah 11, where the Branch is said to "strike the earth by the power of His command, killing the wicked with the breath of His lips" (Isaiah 11:4). As such, it seems far more likely that the Branch of David is *doing* the killing, not *being* killed. Even if the fragment *did* describe the Branch as being killed, the context describes death in battle, not a voluntary sacrifice of the sort that's attributed to Jesus in the Gospels.

According to Baigent and Leigh, the parallels between Christianity and the Qumran community prove that Christians borrowed their faith from Qumran. That's why, the conspiracy theorists claim, the Dead Sea Scrolls were suppressed. Yet all that the parallels prove is that the Qumran community and earliest Christians shared common roots—a supposition that shouldn't surprise anyone, since the Hebrew Scriptures and Jewish traditions formed the essential foundation of both groups.

Was the suppression of the Dead Sea Scrolls a scandal? Certainly, but it wasn't the content of the scrolls that created the scandal. It was the selfishness of a few scholars who wanted to keep the scrolls to themselves while the world waited.

KNOW MORE

Reconstruction of supposed "Dying Messiah" fragment:

"As it is written in the book of Isaiah the prophet, 'He will cut down the thickets of the forest with an axe, and Lebanon will fall by the Majestic One. A sprig will spring from the stump of Jesse, and a branch from his roots will bear fruit.' [...][51] ...the Branch of David, and they will enter into judgment with [...]...and the leader of the congregation, the Branch of David will kill him with blows and with wounds."

—AUTHOR UNKNOWN, 4Q285
(first century B.C. or first century A.D.)

CLUE NUMBER 2: The peshers have problems.

So what about the peshers? When the Gospels are read according to the pesher method, doesn't that reveal some hidden truths about Jesus? And isn't the pesher method rooted in the Dead Sea Scrolls?

Not even close.

Despite Barbara Thiering's claims to the contrary, the results of her "pesher method" represent sheer speculation. In the first place, her pesher method has nothing to do with the peshers in the Dead Sea Scrolls—nothing beyond her own choice to use the word *pesher* to describe her methodology. The Qumran commentators took familiar ancient texts and applied the texts to the writers' present circumstances. Thiering claims that the New Testament authors wrote peshers *not* to apply an ancient text to their present lives but to encode events that occurred in relatively recent memory, which would mean that these writers weren't actually writing peshers in the first place! Peshers were never penned to conceal certain truths in a document; they were written to reveal truths that might not otherwise be apparent.[52]

How does Thiering come up with the substituted word meanings that she presses into the New Testament texts? For example, how does she know that even though the Greek word *mello* means "about to" in thousands of ancient Greek texts, *mello* somehow implies "three" in the New Testament? How does she know that despite the fact that *limos* means "famine" everywhere else in the ancient world, it carries the obscure implication of "three and one-half years between a north solar year and a south solar year" in the New Testament? How does she move from an angel with an appearance like lightning in Matthew 28 to Simon Magus dubbing himself "Pope Lightning" and turning a stone into his throne?

The Qumran peshers were penned in Hebrew and Aramaic, not Greek. So these redefinitions of Greek words certainly don't come from Qumran! In truth, each of these interpretations seems to stem from one single source—Barbara Thiering's imagination. Her redefinitions simply have no substantive foundation in any historical texts.

Despite my skepticism about these historical reconstructions, I must admit this, though: I *do* like the idea of Simon having the alter ego of "Pope Lightning." I mean, wouldn't "Pope Lightning" make a great superhero? Maybe he could be a cross between Merlin the wizard and a monk with some amazing martial arts moves. "Holy throne of stone, Batman!" Robin would say, "It's Pope Lightning!"

Then, perhaps these supposed peshers could be shelved where their content fits best—with the comic books.

KNOW MORE

In the 1970s and again in the 1990s, some well-intended scholars—Jose O'Callaghan and Carsten Peter Thiede— claimed that Qumran fragment 7Q5 preserved part of Mark 6:52–53 and that remnants of Mark 4:28 could be found in 7Q6.[53] Yet both bits of text are far too fragmentary to make such identifications. 7Q6 preserves only seventeen letters with only one complete word—the Greek word that means "and"! As a result, other scholars have universally dismissed the claims of O'Callaghan and Thiede.[54]

CLUE NUMBER 3: James probably wasn't the "Righteous Teacher" of Qumran.

Did Paul's proclamation about Jesus really differ radically from the first followers of Jesus? Did Paul's reworking of the story of Jesus cause James to be written out of the New Testament texts? What about James's broken leg? Did the apostle Paul actually slam James down the temple stairs? If so, why couldn't they have settled their differences over a friendly round of rock, papyrus, and scissors instead?

To understand the strengths and weaknesses of these claims, it's important to notice *where* the critics find their supposed facts. First, there are the references to the Righteous Teacher in the Dead Sea Scrolls. A few theorists identify this mysterious figure with James the brother of Jesus and suggest that the Dead Sea Scrolls represent a reaction to Paul's version of Christianity.

If the scrolls did date from the first century A.D.—a suggestion that remains far from certain—it *might* be possible that "Righteous Teacher" referred to James.[55] The primary problem for this position is that one document from the Dead Sea Scrolls actually states when the Righteous Teacher's ministry began. Here's what the Damascus Document has to say about the rise of the Righteous Teacher:

> In the age of wrath, 390 years after God handed [Israel] over to King Nebuchadnezzar of Babylon, he visited them and caused a branch to spring from Israel and Aaron to inherit his land and to prosper in the good things of the earth. They recognized their iniquity, and they saw that they were guilty; still, they remained like the blind, groping for their way, for 20 years. God saw their deeds, how they searched for him with a whole heart, and he raised for them a Teacher of Righteousness.[56]

Nebuchadnezzar destroyed Jerusalem in 586 B.C. Three hundred ninety years after that event would be 196 B.C.; another two decades would place the rise of the Righteous Teacher around 176 B.C.—more than two hundred years before the death of Jesus, when James became a leader in the Jerusalem church!

Now, it's true that Jewish writers often rounded and estimated numbers of years, especially in prophetic and apocalyptic writings. So, no one believes that the Righteous Teacher's ministry began precisely in 176 B.C. Yet, based on the dates in the Damascus Document, the most sensible suggestion is that the Righteous Teacher led the Qumran community at some point in the second or first century B.C., several decades before James enjoyed any prominence among the Jewish people.[57]

KNOW MORE

James the brother of Jesus—later known as "James the Just" or "James the Righteous One"—was one of the most revered leaders among the first Christians.[58] He was:

An early eyewitness of the risen Lord (1 Corinthians 15:7)

Pillar of the Jerusalem church (Galatians 2:9)

The leader who issued the authoritative decree about how non-Jews should demonstrate their faith in the Jewish Messiah (Acts 15:13)

Sought out by Paul when Paul arrived in Jerusalem (Acts 21:18; Galatians 1:19)

Said to have been allowed to serve as a priest in the Jerusalem temple[59]

Stoned to death in A.D. 62, following a trial instigated by a corrupt high priest named Ananus

CLUE
NUMBER 4: **Paul couldn't have created Christianity.**

Even if James *could* somehow be identified with the Righteous Teacher—which is, as we've already seen, problematic—the second part of Eisenman's reconstruction remains even more problematic than the first part of his reconstruction. Eisenman, as well as Michael Baigent and Richard Leigh, repaints Paul as James's enemy as the creator of a rival Christianity. Yet this reinterpretation simply cannot muster enough historical evidence to stand.

The primary source for Eisenman's conspiratorial claims is known as *Recognitions of Clement*. This text is attributed to Clement of Rome, a leading pastor of the Roman church in the late first century A.D. The style and content of *Recognitions* clearly suggest that this connection is false. That's why most scholars refer to the work as the *Pseudo-Clementine Recognitions*—in other words, a book that was falsely published under Clement's name. In truth, no one knows who wrote *Recognitions*. The text seems to have emerged sometime in the late second century A.D., perhaps later, from an offshoot of the church known as the Ebionites.

So what does *Recognitions* have to do with James and Paul? Here's what *Recognitions* has to say about James and a certain mysterious "Enemy" at one point in the book:

> The Enemy opposed James on the temple steps....Seizing a burning torch from the altar, the Enemy set an example by lashing out....Much blood was shed, and people fled in confusion. In the midst of the confusion, the Enemy attacked James, knocking him headlong from the top of the stairs. Thinking he was dead, he did not try to inflict any further injury on him....After three days, one of the brothers came to us from Gamaliel; he brought this secret news: The Enemy had received a commission from Caiaphas, the high priest, to go to Damascus with letters of approval. There, with the help of other unbelievers, he would wreak havoc among the believers.[60]

Throughout *Recognitions*, Paul "the Enemy" is the nefarious nemesis of truth while James is the hero, the representative of true faith in Jesus.

Combining texts such as this one with the supposition that the Qumran community's Righteous Teacher was actually James, Robert Eisenman develops the thesis that Paul and James developed two variant versions of Christianity. Through the power of violence and political machinations, Paul turned his version of Jesus into the winner. Luke and other New Testament authors became accomplices in Paul's plot, virtually writing James out of the church's story.

So what's the problem with Eisenman's reconstruction?[61]

Look carefully at some of the primary sources that support his hypothesis: First, there's *Recognitions*, a falsely ascribed document from an unknown author, penned in the late second or early third century A.D. Then, there are some superficial similarities between James the brother of Jesus and the Righteous Teacher. Yet the sole appearances of the Righteous Teacher are in scrolls that were probably written decades before James was even born!

Here's what I find most perplexing in Eisenman's reconstruction: He has taken the *Pseudo-Clementine Recognitions* to present a more accurate picture of the earliest Christians than the New Testament Acts of the Apostles, despite the fact that Acts was written less than a generation after the actual events. *Recognitions*, on the other hand, didn't emerge until the late second, perhaps even the *third*, century A.D.! On the basis of sources such as *Recognitions*—coupled with circumstantial connections between names and events in historical and biblical sources—Eisenman expects us to believe that the New Testament Acts represents an encoded overwriting of the *real* history of the early church.

If Paul and Luke had been the only people to proclaim Jesus as the risen Lord, perhaps Eisenman's reconstruction might seem a little more convincing. Maybe the dynamic duo of a mission-minded Pharisee and his Greek physician could have hatched an alternative vision of the Messiah and proclaimed this fiction throughout the Roman Empire. Yet Paul and Luke *weren't* the only witnesses to the understanding of Jesus that's found in the New Testament. In his first letter to the Corinthians, Paul summarized the story of Jesus in an oral history that had already circulated in Judea prior to Paul's conversion to Christianity (1 Corinthians 15:3–7).[62] The Gospel according to Mark—written in the A.D. 60s and treated even in the first century A.D. as the eyewitness testimony of Simon Peter[63]—clearly depicted Jesus as the risen Lord (Mark 8:31; 9:9, 31; 10:34). What about John's Gospel, a text that included clear, first-century testimony to the divine nature of Jesus (John 20:28)?

If Paul plotted to create a Christianity that differed from James's interpretation, how did Paul pull the apostle John, Mark the Gospel writer, and perhaps even Peter into his plot? The most probable answer is that *he didn't*, because there was no plot to rework the story of the earliest Christians. Paul did not create Christianity. What created Christianity was the shared testimony of hundreds of women and men who saw Jesus alive in the days after His death.

There is one sliver of truth in what Robert Eisenman has to say, though: The New Testament texts *did* downplay the role of James the brother of Jesus, but not for the reasons that Eisenman suggests. The New Testament Gospels and Acts were written primarily for believers in imperial metropolises such as Ephesus and Corinth and Rome, places where Paul had planted churches and where Peter had visited on the way to Rome. So, why do these texts downplay the role of James? As far as anyone knows, James never journeyed beyond the regions around Galilee and Judea.[64] He died in Jerusalem in A.D. 62 at the hands of the high priest Ananus, far from any central cities of the Roman Empire. Who were the primary people to mourn his death? The Jewish citizens of Jerusalem, many of whom were slaughtered or enslaved when the Romans ravaged Judea in A.D. 70. So which apostles' adventures ended up in the literary limelight? Paul's and Peter's, but not because of any theological plotting. It was simply because Paul and Peter were the apostles whom the readers of the Gospels and Acts knew best.[65]

So what about James's tumble down the temple steps?

Who knows?

Perhaps *Recognitions* preserves an authentic oral history at this point. Paul admitted that before he became a believer, he "violently persecuted God's church" in Jerusalem with "a raging fury" (Acts 26:11; Galatians 1:13; Acts 9:1; 22:4; 1 Corinthians 15:9). Perhaps Paul, prior to his experience with Jesus on the Damascus road, *did* attack James. Perhaps this incident from the past pained Paul so deeply that neither he nor Luke ever recorded what happened. If so, it still wouldn't turn Paul into the creator of a version of Christianity that contradicted the faith of the original Christians. It would simply remind us that the biblical writers didn't record everything that may have occurred and that God possesses the power to transform any human heart.

KNOW MORE

The original form of *Pseudo-Clementine Recognitions* seems to have included a second-century A.D. document now known as *Ascents of James*. Although *Ascents* has been lost, it could have included some authentic historical information. In the third century, a Syrian sect with some anti-Paul tendencies turned *Ascents* into a prolonged work of fiction—the text that we know as *"Pseudo-Clementine Recognitions"*—that disparaged Paul and claimed to come from a first-century pastor named Clement of Rome.[66]

CRACKING THE DEAD SEA SCROLLS CONSPIRACY

It has been claimed that the Dead Sea Scrolls could spell the end of Christian faith, but, in truth, what the scrolls provide is a clearer picture of the context that birthed Christianity. It has been claimed that Paul created Christian faith as we know it, but the New Testament texts testify to a message about the risen Lord that preceded Paul's proclamation. It has been claimed that the New Testament is a code, waiting to be decrypted, but the codes turn out to be less believable than the New Testament texts. In the end, the Dead Sea Scrolls provide no compelling reason to doubt the New Testament testimony about Jesus Christ.

HOW TO PREPARE FOR FUTURE CHRIST CONSPIRACIES

The Dead Sea Scrolls *don't* provide scandalous information about Jesus and the earliest Christians; that much is clear. What the Dead Sea Scrolls *do* provide for contemporary believers is a demonstration of how carefully the Jewish people preserved the Hebrew Scriptures. When the Isaiah scroll from Qumran was compared with a copy of Isaiah's prophecies that had been made a millennium later, the two scrolls were nearly identical. The only changes that had emerged in one thousand years of copying the text had to do with spelling and vowel marking. Some other biblical books uncovered at Qumran demonstrated slightly higher frequencies of variance. Yet, even in these scrolls, nothing had changed that might affect any vital belief of Christians or Jews.

Conspiracy Number Eight

JESUS, MARY, AND THE HOLY GRAIL

WHAT'S the CONSPIRACY?

J ESUS MARRIED MARY MAGDALENE, AND THIS LONG-SUPPRESSED information could be entwined with the legend of the Holy Grail.

WHO SAYS SO?

- Dan Brown, *The Da Vinci Code*

- Michael Baigent, Richard Leigh, and Henry Lincoln, *Holy Blood, Holy Grail* and *The Messianic Legacy*

- Laurence Gardner, *The Magdalene Legacy*

- Charles Pellegrino and Simcha Jacobovici, *The Jesus Family Tomb*

- Margaret Starbird, *The Woman With the Alabaster Jar* and *Mary Magdalene, Bride in Exile*

Fully human yet fully God.

It's one of the most confusing paradoxes of Christian faith. How could Jesus be "Light from Light, true God from true God" yet also truly human?[1]

So, just how human *was* Jesus?

Well, if the New Testament is to be believed, He entered this world through human birth (Galatians 4:4), and He endured childhood and puberty (Luke 2:40, 52). He was known for dining with all sorts of people (Matthew 11:19; Luke 24:42)—and it's safe to assume that His deity didn't change how His body dealt with food and drink. Jesus passed gas and fluids and solids just as you do. Though He never failed to follow His Father's will, Jesus was tempted to sin (Hebrews 4:15).

Was He married?

If the New Testament Gospels are to be believed, Jesus certainly *talked* a lot about weddings. He called Himself a "bridegroom" (Matthew 9:15). He compared His kingdom to a wedding feast (Matthew 22:1–11). He performed His first miraculous sign at a wedding (John 2:1–11).

136

Was He ever the bridegroom at a wedding? Did He have a wife? Did He father children?

More than a few conspiracy theorists think so. In fact, many of these theorists are certain that they know not only the marital status of Jesus but also the identity of His wife. Who was the mysterious Mrs. Jesus?

It was Mary Magdalene.

Yes, that's right.

The woman from whom Jesus cast seven demons and who watched Jesus as He died (Matthew 27:55–56; Luke 8:2) was also the woman who shared His bed. In fact, according to one author, the union of Jesus and Mary is "part of the historical record."[2]

Yet if the marriage of Jesus is "part of the historical record," why don't Christians celebrate their Savior's wedding anniversary? I mean, wouldn't it make sense to have a certain Sunday set aside—"Jesus and Mary Anniversary Sunday," perhaps—for spouses to exchange gifts and cards? Why isn't the marriage of Jesus and Mary an essential part of the church's beliefs and practices?

According to the conspiracy theorists, here's why: *early church leaders suppressed the truth about the Messiah's marriage to Mary Magdalene.*

KNOW MORE

Mary Magdalene (biblical character): Disciple of Jesus from whom Jesus cast "seven demons" (Luke 8:2). She witnessed the Crucifixion and empty tomb (Matthew 27:56; Luke 24:10). She may have been from Magadan, a village on the western shore of the Sea of Galilee (Matthew 15:39). It was from the name of this village that Mary would have received the moniker "Magdalene." A tradition arose in the third or fourth century that Magdalene may have been the woman described in Luke 7:36–50 and perhaps the woman caught in adultery in John 8:1–11. In A.D. 591, Gregory, bishop of the Roman church, included these traditions in a sermon.

> It is an embarrassing insight into human nature that the more fantastic the scenario, the more sensational is the promotion it receives and the more intense the faddish interest it attracts. People who would never bother reading a responsible analysis of the traditions about how Jesus was crucified, died, was buried, and rose from the dead are fascinated by the report of some "new insight" to the effect he was not crucified or did not die, especially if his subsequent career involved running off with Mary Magdalene to India.[3]
> —RAYMOND E. BROWN, *The Death of the Messiah* (1994)

THE MAGDALENE CONSPIRACY

That's right, sometime in the early centuries of Christianity, church leaders censored knowledge of this historical event. According to *Holy Blood, Holy Grail* coauthor Michael Baigent, the marriage of Jesus and Mary "is tangled up with secrets about Jesus that the Church is at pains to conceal, and at pains to keep concealing."[4] These secrets include not only the possibility that Jesus married Mary Magdalene but also Mary's subsequent place as leader of the church.

Why was it so crucial to conceal these supposed historical truths? *Because the church's leaders wanted more power for themselves and for the church.* As part of their plan to multiply their power, church leaders worked to portray sex as evil and to place men in positions of control.

If people knew that Jesus had been married, this would have complicated plans to recast sex as sinful, and if Mary had once been head of the church, it would be difficult to relegate women to secondary roles. So, in the words of a character from *The Da Vinci Code*, the early church launched "a smear campaign...to defame Mary Magdalene [and] to cover up her dangerous secret."[5]

Put another way, once upon a time, Christians knew Mary Magdalene as the lover of Jesus and leader of the church, but church leaders twisted the true memories of Mary into fictitious tales that portrayed her as a penitent prostitute. In the process, church leaders also wiped out feminine elements from the Christian faith and "worked hard to demonize sex and recast it as a disgusting and sinful act."[6]

Censored information about Jesus?

The beauty of human sexual expression distorted into something repulsive and vile?

History rewritten to suppress a sordid secret buried somewhere in the church's past?

Sounds like another conspiracy, doesn't it?

What's the proof for such conspiratorial suppositions?

Well, it's in the Bible.

What? You missed that part of the Gospels?

So have most people, but according to some conspiracy theorists, it's possible to reconstruct the remnants of Mary's former position from the Gospel texts.

The wedding at Cana that is described in John 2? That was a wedding dinner[7]—or perhaps a betrothal banquet[8]—for Jesus and Mary Magdalene! The very name *Magdalene* supposedly points to a powerful union between Jesus and Mary. *Magdalene* comes from *migdal*, a Hebrew term that means "powerful tower." Therefore, it is claimed that Mary Magdalene must have been a member of a Jewish royal family that established a dynasty by marrying Magdalene to the Messiah.[9]

What's more, since first-century Jewish males almost always married, Jesus must have been wedded to *someone*—or so some theorists say. Here's how Michael Baigent and Margaret Starbird make this portion of their case for the marriage of Jesus:

> The position of the Pharisees, one of the major groups within Judaism in the first century A.D., was that "it was a man's unconditional duty to marry." The contemporary Rabbi Eliezer is credited with stating: "Whoever does not engage in procreation is like someone who spills blood." So if Jesus was unmarried, as the Church would have us believe, why didn't his Pharisee opponents—of which there were many noted in the New Testament—use his unmarried state as a further criticism of him and his teachings? Why didn't the disciples who were married ask Jesus to explain his failure to marry?[10] . . .
>
> The obligation to marry and to have children was taken seriously, especially among descendants of the Davidic bloodline, from whom the Messiah was expected to stem.[11]

The Gospels never mention any criticism of Jesus's unmarried status. Therefore, the conspiracy theorists reason, Jesus had to have been married.

Quotations from "lost Gospels" provide the conspiracy theorists with further fodder for their claim that Jesus married Mary Magdalene. The Gospel of Mary—a Gospel that a character in *The Da Vinci Code* dubs "a gospel . . . in Magdalene's words"[12]—states that Jesus "loved [Mary] more than any of the other women."[13] The Gospel of Philip even declares, "There were three who had been walking with the Lord in every time: Mary his mother, his sister, and Magdalene—the one they call his companion. . . . The Messiah loved [Mary Magdalene] more than all the disciples, and he was kissing her."[14]

According to several popular writers, the Coptic term translated "companion" comes from a Greek word (*koinonos*) that means "consort" or "spouse"![15]

How might all of this be entwined with the Holy Grail? Well, sometime in the late twelfth century A.D., someone named Chrestien de Troyes penned a poetic novel named *Perceval*, recounting an early version of the legend of the Holy Grail.[16] (This version of the Grail legend was so early, in fact, that it lacked any references to holy hand grenades, killer bunnies, or the airspeed velocity of English swallows.[17])

A century after the publication of *Perceval*, a monk named Jacob de Voragine expanded some medieval stories about the saints into a series of fantastic tales entitled *Legenda Aurea* ("Golden Legend").[18] Voragine's tale located Mary Magdalene, Martha, Lazarus, and several other believers on a boat that drifted from southwestern Asia to southern France sometime in the first century A.D. From their readings of *Perceval*, *Legenda Aurea*, and other medieval myths, conspiracy theorists such as Margaret Starbird, Michael Baigent, and Laurence Gardner have surmised that one person in the boat must have been a child—the offspring of a royal union between Jesus and Mary Magdalene—and that the bloodline represented by this child *was* the Holy Grail.[19]

Archaeological confirmation of the union of Jesus and Mary seems to be available now too. A few weeks before Easter 2007, filmmakers James Cameron and Simcha Jacobovici came up with a somewhat surprising revelation: *In the early 1980s, not far from Jerusalem, Mary Magdalene's bones were discovered near the remains of her husband Jesus.* In 1980, construction workers had accidentally unearthed a tomb that contained several ancient *ossuaries* or "bone boxes." According to a few theorists, these bone boxes contained the remains not only of Jesus and Mary Magdalene but also of someone named "Judas son of Jesus."

Not only was Jesus married; He was a *father*.

Most distressing for the Christian faith, He was still dead.

Nearly two thousand years after Jesus walked and talked with His disciples on this planet, the family tomb of Jesus—complete with the remains of Jesus Himself—had been found. Despite the testimony of the New Testament, it seemed that Jesus was not physically raised from the dead never to die again.[20]

In the face of evidence such as this, what are the possibilities for the future of Christian faith? After all, if the remnants of Jesus's earthly body *did* find their final resting place in an ossuary a few miles outside of Jerusalem, Christian faith is nothing more than a fool's legend. If the remains of Jesus once lay in that bone box, the case for Christianity is closed—and *not* in favor of Christian faith.

CLUES TO CRACK THE MAGDALENE CONSPIRACY

Maybe there's more to the story than the conspiracy theorists have tended to tell. What if, for example, the supposed facts that support a "Jesus family tomb" were spun for the sake of crafting a sensational documentary? What if the evidence for a mortal Messiah isn't quite as strong as it seems at first? What if there was never a scandal that church leaders needed to hide in the first place? These are possibilities that are, at the very least, worth examining a little more closely.

CONSPIRACY NUMBER EIGHT

Jesus married Mary Magdalene and founded a physical dynasty—and this long-suppressed information may be entwined with the legend of the Holy Grail.

The TRUTH BEHIND the CONSPIRACY

The evidences for this claim come from legendary sources that were written long after the New Testament.

KNOW MORE

Holy Grail (from Latin *Gradale* "platter" and Middle English *Sankgreall* "Holy Vessel"): the Holy Grail has been traditionally understood as the cup from which Jesus drank during the Last Supper as well as a vessel that held His blood. It was suggested in some legends that the Grail had a supernatural capacity to grant life and healing. *Holy Blood, Holy Grail* authors Michael Baigent, Richard Leigh, and Henry Lincoln suggest that the French term *Sangreal* ("Holy Grail") derives from *sang real*, which means "royal blood," providing one more supposed connection to the bloodline of Jesus, but "royal blood," in French, would be "*le sang royal*," not "*sang real*."

ossuary (from Latin *os*, "bone"): a box that, in the burial practices of some wealthy Jews of the first century B.C. and the first century A.D., contained the bones from a loved one's body. In this short-lived procedure for preserving the remains of loved ones, the corpse remained in the outer chamber of a family tomb until the flesh decomposed.

Family members then arranged the bones in a limestone box, or ossuary; the ossuary was placed in one of the tomb's inner chambers. Often, the bones from several bodies were placed in a single ossuary. In the supposed "Jesus family tomb," for example, only ten ossuaries were found in a tomb that may have contained the remains of thirty-five persons.

CLUE NUMBER 1: The tomb of Jesus? Probably—but not *that* Jesus.[21]

Let's suppose that you're walking the streets of Jerusalem in the first century A.D. Maybe you're searching for someone named "Mary." If you shouted "Mary!" in a crowded marketplace in the first century, what do you suppose would have happened?

More than *one-fifth* of the women would have turned and looked at you—well, that and several dozen husbands would probably have leaped out of the crowd and pounded you into a pulp for yelling at their wives. As such, to discover just how many Marys would have been part of a typical crowd, perhaps it would be more profitable for you to keep quiet and to take a look at these two tables instead:[22]

TOP TEN WOMEN'S NAMES AMONG PALESTINIAN JEWS AROUND THE TIME OF JESUS

Names in Order of Popularity	Percentage of Female Population
Mary	21.3 percent
Salome	17.7 percent
Martha (including diminutive form Mara)[23]	8.3 percent
Shelam-Zion	7.3 percent
Joanna	3.6 percent
Sapphira	3.6 percent
Bernice	2.4 percent
Imma	2.1 percent
Cyprus	1.8 percent
Sarah	1.8 percent

Now, look at the names of the people who would have beaten you up for yelling at their spouses:

TOP TEN MEN'S NAMES AMONG PALESTINIAN JEWS AROUND THE TIME OF JESUS

Names in Order of Popularity	Percentage of Male Population
Simon	9.3 percent
Joseph (including diminutive forms Joses, Joseh, Josah)	8.3 percent
Lazarus	6.3 percent
Judas	6.3 percent
John	4.7 percent
Jesus	3.8 percent
Ananias	3.1 percent
Jonathan	2.7 percent
Matthew	2.4 percent
Menaen	1.6 percent

Clearly, first-century Jewish parents could have been a bit more creative when choosing their children's names. Nearly half of all females were named Mary, Martha, or Salome, and more than one-fourth of the men were known as Simon, Joseph, Lazarus, or Judas! Not surprisingly, many variations of these names emerged, probably for the purpose of reducing confusion at family reunions. For example, someone named Martha might be dubbed Mara to distinguish her from dozens of other Marthas, while boys named Joseph could end up being called Joses or Joseh.

In such a context, suppose that you located a first-century family tomb that contained ten bone boxes. Now, let's suppose that you saw these names inscribed on six of the ossuaries:

- Mariamne Mara

- Judas son of Jesus

- Matthew

- Joseh[24]

- Mary[25]

- An obscured name that probably reads "Jesus" immediately before the words "son of Joseph"

Most likely, here's how you'd respond: you would recognize that these names—with the possible exception of Mariamne, a rare variant of Mary—were common names in first-century Judea. So common, in fact, that definite conclusions about these people's identities would be impossible.

Unless, of course, you're a filmmaker with little knowledge of ancient history but lots of imagination.[26]

If that's the case, you might concoct a sensational documentary about the ossuary inscriptions. In this documentary, you might conveniently downplay the actual inscriptions, opting instead for a string of vague literary connections that would be laughable except for the fact that so many people might take the connections seriously. Perhaps you would even try to turn your documentary into a faith-shaking moneymaker, released a few weeks before a celebration of Jesus's resurrection.

That is precisely what the producer and director of the documentary film *The Jesus Family Tomb* chose to do.

Here's a taste of what *The Jesus Family Tomb* suggests about these ancient ossuaries:

■ Mary Magdalene's "real name" was Mariamne;[27] therefore, the bones in the ossuary marked "Mariamne" must have belonged to Mary Magdalene.

■ DNA comparison of the physical remains of Mariamne and Jesus son of Joseph demonstrated that these two individuals did not have the same mother; therefore, Mariamne and Jesus would "most likely have been husband and wife."[28]

■ The clustering of names on the ossuaries in this family tomb is so unique that the connection to the family of Jesus Christ of Nazareth is virtually certain.[29]

What historical evidence do the producers of *The Jesus Family Tomb* produce to support these claims?

Well, here's how director Simcha Jacobovici describes his discovery of the link between Mariamne and Mary Magdalene:

I said, "See if there's a connection between Mariamne and Magdalene."

"Well," Ron smiled a toothless grin, "today we have the Internet. Why don't we look into it right now?" He googled "Mariamne" and then turned slightly pale. "Look, Simcha," Ron exclaimed. Over his shoulder I peered at the screen and the article his search had led him to. "According to modern scholarship," he read out loud. "Mary Magdalene's real name was Mariamne."[30]

After reading this paragraph in *The Jesus Family Tomb*, I "turned slightly pale" too, but that was primarily because I was laughing so hard that it became difficult to breathe. Here's why: the source of this supposed connection is a gnostic tract known as the Acts of Philip.

When was the Acts of Philip written?

Sometime in the *fourth century* A.D.

That's right. In the book *The Jesus Family Tomb*, the theory that Mariamne was Mary Magdalene hinges on a literary link between a first-century tomb inscription and a fourth-century gnostic writing! In the documentary film, this connection becomes even more comical. The narrator intones at one point in *The Jesus Family Tomb* that "from the second century when church fathers began suppressing dozens of early Christian writings, the church rejected two writings that held Mary Magdalene in highest regard: the Gospel of Mary Magdalene and a text describing her brother's ministry, the Acts of Philip."

How *second-century* Christian leaders could have suppressed a *fourth-century* gnostic text, I do not know. Perhaps the sequel to *The Jesus Family Tomb* will offer a few more details about how church leaders squelched a text two centuries before the text even existed. Until that time, I will simply have to stand amazed at these time-traveling theologians of the early church.

Even more problematic for the hypotheses of *The Jesus Family Tomb*, Mariamne is *never* clearly identified in the Acts of Philip as Mary Magdalene![31] The portrayal of Mariamne in the text *does* parallel the descriptions of Mary Magdalene in a few other gnostic texts, but no explicit identification is ever made in the text. Interesting literary connections? Perhaps, but such parallels are far from proof that Mary Magdalene's real name was Mariamne![32]

Perhaps most ridiculous is the claim that because DNA analysis failed to make a maternal connection between Mariamne and Jesus, the two must have been married. I must admit, this one left me scratching my head. Even without the capacity for careful scholarly research, someone should have seen several possibilities beyond husband and wife. What about father and daughter? Paternal uncle and niece? Sister and adopted brother? Paternal grandfather and granddaughter? In a family tomb that could have originally contained the remains of more than thirty kin,[33] the fact that two people were unrelated on their mother's side means only that Mariamne and Jesus were not biological siblings—nothing more.

In the end, though, it's the sheer commonness of the names on the ossuaries that shatters the claims of *The Jesus Family Tomb*. Every name found in the tomb stands among the most popular names for first-century Judeans. Of the forty thousand or so men from multiple generations who would have lived in Jerusalem around the time of Jesus, approximately *fifty-six hundred* would have borne the title "Jesus son of Joseph"! Of these, at least twenty would have had a brother named James.[34] Despite the convoluted statistics that the producers of *The Jesus Family Tomb* have manipulated to confirm their case,[35] the clustering of names in the tomb is simply not sufficiently unique to substantiate their claims.

Not far from the site of the supposed Jesus family tomb, another tomb has also been unearthed and dubbed *Dominus Flevit*.[36] What names were inscribed on the bone boxes inside the tomb? On the ossuaries, archaeologists found names such as Joseph, Judas, Mary, John, Lazarus, Martha, Matthew, Salome, Simon son of Jonah, and Jesus.

Another tomb filled with familiar names from the New Testament? A tomb that once contained the corpse of someone named Jesus, the sixth most common name among first-century Judean males?

Well, yes, but just like the tomb featured in *The Jesus Family Tomb*, it isn't the tomb of *that* Jesus, the one known as "Jesus the Messiah." These names were too common in the first century for contemporary scholars to make any reasonable connections between the tomb and biblical texts.

This much seems clear, though: if the body of Jesus Christ *had* remained in a tomb after His disciples declared that they had seen Him alive, the religious authorities of first-century Jerusalem would have located the body, silencing all claims that this man might have risen from the dead. Yet they didn't for one single reason: the tomb was *empty*.

KNOW MORE

Acts of Philip (Christian writing, fourth century A.D.): in this text, Jesus sends Philip and His sister Mariamne to proclaim the gospel throughout the world. François Bovon, who discovered the most complete surviving manuscript of the Acts of Philip, stated that Mariamne in the Acts of Philip seems to serve the same literary function as Mary Magdalene in the Gospel of Mary. Simcha Jacobovici, director of *The Jesus Family Tomb*, misconstrued this literary parallel to mean that Mariamne and Mary Magdalene represented the same historical person.[37]

Gospel of Mary (gnostic writing, mid to late second century A.D.): though often known as the the Gospel of Mary Magdalene, it is not clear if Mary Magdalene is the primary Mary in this fragmentary Gospel. The text seems to provide imaginative reworking of a postresurrection appearance of Jesus.

> Gospel of Philip (gnostic writing, late second or early third
> century A.D.): not a narrative Gospel but a collection of
> excerpts from various gnostic teachers, influenced by the
> teachings of a second-century gnostic named Valentinus.

CLUE NUMBER 2: No ancient historical record clearly suggests that Jesus married Mary Magdalene.

So what about the New Testament Gospels? Couldn't the wedding at Cana have been the marriage banquet of Jesus and Mary Magdalene? Even if Jesus Christ *wasn't* buried with Mary in a family tomb, isn't it possible that the Gospels imply a marriage between Jesus and Mary Magdalene?

It's *possible*, but before buying into this theory, let's look carefully at the evidence for this supposed union. Michael Baigent and others have repeatedly suggested that the wedding at Cana was the marriage of Jesus and Mary. "That would explain," Baigent claims, "why he was 'called' to the wedding [John 2:2] and subsequently had the responsibility over the wine."[38] In actuality, the presence of the word *call* suggests the precise opposite! Among first-century Jews, it was *guests* who received a call to a feast. Jesus set up His parable about a wedding feast with these words: "The kingdom of the heavens is like a certain king who arranged a marriage for his son. He sent out his slaves *to call the ones that were called to the marriage*"[39] (Matthew 22:2–3, emphasis added). Throughout the Gospels, it's clear that when it came to feasts and wedding banquets, the ones who received the "call" were guests, *not* the bride or groom or host! (See also Matthew 22:8–9; Luke 14:8, 12–24.)[40]

What about the fact that Jewish males almost always married, especially if they descended from King David? That's true, but it's also true that first-century Jews admired celibacy for the sake of devotion to a divine task. In fact, some members of a Jewish sect known as "Essenes" remained unmarried. The first-century Jewish philosopher Philo celebrated their lifestyle with these words:

> The Essenes…reject marriage, practicing an eminent degree of self-
> control.… This is the commendable lifestyle of these Essenes. Not only
> ordinary individuals but also mighty kings admire these men, revere
> their sect, and increase their dignity and majesty in ever-higher degrees
> by their approval and by the honors that they confer on them.[41]

Yes, most Jewish males married, but some Jews also willingly committed themselves to become, in the words of Jesus, "eunuchs for the sake of the kingdom of the heavens" (Matthew 19:12). Because of this commitment, these persons—at least among the Essenes—received respect from the masses and support from the wealthy. In such a context, the silence of the Gospels regarding Jesus's marital status neither confirms nor denies the Savior's singleness.

The sole ancient texts that *might* suggest some intimate relationship between Jesus and Mary are the Gospel of Mary and the Gospel of Philip. According to the Gospel of Mary, Jesus "loved [Mary] more." *The Da Vinci Code* suggests that this writing was "a gospel…in Magdalene's words,"[42] even though the Gospel of Mary never actually states that the primary Mary in the text is Mary Magdalene. Even if the text *did* denote itself as the testimony of Mary Magdalene, this claim still could not stand. The style and substance of the Gospel of Mary point clearly to an origin in the mid to late second century A.D., long after the death of Mary Magdalene![43] More important, even if Jesus *did* love Mary "more" than the other disciples, this doesn't require a sexual relationship, as the conspiracy theorists imply.

The Gospel of Philip emerged even later than the Gospel of Mary—in the late second century at the earliest, more likely in the third century.[44] So, even if the Gospel of Philip did claim that Jesus married Magdalene, the testimony couldn't be connected reliably to any eyewitnesses of Jesus's ministry. As it turns out, though, the Gospel of Philip never identifies Jesus and Mary as an intimate couple in the first place.

According to the Gospel of Philip, Jesus "was kissing" Mary Magdalene.[45] At this point in the Gospel of Philip, a small hole appears in the text. As such, it's impossible to know *where* Jesus supposedly kissed Mary. In a culture where kissing served as a common greeting among friends (Acts 20:37; Romans 16:16; 1 Corinthians 16:20; 2 Corinthians 13:12; 1 Thessalonians 5:26; 1 Peter 5:14), kissing would have suggested close friendship but not necessarily a sexual or marital connection.

The Gospel of Philip also refers to Mary Magdalene as "companion" of Jesus. The term translated "companion" is a Coptic derivative of the Greek word *koinonos*. Several conspiracy theorists—Michael Baigent, Margaret Starbird, Laurence Gardner, and Dan Brown among them—claim that *koinonos* meant "consort" or "spouse" in the ancient world.[46] The problem for these conspiracy theorists is that the word *koinonos* never consistently implied such a relationship. In fact, what *koinonos* denoted was *a fellow participant in a shared goal*. The term appears ten times in the New Testament, and not once does it even vaguely imply a sexual or marital relationship. James and John shared a *koinonos* relationship with Simon Peter (Luke 5:10); Paul had *koinonos* connections with Titus, Philemon, and the entire church at Corinth (2 Corinthians 1:7; 8:23; Philemon 17); and Simon Peter called himself a *koinonos* in God's glory (1 Peter 5:1). Somehow, the conspiracy theorists' sexualized definitions of *koinonos* don't seem to work in any of these instances—or in the Gospel of Philip, for that matter. (For further examples of the functions of *koinonos* in Christian literature, see Matthew 23:30; 1 Corinthians 10:18, 20; Hebrews 10:33; 2 Peter 1:4.)

What about supposed links between Mary Magdalene and the Holy Grail? No ancient evidence whatsoever exists to support such suppositions. The earliest reference to the existence of a Holy Grail emerged more than a millennium after the time of Jesus in a novel penned by Chrestien de Troyes. Another century passed before anyone attempted to place Mary Magdalene on a boat that might have held the legendary Grail.

So who originated the claim that Mary Magdalene *was* the Holy Grail and that she preserved the bloodline of Jesus? This claim can be traced to some bizarre reinterpretations of the life of a nineteenth-century priest named Béranger Saunière. This priest—who served a Roman Catholic congregation in a tiny French village known as Rennes le Chateau—was said to have possessed positive proof of some long-suppressed secret about Jesus. Saunière supposedly used this secret to blackmail the Roman Catholic church. In the early 1980s, these hypotheses formed the backbone of the best-selling books *Holy Blood, Holy Grail* and *The Messianic Legacy*.[47]

What's the problem with these claims? The documents that seemed to support these connections came from a Frenchman named Pierre Plantard who evidently aspired to become the king of France. Plantard's documents traced a royal bloodline from Jesus and Mary Magdalene through the kings of France to Pierre Plantard himself—and all of his supposed proofs were forged. In 1993, Plantard admitted, under oath, that his claims had been completely false.[48]

Despite the clamoring of conspiracy theorists to the contrary, the marriage of Jesus and Mary Magdalene is *not* "part of the historical record"[49]—unless, of course, your definition of a "historical record" consists of frail literary parallels, forged documents from a French megalomaniac, and medieval legends of a Holy Grail.[50] Otherwise, this supposed union simply cannot survive any test of historical probability.

KNOW MORE

According to one of the protagonists in *The Da Vinci Code*, the major religions of the world have "worked hard to demonize sex and recast it as a disgusting and sinful act."[51] A glance at the Old and New Testaments quickly calls this claim into question: "Rejoice in the wife of your youth," one Jewish sage commanded, "let her breasts fill you with delight" (Proverbs 5:18–19). According to the apostle Paul, the only reason for a wife and husband *not* to have sex consistently was if they had agreed to "devote [themselves] to prayer for a limited time" (1 Corinthians 7:3–5). Even in the second century, church leaders viewed sexual expression within marriage in positive terms: "Through his Son, God is with those who have solemnly married and produced children," Clement of Alexandria wrote. "By the same word of reconciliation, the same God is also with the one who reasonably exercises celibacy."[52]

KNOW MORE

Why does the quest for the Holy Grail continue to capture people's imaginations? Even if they don't desire to admit it, every person longs to make contact with something that comes from God. In every human heart, there is a longing for that which is eternal (Ecclesiastes 3:11). The bad news is that even if someone found the Holy Grail, it still wouldn't satisfy this longing. The good news is that God *has* provided a way for humanity to experience the eternal realm. Through faith in Jesus Christ as your Lord and God, you can directly experience the Spirit of God. This Spirit, dwelling in the hearts of believers, "testifies with our spirits that we are God's children" (Romans 8:16). In this way, each of us can become a "Holy Grail"—a recipient of the very presence of God.

CRACKING THE MAGDALENE CONSPIRACY

A few years ago, *The Da Vinci Codebreaker*—a book I cowrote with my friend Jim Garlow—hit the best-seller lists about the same time that Sony Pictures released the movie *The Da Vinci Code*. As a result, nearly one hundred television and radio stations interviewed one or both of us in the space of a few weeks. At some point during that flurry of interviews, one interviewer asked me, "Why are you so against the idea that Jesus was married?"

"I'm not," I replied after a second or two of reflection. "If I woke up tomorrow morning and heard that archaeologists had exhumed incontrovertible evidence that Jesus married Mary Magdalene, it wouldn't affect my faith in the least. The New Testament neither affirms nor denies the singleness of Jesus. Whether Jesus was a lifelong bachelor or a devoted husband, He was still God in human flesh, a sinless sacrifice, and the risen Lord. As I examine the historical evidence, I find absolutely no substantial evidence to suggest that Jesus was married. I find even less evidence of some sort of churchwide cover-up. If Jesus did marry Mary Magdalene or anyone else, it seems that the Gospels would have specifically mentioned this woman as His wife. When the church fathers first mentioned the marital status of Jesus in the second century, they assumed that Jesus was single—it's not something they felt compelled to defend. I'm not against the idea that Jesus was married. What I'm against is the weak historical basis of such a supposition."

The idea of a married Messiah wasn't rejected because such a revelation might cause the Christian faith to fall apart—it wouldn't. It wasn't rejected because the earliest Christians wanted to degrade human sexuality or to demonize women, as *The Da Vinci Code* claims,[53] and there is no proof whatsoever of a conspiracy to hide this information. The marriage of Jesus didn't become part of the church's story of Jesus for a single reason: no reliable proof exists for such a marriage.

HOW TO PREPARE FOR FUTURE CHRIST CONSPIRACIES

Why, even after being debunked hundreds of times, does the idea of a long-suppressed marriage between Jesus and Mary Magdalene still catch people's attention? I suppose it's because everyone would like to discover something that's been hidden. That's why murder mysteries, conspiracy theories, and tales of hidden treasure still show up on the best-seller lists. What could possibly be more intriguing than the thought that there has been a conspiracy hidden in a place that we would never suspect—in the pages of the New Testament?

This conspiracy will, without a doubt, surface again and again. Each time, consider carefully the sources of the supposed information. Do the sources represent eyewitness testimony about Jesus? Have the creators of the conspiracy theory derived their data from first-century sources? Do their conclusions represent reasonable deductions from their data? Or have they selected only the most sensational scenario from several possibilities?

Conspiracy Number Nine

THE DOGS BENEATH
THE CROSS

WHAT'S the CONSPIRACY?

JESUS WAS NEVER BURIED, AND HE WAS NEVER RAISED FROM THE DEAD. Dogs and other wild animals consumed His body.

WHO SAYS SO?

- John Dominic Crossan, *Jesus: A Revolutionary Biography, Who Killed Jesus?* and *The Historical Jesus*

- Gerd Lüdemann, *What Really Happened? A Historical Approach to the Resurrection*

So much can depend on the answer to a single question.

"Will you marry me?"

"Did he get the job?"

"Was I accepted into the program?"

"Did she survive?"

"Will you forgive me?"

Sometimes everything comes together—or falls apart—in the shadow of a single question.

Christian faith is that way.

In the case of Christianity, everything depends on one question: What happened after Jesus died? If Jesus returned to life after He died, there is every reason to entrust my entire existence to Him. If Jesus is still dead, Christianity is the most far-fetched lie that the world has ever known.

So, what did happen after Jesus died? Here's one possibility that several scholars have proposed: Suppose that the body of Jesus never made it to a tomb. What if the Romans left Him on the cross? What if His remains became food for birds and beasts? What if He was never raised from the dead because there was no body left to be resurrected?

152

```
CONSPIRACY NUMBER NINE
```

Jesus was never buried, and He was never raised from the dead. Dogs and other wild animals consumed His body.

```
The TRUTH BEHIND the CONSPIRACY
```

Roman and Jewish legal codes would have required Jesus's burial. Five independent witnesses testify together that Jesus was crucified and raised from the dead.

The CARRION CONSPIRACY[1]

With few exceptions, even skeptical scholars admit that Jesus was crucified—and for good reason. Not only Christian authors but also the Roman historian Tacitus mention the crucifixion of Jesus. It's highly unlikely that first-century Christians would have fabricated such a shameful fate for the founder of their faith. In the first century A.D., crucifixion represented the darkest possible path to death.

The Roman philosopher Seneca described what he witnessed at a crucifixion with these words: "I see the stakes there—not of one kind but of many. Some victims are placed head down; some have spikes driven through their genitals; others have their arms stretched out on the gibbet."[2] Beginning in the third century B.C., the very word *crucify* was a vulgarism that did not pass freely between the lips of cultured people. In one ancient document, a Roman prostitute hurled this insult—perhaps the lewdest curse in her vocabulary—at an uncouth patron: "Go get yourself crucified!"[3]

That's why first- and second-century folk referred to the worship of a crucified God as "foolishness," "insanity," and "idiocy." In fact, one of the earliest graphical depictions of such worship is a scrap of late second-century graffiti, uncovered near Rome in a palace where slaves trained to serve the imperial family.

In this graffito, a man with the head of a donkey dangles naked from a cross. At the foot of the cross, someone kneels, surrounded by these rough-scrawled words: *Alexamenos sebete theon*. "Alexamenos worships God."[4] Evidently, someone—perhaps a servant training to serve Caesar himself—was ridiculing a young man named Alexamenos because Alexamenos had embraced a new religion, a faith centered around a deity who suffered the punishment for humanity's sin on a cross.

And no wonder.

The shame of crucifixion ran deeper than the nakedness, the torture, and the taunting. In most cases, crucified bodies were not even buried. Instead, in the days that followed the deaths of the crucified, the beaks of vultures and the teeth of wild dogs tore the corpses to shreds and scattered their remains across the countryside.

> Roman crucifixion was state terrorism;…its function was to deter resistance or revolt and…the body was usually left on the cross to be consumed eventually by the wild beasts….The norm was to let the crucifieds rot on the cross or be cast aside for carrion.[5]

According to such critics as John Dominic Crossan, that's what happened to Jesus too. Consumed by birds and beasts, the flesh of Jesus degenerated inside the stomachs of wild creatures and became the dung that decayed in the sun in the alleys of Judea.

Not a pleasant thought, is it?

Not the end that you'd imagined for someone as celebrated as Jesus.

But what if it's true?

Crossan does, after all, have some archaeological and literary evidence that stands on his side. For example, not long after the birth of Jesus, the Roman general Varus crucified two thousand Jewish rebels at once.[6] While besieging Jerusalem in A.D. 69 and 70, the Roman general Titus crucified Jewish captives in view of the denizens of Jerusalem.[7] In each of these cases—and in many, many other instances of mass execution—it seems that the bodies remained on crosses. There, weather and wild creatures reduced their flesh to dust and dung.

The fate of crucified corpses is mentioned in many literary texts too. Suetonius wryly noted regarding a crucified man, "The carrion-birds will quickly take care of his burial." "The vulture hurries," the satirist Juvenal claimed, "from dead cattle to dead dogs to crosses."[8] The epitaph of a second-century murder victim includes this haunting clause: "My murderer was suspended from a tree, while still alive, for the benefit of beasts and birds."[9]

Crossan seems to have a bone that supports his argument too—a heel bone with a spike in it, to be exact. Over the span of four centuries, the Romans crucified tens of thousands of murderers, revolutionaries, and persons trapped on the wrong side of the political tides. Yet all that seems to have survived from these thousands of cadavers is one single heel bone, still pierced by a spike.[10] According to the inscription on the side of this man's ossuary, his name was John. He was a Jew.

Why have the remains from only one crucified body survived? According to Crossan, it's because, in nearly all cases, weather and wild creatures dealt with the corpses of the crucified. Crossan declares:

I keep thinking of all those other thousands of Jews crucified around Jerusalem in that terrible first century from among whom we have found only one skeleton and one nail. I think I know what happened to their bodies, and I have no reason to think Jesus' body did not join them.[11]

The body of Jesus became carrion for wild beasts. And what of the Resurrection? From Crossan's perspective, it was a hallucination that emerged from the disciples' deep-seated hopes and dreams.

> In the ancient mind, the supreme horror of crucifixion was to lose public mourning, to forfeit proper burial, to lie separate from one's ancestors forever....In normal circumstances the soldiers guarded the body until death and thereafter it was left for carrion crow, scavenger dog, or other wild beasts to finish the brutal job. That nonburial consummated the authority's dreadful warning to any observer and every passerby.[12]
>
> —JOHN DOMINIC CROSSAN, member of the Jesus Seminar

CLUES TO CRACK THE CARRION CONSPIRACY

So what *did* happen to the body of Jesus? Does any reliable evidence exist to suggest that beasts and carrion fowl *didn't* feed on His flesh? And what of the disciples' visions of the risen Lord? Can these be explained as hopeful hallucinations?

That's possible, but Crossan's case isn't quite closed yet. There are other evidences that point to several alternative possibilities—possibilities that are more probable than any of Crossan's claims. Even if you aren't convinced that Jesus was the risen Lord, at least take a look at a few of these possibilities and see where they may lead.

CLUE NUMBER 1: **The Jews would have wanted the body of Jesus to be buried.**

In most areas of the Roman Empire, crucified bodies became pickings for vultures and dogs.

But not always, and not everywhere.

In Judea—and especially around Jerusalem—there was a law that, from the Jews' perspective, came from a higher source than Caesar. In this law, God commanded the Israelites:

If someone commits a capital crime for which he is executed and if you hang him on a tree, his body shall not remain all night upon the tree. You shall bury him the same day, for anyone hanged from a tree is damned by God. You shall not defile your land that the Lord your God is giving you as an inheritance.

—DEUTERONOMY 21:22–23; see also EZEKIEL 39:14–16

The Temple Scroll from Qumran testifies to how seriously Jews took this command in the centuries before Christ: "You shall not allow bodies to remain on a tree overnight; most assuredly, you shall bury them, even on the very day of their death."[13] The Jewish Book of Tobit—an entertaining little text, penned in the time period that stands between the Old and New Testaments—identifies the burial of abandoned corpses as an act of supreme piety.[14]

Near the end of the first century A.D., the Jewish historian Josephus contrasted the Jewish perspective on crucified bodies to typical Roman practices. According to Josephus, "Jews are conscientious about their burial practices—so much so that even criminals sentenced to crucifixion are removed and buried before the sun sets!"[15] In another writing, Josephus stated, "[Jews] must furnish fire, water, and food to anyone who asks, giving directions to the right road, *never leaving a corpse unburied.*"[16] Later rabbis echoed this concern for the deceased. According to the rabbis, although the bodies of criminals might not immediately be placed with the bodies of their ancestors, even criminals had to be buried. After their flesh decomposed, even the bones of criminals were placed in a family tomb.[17]

Especially on the eve of a festival as important as Passover, someone would have wanted the body of Jesus removed from the cross. In the case of a figure as popular and potentially problematic as Jesus, it's likely that someone would have been willing to bury Him, even if that act rendered the person ceremonially unclean during the Passover celebration.

In this context, the request of Joseph of Arimathea makes complete sense (Mark 15:43–45). To be sure, Joseph wanted to honor the body of Jesus, but from the perspective of Pontius Pilate and fellow members of the ruling council, here's how his motive would have appeared: As a member of the ruling council, Joseph of Arimathea wanted the corpse removed before sundown to avoid any defilement in the land of Israel (Deuteronomy 21:23). A burial overseen by the Jewish ruling council also fits with the assumptions of the Gospel of Peter—a Gospel that, though written several decades after the apostolic eyewitnesses, may well retain remnants of an ancient retelling of the resurrection narrative, independent of the New Testament Gospels.[18]

Someone would have wanted to bury the body of Jesus; that much seems certain. Both the Roman authorities and the ruling council would have wanted to stifle any loyalty to this would-be Messiah as soon as possible. Furthermore, from a Jewish perspective, *not* to bury His body would have violated the law of God. So, the question isn't whether anyone would have requested the body of Jesus; someone would have. The question is, Would the Romans actually have granted such a request?

 **Roman law required Pontius Pilate to hand over the body of Jesus.**

In times of rebellion and war, Romans ignored the native practices of occupied nations. That's why, when crushing the Jewish independence movement in A.D. 70, the Romans crucified thousands of Jews and left the corpses to rot on their crosses.

Jesus wasn't crucified in a time of war.

He was, in fact, crucified during a relatively peaceful period in the history of Judea.

In times of relative peace, Romans consistently respected the laws of occupied nations. "The Romans," Josephus contended, "do not require...their subjects to violate their national laws."[19] The Jewish philosopher Philo of Alexandria described Roman practices among the Jews in this way: "I've known cases when, on the eve of a holiday of this sort, people who have been crucified were taken down, their bodies being handed over to their families, because it was considered good to give them burial and allow them ordinary rites. It was appropriate that the dead also should have the advantage of kindness upon the emperor's birthday and also that the sanctity of the festival should be maintained."[20]

As part of this pattern of toleration for local peculiarities, Pontius Pilate would probably have granted the body of a deceased Jew to his own people, even if Roman law didn't demand it. After all, hadn't Herod Antipas given the body of John the Baptist to his disciples after he beheaded the popular prophet?[21] During a potentially volatile religious festival, Pilate had an even greater reason to respect local customs. Pilate's desperate determination to maintain peace during the Passover would probably have persuaded the governor to hand over the body of Jesus for burial.

There's even more to the story, though; such concessions weren't just Roman practice. They were Roman *law*.

Here's what *Pandectae*—a summary of the Roman legal code—declared about the bodies of crucified criminals:

> The bodies of those who are condemned to death should not be refused their relatives; and [Caesar] Augustus the Divine, in the tenth book of his *Vita*, said that this rule had been observed.

> At present, the bodies of those who have been punished are only buried when this has been requested and permission granted; and sometimes it is not permitted, especially where persons have been convicted of high treason.... The bodies of persons who have been punished should be given to whoever requests them for the purpose of burial.[22]

This fits perfectly with the description in the New Testament Gospels. Roman law called Pilate to provide the body of Jesus "to whoever" requested it "for the purpose of burial." When Joseph of Arimathea requested the body of Jesus, Pilate verified that Jesus was dead. He had already dealt with Jesus once, and he didn't want to deal with Him again if His followers somehow resuscitated Him. That's why theories claiming that Jesus somehow survived the Crucifixion can be readily written off. If someone had rallied supporters in a way that might result in a revolt under the right circumstances, the Romans would have made certain that this rabble-rouser couldn't come back. Once the centurion confirmed that Jesus was dead, Pilate granted Joseph's request.

"Roman legal practice," Gerd Lüdemann claims in the book *What Really Happened? A Historical Approach to the Resurrection*, "provided for someone who died on the cross to rot there or be consumed by vultures, jackals or other animals."[23] Despite the confident title of Lüdemann's text, this was *not* "what really happened"; Roman legal practice explicitly provided for the precise opposite. Other than mass crucifixions during times of war or revolt, it was only when a Roman official was executed for high treason that burial was forbidden—a category that the crucifixion of Jesus certainly didn't fit.[24]

CRACKING THE CARRION CONSPIRACY

So, why—if families could request an executed corpse—does Roman literature include so many references to the consumption of crucified corpses by birds and beasts? And why has only a single heel bone from one crucified man survived?

Don't forget this crucial fact: crucifixion constituted the supreme dishonor in the ancient world. The very word *crucify* remained unmentioned in polite company. Among Romans, suicide was to be preferred above a cross.[25] As such, beyond the borders of the Jewish provinces, it would have been highly unusual for a family to reclaim the corpse of their crucified kin; families would have disowned this person because of the shame that the accused criminal's actions had brought on their family's name. These forsaken bodies—the vast majority of the victims of Roman crucifixion—remained on their crosses to be consumed.[26] Thus their remains disintegrated into the dust of the Roman Empire. The case of Jesus—a Jew, crucified near Jerusalem on the eve of a popular religious festival—doesn't fit the typical pattern. The Jews would have wanted Jesus buried, and Roman law required Pontius Pilate to grant this request.

> ## KNOW MORE
>
> In *The Jesus Papers*, Michael Baigent claims to have seen a letter from Jesus Himself that was written in Aramaic and sent to the Jewish ruling council. According to Baigent, the letter proves that Jesus faked His death and fled to Egypt. The problem is, Baigent himself admits that he can't read Aramaic, so he had to rely on the word of an antiquities dealer to determine the content of the letter. But the antiquities dealer to determine the content of the letter, but the antiquities dealer couldn't read Aramaic either and Baigent refuses to provide his name. The two scholars who supposedly authenticated the letter? They died before Baigent's book was published. In the words of Christian scholar Craig Evans, "No living, qualified expert has seen these documents, and the two who say they have seen them—and are still living—cannot read them.... Baigent neglects to mention that archaeologists and papyrologists will tell you that no papyrus...can survive buried in the ground, in Jerusalem, for two thousand years.... Jerusalem receives rainfall every year; papyri buried in the ground, beneath houses or wherever, decompose quickly. So whatever Baigent saw, they were not ancient papyri found beneath somebody's house in Jerusalem, and they were not letters Jesus wrote."[27]

HOW TO PREPARE FOR FUTURE CHRIST CONSPIRACIES

Carefully study several sources that explore the historical backgrounds of the death of Jesus. I especially recommend these texts: *The Resurrection of the Son of God* by N. T. Wright, *The Resurrection of Jesus* by N. T. Wright and John Dominic Crossan, and *Jesus' Resurrection: Fact or Figment* by William Lane Craig and Gerd Lüdemann. Be absolutely certain that you possess an adequate answer to the question: How do you know that Jesus died and that He was buried?

Conspiracy Number Ten

NO PLACE FOR THE EVIDENCE

WHAT'S the CONSPIRACY?

H ISTORY DEALS WITH WHAT PROBABLY HAPPENED. SINCE MIRACLES are always improbable, the resurrection of Jesus cannot be considered a historical event, regardless of how much historical evidence supports the Resurrection.

WHO SAYS SO?

- Bart Ehrman, *Jesus: Apocalyptic Prophet of the New Millennium*

- James Tabor, *The Jesus Dynasty*

Jesus died and was buried...but what happened three days later?

Everything in Christian faith hinges on the answer to that single question. So, what's the answer?

Might the disciples have experienced hopeful hallucinations of their late leader in the months after His death? Not likely. News of the Resurrection began to be recounted very quickly after the death of Jesus[1]—at a time when the body could still have been found in the tomb if Jesus were indeed dead. If news of the Resurrection really resulted from hallucinations, Jewish and Roman rulers could have easily silenced the disciples' claims by producing a deceased body. Yet they didn't, which suggests that the tomb must have been empty.

Could the disciples have stolen the body of Jesus? In light of the later fates suffered by the apostles, body snatching doesn't seem very likely either. Paul's letters—penned less than two decades after the death of Jesus—refer to Peter, John, and James the brother of Jesus as pillars of the early Christian movement (1 Corinthians 15:5, 7; Galatians 1:18; 2:9). It seems that Peter, John, and the brother of Jesus, at the very least, would have known about such a plot.

That's precisely why I find it highly unlikely that the first followers of Jesus would have hatched or even known about a plot of this sort: multiple independent sources suggest that Simon Peter received the death sentence because of his testimony about Jesus,[2] and other apostles seem to have suffered similar fates. According to the report of the Jewish historian Josephus, James the brother of Jesus was stoned to death.[3]

If the apostles *did* steal the body of Jesus and fabricate the stories of His resurrection, would they have continued to proclaim these known falsehoods even after their proclamation could lead to exile or execution? I don't think so. To be sure, people *have* sometimes died for a lie, but not typically if they *knew* it was a lie. If the first followers of Jesus had stolen His body, Peter and his fellow apostles would have gotten wind of the plot. As they suffered torture and death for their faith in Jesus, they would have known that their claims about Jesus's resurrection were false. It is utterly implausible that such persons would have died for this story while knowing that it was a falsehood.

Could someone have simply moved the body?[4] That might account for the empty tomb, yet such a supposition cannot explain the disciples' experiences with someone whom they identified as Jesus—experiences so vivid that they were willing to leave their vocations and even suffer agonizing deaths for the sake of sharing these experiences with others.

If none of these scenarios seem likely, what could *possibly* have happened after Jesus died?

I do have one last suggestion.

Maybe Jesus really rose from the dead.

Typically, when several independent sources agree about a certain claim, that claim merits some serious historical consideration. If there's something in the story that *no one* would have fabricated—suppose, for example, that the first witness of the event was a woman, in a culture that would have disdained a woman's witness[5]—the event would be considered even *more* likely to have occurred. If these claims were made while eyewitnesses were still alive, the historical foundations of the supposed event would seem to be secure.

That's precisely what we find in ancient accounts of the resurrection of Jesus Christ.

All four New Testament Gospels—as well as the Gospel of Peter, for that matter—make this claim: *Mary Magdalene went to the tomb where Jesus had been buried and found the tomb empty.* Even a scholar as skeptical as Bart Ehrman recognizes the implications of this consistency. He writes:

> I am struck by a certain consistency among otherwise independent witnesses in placing Mary Magdalene both at the cross and at the tomb on the third day. If this is not a historical datum but something that a Christian storyteller just made up and then passed along to others, how is it that this specific bit of information has found its way into accounts that otherwise did not make use of one another? Mary's presence at the cross is found in Mark (and in Luke and Matthew, which used Mark) and also in John, which is independent of Mark. More significant still, all of our early Gospels—not just John and Mark (with Matthew and Luke as well) but also the Gospel of Peter,

which appears to be independent of all of them—indicate that it was Mary Magdalene who discovered Jesus' empty tomb. How did all of these independent accounts happen to name exactly the same person in this role? It seems hard to believe that this just happened by a way of a fluke of storytelling. It seems much more likely that, at least with the traditions involving the empty tomb, we are dealing with something actually rooted in history.[6]

Even though he ultimately rejects the historical resurrection of Jesus, Ehrman admits that when it comes to the empty tomb of Jesus, historians are "dealing with something actually rooted in history."

In light of the historical evidences, these accounts must indeed be rooted in real history.

When the oral history recorded in 1 Corinthians 15:3–7,[7] four independent witnesses report that Jesus was crucified and later rose from the dead.[8]

It is possible that the the longer ending of Mark's Gospel—the one that now appears in Mark 16:9–20—originally circulated on its own, independent of the other Gospels. If this longer ending *does* represent another testimony to the resurrection of Jesus, *five* independent witnesses testify to the resurrection of Jesus. Four of these witnesses add the detail that Mary Magdalene was the first person to find the tomb empty—a point of agreement that cannot be reasonably attributed to a fluke of fabrication. And most of these testimonies—perhaps all of them—emerged in the lifetimes of the eyewitnesses!

CONSPIRACY NUMBER TEN

History deals with what probably happened. Since miracles are always improbable, the resurrection of Jesus cannot be considered as a historical event, regardless of how much historical evidence supports it.

The TRUTH BEHIND the CONSPIRACY

If the best available historical evidences about Jesus point to His resurrection, His resurrection ought to be considered as a historical event.

QUICK GUIDE

FIVE INDEPENDENT WITNESSES

Where is the witness?	When did the witness emerge?	What does the witness claim?
1 Corinthians 15:3–7	Emerged as an oral history in the early A.D. 30s, recorded in Paul's letter to the Corinthians in A.D. 55	Jesus died and was raised from the dead three days later. Many people saw Him alive.
Mark 16:1–8 (duplicated with minor adaptations in Matthew 28:1–4 and Luke 24:1–4)	Written between A.D. 65 and 69, based on earlier tradition	Jesus died and was raised from the dead three days later. Mary Magdalene discovered the empty tomb.
John 20:1–18	Written in the mid to late first century, based on earlier tradition	Jesus died and was raised from the dead three days later. Mary Magdalene discovered the empty tomb.
Mark 16:9–20	Added to Mark's Gospel in the second or third century A.D., probably based on earlier tradition	Jesus died and was raised from the dead on the first day of the week. Mary Magdalene was the initial witness of the Resurrection.
Gospel of Peter (Papyrus Cairo 10759)	Composed in the mid-second century; probably based on earlier tradition	Jesus died and was raised from the dead three days later. Mary Magdalene discovered the empty tomb.

It will not do...to say that Jesus' disciples were so stunned and shocked by his death, so unable to come to terms with it, that they projected their shattered hopes onto the screen of fantasy and invented the idea of Jesus' "resurrection" as a way of coping with a cruelly broken dream. That has an initial apparent psychological plausibility, but it won't work as serious first-century history. We know of lots of other messianic and similar movements in the Jewish world roughly contemporary with Jesus. In many cases the leader died a violent death at the hands of the authorities. In not one single case do we hear the slightest mention of the disappointed followers claiming that their hero had been raised from the dead. They knew better. "Resurrection" was not a private event. It involved human bodies. There would have to be an empty tomb somewhere. A Jewish revolutionary whose leader had been executed by the authorities, and who managed to escape arrest himself, had two options: give up the revolution, or find another leader. We have evidence of people doing both. Claiming that the original leader was alive again was simply not an option.

Unless, of course, he was.[9]

—N. T. WRIGHT, *Who Was Jesus?* (1992)

THE **CONSPIRACY** OF **HISTORICAL PROBABILITIES**

"And still some doubted" (Matthew 28:17), Matthew's Gospel tells us, even as they stood in the shadow of the risen Lord.

Some people still do today.

When we're dealing with a claim as incredible as resurrection from the dead, we *should* be skeptical. After all, in case you hadn't noticed, dead people do have a tendency to stay dead.

What if multiple independent witnesses testify together to the truth of this event?

What if these witnesses emerged while eyewitnesses of the original events were still alive?

What if these eyewitnesses were willing to endure torture and death for their claim that Jesus was alive?

What if none of the alternative hypotheses possessed greater explanatory power than the simple proclamation that Jesus returned to life?

At the very least, shouldn't the resurrection of Jesus be considered as one very probable possibility?

It seems to me that it should.

According to some skeptics, a miraculous event can never be considered as a historical possibility, regardless of how much evidence may stand in support of the miraculous event. Here's how Bart Ehrman has summarized this position:

> The resurrection claims are claims that not only that Jesus' body came back alive; it came back alive never to die again. That's a violation of what naturally happens, every day, time after time, millions of times a year. What are the chances of that happening? Well, it'd be a miracle.

> In other words, it'd be so highly improbable that we can't account for it
> by natural means.... So, by the very nature of the canons of historical
> research, we can't claim historically that a miracle probably happened.
> By definition, it probably didn't. And history can only establish what
> probably did [happen].[10]

Another skeptic puts it this way: "Historians are bound by their discipline to
work within the parameters of a scientific view of reality." How does he define
a "scientific view of reality"? "Dead bodies don't rise—not if one is clinically
dead—as Jesus surely was after Roman crucifixion and three days in a tomb."[11]

Rudolf Bultmann, a New Testament scholar from the first half of the twentieth century, bears much of the responsibility for turning this assumption
into a supposed "canon of historical research." Bultmann says:

> History is...a closed continuum of effects in which individual events
> are connected by the succession of cause and effect.... This closedness
> means that the continuum of historical happenings cannot be rent by
> the interference of supernatural, transcendent powers.[12]

In the simplest possible terms, here's what each of these scholars claims:
If science cannot explain how an event happened, the event must not have
occurred, and any historical witnesses to the contrary should be ignored.

CRACKING THE HISTORICAL PROBABILITY CONSPIRACY

I would like to suggest an alternative canon for historical research: Follow the
best available evidence, regardless of where it takes you.[13] After examining the
most reliable records from the first four centuries of Christianity, here's what
has become clear not only to me but also to billions of others. The tomb was
empty because what appeared to be the end of the story was actually the birth
of a new beginning, because death was turned into life. What was least probable of all became possible and real and true.

So, to return to the question that kicked off this chapter, what happened
after Jesus died?

According to the earliest and most reliable witnesses, Jesus was crucified, He
was buried, and He rose again. Or, as the ancient tradition is recited among
the Maasai people in the savannahs of Africa:

> We believe that God made good his promise by sending his Son, Jesus
> Christ, a man in the flesh, a Jew by tribe, born poor in a little village,
> who left his home and was always on safari doing good, curing people

by the power of God, teaching about God and humanity, showing the meaning of religion is love. He was rejected by his people, tortured and nailed hands and feet to a cross, and died. He lay buried in the grave, but the hyenas did not touch him, and on the third day, he rose from the grave. He ascended to the skies. He is the Lord.[14]

I began this book with an invitation. My invitation was simply this: join me on a journey. Thus far, this journey has taken us from the deserts of Egypt to the limestone cliffs that line the Dead Sea, from a nail-pierced heel in a box of bones to the hazy interiors of cryptic tombs. You've considered ancient fragments of parchment and papyrus, of stone and clay. Through these artifacts, you've heard the words of long-forgotten women and men, believers and heretics, sinners and saints.

The journey isn't over.

Where the journey leads next is, however, up to you.

It has been my hope that this journey would lead you from blind belief to thoughtful trust. Even if you haven't found yourself at a point of thoughtful trust in Jesus Christ, I leave you with this bit of encouragement: *Don't stop searching.* Keep looking at every available evidence of truth; then, follow wherever the truth leads. The more I have searched, the more I have become convinced that truth is not an idea but a person, a person who endured the darkest possible death and who returned to life again. Though my mind can never completely capture such infinite and wonderful truth, I have come to trust that this Truth has captured me.

HOW TO PREPARE FOR FUTURE CHRIST CONSPIRACIES

The resurrection of Jesus Christ is the crucial point at which Christianity stands or falls. Rehearse with a friend how you might respond to someone who claims, "The Resurrection can't be considered a historical event because history only deals with what is probable, and no matter how much evidence there may be for resurrection, someone coming back from the dead is always highly improbable." If you are in a small group, role-play this discussion several times until you are comfortable with your capacity to defend the historicity of Jesus's resurrection. If you are interested in researching this topic more thoroughly, study these excellent books: *The Jesus Legend* by Paul Eddy and Gregory Boyd, *The Resurrection of Jesus* by N. T. Wright and John Dominic Crossan, and *Jesus' Resurrection: Fact or Figment* by William Lane Craig and Gerd Lüdemann.

Appendix

PHOTOGRAPHS OF FIRST-CENTURY CHRISTIAN ARTIFACTS

FRAGMENTS FROM the FIRST CENTURIES of CHRISTIAN FAITH

Papyrus 52/ John Rylands Papyrus 457

Papyrus 52 is the earliest known fragment of the New Testament. P52 was found in Egypt; the fragment preserves a portion of John 18. The handwriting found in P52 is strikingly similar to a bit of papyrus known as Papyrus Fayyum 110. Papyrus Fayyum 110 is dated in "the fourteenth year of the reign of Emperor Domitian"—the year A.D. 94. The strong similarity between the writing styles of the two fragments suggests that the Gospel according to John was in wide circulation by the late first or early second century A.D. *(Scanned from public domain volume,* Our Bible and the Ancient Manuscripts, *Frederick Kenyon (1939) 128, plate XIV.)*

MS2752

A few fragments of otherwise-unknown sayings of Jesus—such as this one from Egypt—might represent first-century traditions about Jesus. Yet these texts are too fragmentary to be certain about their origins or their portrayal of Jesus. Most of these tidbits seem to represent variations of stories already found in the New Testament. *(Courtesy of the Schowyen Collection, Oslo and London)*

MS2649

A second-century fragment of the Greek translation of the Old Testament, known as the Septuagint. Copies of the Septuagint would have been found in the armaria ("book-chests") of the earliest churches. *(Courtesy of the Schoyen Collection, Oslo and London)*

MS021

Medieval copy of messages that a Christian leader named Origen of Alexandra proclaimed in the third century A.D. According to conspiracy theorist Michael Baigent, "The Council of Nicea created the literally fantastic Jesus of faith" in the fourth century A.D. Yet, a century before the Council of Nicea, Origen repeated the same truth about Jesus that the apostolic eyewitnesses had spoken in the first century A.D.: "The Messiah Jesus was truly God's Son" (*Contra Celsum, 57*). *(Courtesy of the Schoyen Collection, Oslo and London)*

MS2634/1

The oldest known fragment of Acts of Paul, copied in the third century A.D. A Christian elder in Asia composed this fictional text "out of love for Paul" in the second century A.D. Because the book could not be connected o eyewitness testimony about Jesus or His first followers, early Christians rejected Acts of Paul as an authoritative writing. *(Courtesy of the Schoyen Collection, Oslo and London)*

Shepherd of Hermas in Codex Sinaiticus

Though a popular text among second-century Christians, *Shepherd of Hermas* was rejected as an authoritative text because, "Hermas composed *The Shepherd* quite recently.... So, while it should indeed be read, it ought not to be read publickly for the people of the church—it is counted neither among the [Old Testament] prophets (for their number has been completed) nor among the apostolic eyewitnesses (for it is after their time)." *(Courtesy of CSNTM.org)*

LITERACY and SCRIBAL PRACTICES in the FIRST CENTURY A.D.

MS140 and MS150

Some skeptics claim that the Gospels cannot represent eyewitness testimony because the apostolic eyewitnesses were illiterate. Yet thousands of tax receipts—such as these papyri from the centuries before Jesus Christ—demonstrate that tax collectors, such as the apostle Matthew, were in fact literate. *(Courtesy of the Schoyen Collection, Oslo and London)*

MS1835 and MS5095/3

Tax collectors were known to carry *pinakes*, wooden tablets coated with beeswax into which they used styli to inscribe notes. It is possible that someone such as Matthew might have originally recorded the teachings of Jesus using tablets and styli similar to the ones pictured here. *(Courtesy of the Schoyen Collection, Oslo and London)*

MS2634/3

Ancient physicians—such as Luke, author of the third New Testament Gospel—were frequently, though not universally, literate. Literate physicians referred to summaries of the medical practices of Hippocrates, such as the one pictured here, to guide them as they cared for ill patients. *(Courtesy of the Schoyen Collection, Oslo and London)*

Painting of the Poet Sappho

In A.D. 79, the volcanic Mount Vesuvius erupted and destroyed the cities of Pompeii and Herculaeum. This painting of the ancient poet Sappho, found in the ruins of Pompeii, shows Sappho with a *pinax* and stylus, similar to the ones used among tax collectors like the apostle Matthew. *(Public domain)*

Painting of Paquius Proculus and His Wife

This painting of the politican Paquius Proculus and his wife was recovered from the ruins of Pompeii. The painting shows two primary methods for writing in the ancient Roman Empire: In the hand of Paquius is a papyrus roll, on which a scribe might have used a quill and ink to write. The wife of Paquius holds a *pinax*—a wooden tablet with beeswax coating—and a stylus. *(Public domain)*

John 1:18 in Codex Sinaiticus

John 1:18 in Codex Washingtonianus

In *Misquoting Jesus: The Story Behind Who Changed the Bible and Why*, Bart Ehrman claims that there are many places where a miscopied text significantly changes the meaning of the Bible. It's true that differences do exist among the New Testament manuscripts—but the differences aren't nearly as significant as Ehrman supposes. Let's look at a simple example: In Codex Sinaiticus, John 1:18 reads, in Greek, "*monogenes th-s*" ("one and only God" or "only begotten God"). The same text in Codex Washingtonianus reads "*monogenes hu-s*" ("one and only Son" or "only begotten Son"). Yet, in this instance and in thousands of others, the difference does not change any essential belief that Christians embrace regarding Jesus Christ. In fact, *both wordings affirm truths that are clearly expressed throughout John's Gospel.* In support of "one and only God," John 20:28 unambiguuously identifies Jesus as God. In support of "one and only Son," the familiar words of John 3:16 already refer to Jesus as "the only begotten Son" or "the one and only Son." Even though an authentic difference does exist among the manuscripts of John's Gospel, neither possibility contradicts anything in this Gospel or in the remainder of the New Testament. At some point, a tired or careless scribe changed "one and only Son" to "one and only God" or *vice versa*—that much seems certain. Yet, either way, the scribe simply emphasized a truth that was already present in John's Gospel. *(Pictures courtesy of CSNTM.org)*

ANCIENT REFERENCES THAT RELATE to JESUS

MS118

Medieval copy of the writings of the ancient Roman historian Suetonius Tranquillus. Suetonious wrote in the early second century A.D. that "since the Jews were causing disturbances due to a certain *Chrestus*, [Emperor Claudius] expelled them from Rome." With a few exceptions, historians understand *"Chrestus"* to be a misspelling of the title "Christ"—and probably a reference to Jesus. (*Courtesy of the Schoyen Collection, Oslo and London*)

MSi561

Medieval copy of the writings of Jewish-Roman historian Josephus. Josephus lived in the first century A.D. and, at one point, even served as governor of Galilee. Though a Christian copyist expanded one of Josephus's references to Jesus, most scholars recognize that the following statement about James the brother of Jesus is genuine: "The high priest...gathered the legal experts of the Sanhedrin and brought them, with certain others, a man called James, the brother of Jesus who was called the Messiah. Accusing them of having trans-

gressed the law, he delivered them up to be stoned to death." At the very least, Josephus knew that Jesus was a historical figure, believed by some to have been the Messiah. (*Courtesy of the Schoyen Collection, Oslo and London*)

The Alexamenos Graffito

One of the earliest graphical references to Christian worship is this vulgar bit of graffiti, uncovered near Rome in a palace where slaves once trained to serve the imperial family. The caption reads *Alexamenos sebete theon*, "Alexamenos worships God"—probably a derisive statement, ridiculing someone named "Alexamenos" for worshiping Jesus. *(Author's reconstruction)*

ARTIFACTS FROM the DEAD SEA

MS1655/1

One of the jars in which the Qumran community hid their scrolls in limestone caves overlooking the Dead Sea. *(Courtesy of the Schoyen Collection, Oslo and London)*

MS1655/2

An inkwell, probably used by scribes as they copied the Dead Sea Scrolls. Scribes made ink by mixing water, ground gum, and charcoal in inkwells such as this one. *(Courtesy of the Schoyen Collection, Oslo and London)*

MS1909

Fragments of Manual of Discipline from the Dead Sea Scrolls. *(Courtesy of the Schoyen Collection, Oslo and London)*

THE WORLD of the FIRST CHRISTIANS

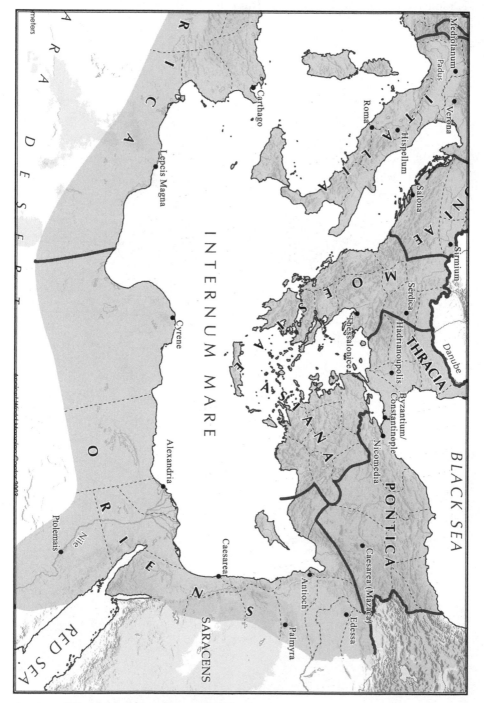

Ancient World Mapping Center 2003

LEARNING SESSIONS STUDY GUIDE

by

Kristi van Dyke

Garrett Fellow School of Leadership and Church Ministry
The Southern Baptist Theological Seminary

Introductory Learning Session

The TROUBLE WITH JESUS

Before the session

- Movies, celebrities, and books have all contributed to the newly popularized genre of speculative biblical history. If the composition of the study group is known before the first session, the study leader may benefit from conducting a quick survey to find out which of the conspiracies named at the beginning of each chapter has influenced the learners. If the group forms at the first session, take an informal survey before beginning.

- Books by Bruce Metzger, C. S. Lewis, and F. F. Bruce helped the author in his quest for truth. In order to help group members with their personal study, the study leaders should become familiar with these resources and should be prepared with some practical advice for where additional helps such as these may be found. You may find help at your church library or a local Christian bookseller.

- Collect index cards and writing utensils for use in the group session. Before beginning, give each member two or three cards for his or her response to the learning activity described below. Have extra cards on hand.

During the session

- Describe a person who you are convinced fully believes in Jesus. What makes their faith strong? What evidence of their faith can you see? Contrast this individual with another person who says they believe in Jesus, but whose faith does not seem to be strong. What do you see as the difference between these two people?

- According to informal interaction with Christians, the author says that believers in Jesus tend to give reasons for their faith that can be categorized by two statements: (1) I know Jesus is alive because I've felt His presence, or (2) the Bible is God's Word, so if the Bible says it, I believe it. Do you agree or disagree with the author that these "are rotten reasons to believe in Jesus"? Why or why not?

- Choose one of the two statements from above. Working with a partner, reconstruct the author's argument for why this is not a good reason to believe in Jesus.

■ The author has a very purposeful intention for his readers. Summarize your own desire for what you hope to learn or gain from reading this book.

■ While relating his personal story about developing a deeper faith, the author reveals areas of personal doubt that haunted him. In a confidential manner, ask the group to identify doubts about Jesus that they have had personally (or ones with which they have come in contact) by writing them on an index card. Collect the cards, and read the responses aloud. (To maintain confidentiality, which will foster the group's internal trust, do not identify members by name.)

■ Of the ten conspiracies, which one is of most interest to you? In other words, about which conspiracy do you want to learn the most?

After the session

■ Consider where you find yourself on the spectrum between "thoughtful trust" and "blind belief." Write a short reflection on these thoughts.

NO ONE KNOWS WHO WROTE THE GOSPELS

WHAT'S the CONSPIRACY?

THE NEW TESTAMENT GOSPELS DO NOT REPRESENT RELIABLE TESTImony about Jesus; they are anonymous, secondhand witnesses to the life of Jesus.

Before the session

- Two early church fathers are named in this chapter. Take time before the study session to find a brief biographical sketch of Polycarp of Smyrna or Papias of Hierapolis. Share this information with the study group.

- Copy below the three main clues that the author gives as the best evidence for when the New Testament Gospels were written.

_____

_____

_____

During the session

- In the digital information age, messages are constantly being received from unnamed sources. This is obvious in e-mail. From other media outlets such as newspaper, magazines, and television, we receive content from an acknowledged author or producer, yet in most of these cases we have no direct relationship with these people. How does this situation differ from the situation of first-century churches that received and circulated written correspondence?

- Distinguish between first- and secondhand testimony. Does it matter which is accepted? Which is better?

- What is a major factor in determining a date for Papyrus 52?

- Have you used a book that is structured as a simple survey of the Bible such as *Talk Through the Bible*? Tell the group how this resource helped you. How might such resources help you as you compare different views of the authorship of the New Testament texts?

After the session

■ Work through the table of contents in your New Testament. For each book in the New Testament, be able to answer this question: "Who was the apostolic eyewitness or close associate of an eyewitness that testified to the truth of this text?"

HOW THE LOST GOSPELS GOT LOST

WHAT'S the CONSPIRACY?

ARLY-CHURCH LEADERS ELIMINATED MANY BOOKS FROM THE NEW Testament; some of these "lost scriptures" were the sacred texts of the earliest Christians.

Before the session

■ Define the word *Gospel* in your own words. Be certain to distinguish *gospel* (the message of salvation in Jesus) from *Gospel* (a text that claims to provide information from the life and teachings of Jesus). Look up the term *Gospel* in several Bible dictionaries. Take a few minutes to contemplate and, if necessary, to revise your definition.

■ Contemporary research on the topics discussed in this book provides new insights and food for thought. Take time before the study session to find a summary of information that you can share with the group regarding one of the following:

  Historical details related to one of the "lost Gospels" and/or its discovery

  Current news about a "lost Gospel"

During the session

■ Treasure hunting is an exciting pastime for many folks, an activity made even more exciting when you are not expecting to make a discovery. Consider your biggest discovery to date. Was it an idea, an object, a location, a person? How was your life changed by the discovery? Imagine how your life would have changed if your discovery had been made years earlier or later. Share this with the group.

■ In pairs or groups of three to four members, allow each member to explain conspiracy number two in their own words.

■ Remain in pairs, and review major documents that are categorized as "lost Gospels." Assign one group member to share two or three important points regarding each of the following:

  Gospel of Thomas

  Nag Hammadi documents

  Gospel of Q

  New Testament Gospels

■ What is the Gospel of Q? Is it really a "Gospel"?

■ Predict the impact of conspiracy number two on Christianity by completing the following sentence starters with your own answers, thoughts, and responses:

  "If Jesus was merely a 'Jewish man of wisdom…'"

  "If the 'lost Gospels' do actually tell us how the earliest Christians understood Jesus, what the New Testament Gospels tell us about Jesus is…"

  "If the 'lost Gospels' are correct, the person who Christians worship as the living Lord is actually…"

■ The author proposes a two-step plan for testing the authenticity of documents that claim to be "lost Gospels." Write these two steps below.

_____

_____

_____

_____

After the session

■ The explanation and defense of the first conspiracy is quite lengthy. How did the author use his own two-step plan for evaluating supposed "lost scriptures"?

■ Write down questions or concerns that require further explanation and study. Was there anything that you did not understand?

_____

_____

_____

IT WAS ALL ABOUT POWER

WHAT'S the CONSPIRACY?

ARLY CHRISTIAN LEADERS SELECTED SACRED BOOKS AND ESSEN-tial beliefs to protect the church's power structures, not to testify to historical truth about Jesus. Other books and beliefs were suppressed, sometimes violently.

Before the session

■ Suppositions and imaginations are fun, so find out about the real-life circumstances for Christians in the second century A.D. by doing a little research. If you are completing this study with a group, ask members to come prepared to briefly share about a topic that interests them, or choose one of the following topics: meeting places of the first Christians, different lists of New Testament books, political structures in the first-century Roman Empire, social structures in the first-century Roman Empire, daily living, travel, education, and religion.

■ Gather felt-tip markers and ensure that one or multiple writing surfaces are available in your meeting area. If your group is large, you may want to organize groups to write on multiple posters.

During the session

■ In pairs or groups, contrast the author's reconstruction of how certain books and beliefs became essential to Elaine Pagels's reconstruction of how these books and beliefs were chosen. (1) Pagels's "conspiracy" claims that sacred books and beliefs were selected by "political power structures." (2) The author claims that the basis of these choices was consistent, reliable, eyewitness testimony to the life and ministry of Jesus. On a poster or dry-erase board, describe the following for each possibility: Who would have been the decision makers? What would have been their primary purpose? When would this process have occurred? What might have been the nega-tive consequences of such a process? What might have been the positive results of such a process?

■ Of all the negative consequences that your group can concoct, would any of these have kept you from possessing or knowing the truth about Jesus?

■ The first two clues to cracking this conspiracy are related to Christian beliefs. Write the Christian belief connected to both clues below:

Clue 1: Belief in _____

Read Acts 2:31 in a New Testament. List some other Bible passages that express this belief.

_____

_____

_____

Clue 2: Belief in _____

Read 1 Timothy 2:5 in a New Testament. List some other Bible passages that express this belief.

_____

_____

_____

■ The third clue to cracking the power conspiracy adds a new guiding principle to your two-step plan for testing the authenticity of documents that claim to be "lost Gospels."

■ Write your personal plan for responding to claims of newly discovered Gospels. Place this list in your Bible; refer to it in the future, as new challenges to Christian faith arise.

_____

_____

_____

After the session

■ Think about it. You have the luxury of reading from many English versions of the Bible along with a multitude of foreign languages of your choice. Recall the Bible-reading challenges of second-century Christians as explained in this chapter. How has the wide availability of literacy and Bibles changed the way we read the Bible today?

_____

_____

■ List one new truth that you learned while reading the chapter. Was it an unexpected discovery?

_____

_____

_____

_____

_____

_____

WHO MISQUOTED JESUS?

WHAT'S the CONSPIRACY?

T HE GOSPELS AND OTHER NEW TESTAMENT WRITINGS WERE COPIED so poorly and edited so thoroughly that the meanings of entire books have changed.

Before the session

■ Reflect on a time when you were misquoted. Were you able to repair the damage from that incident? Your reaction to being misquoted probably indicates a defensive or protective attitude. In your estimation, how does "the copyist conspiracy" attack the integrity of the authors and copyists of the New Testament? What is the best way to defend or protect their integrity?

During the session

■ What questionable connection does Ehrman make between God's work in the inspiration of Scripture, and His work in the preservation of Scripture? What are the problems with making such a connection?

■ One chart in this chapter lists verses that some scholars do not believe were in the original New Testament. Regardless of your personal beliefs about these particular verses, be able to defend why none of these omissions ultimately change what the church confesses about Jesus Christ.

■ Discuss the concept of significance and how it impacts this conspiracy. Is there a scale of significance? Consider a promised birthday celebration. Would it be significant if the location of the party changed? How about if the party was canceled? How does the concept of a significant change relate to the arguments of this chapter?

■ List some honest concessions that Christians can make that relate to our lack of exact copies of the New Testament.

There are variants in documents, but _____

_____ .

_____

A few variants might _____ .

_____

■ In two or three sentences, summarize the author's response to these concessions.

_____

_____

_____

■ How does textual criticism help us to determine the original reading of biblical texts?

_____

_____

_____

After the session

■ In your own words, write a brief response to this statement: "No essential truth in Scripture depends on a disputed verse."

_____

_____

■ The faith of many Christians is shaken because they come into contact with conspiracy theories that they are not equipped to deal with. In what way did this chapter help you be prepared to offer a reasonable response to those who say the Bible is a collection of misquotes?

_____

_____

■ For further study in early church history, seek additional biographical information on the following key figures:

   ■ Tertullian of Carthage

   ■ Origen of Alexandria

GOSPEL TRUTH OR GOSPEL FICTION?

WHAT'S the CONSPIRACY?

WITH FEW EXCEPTIONS, THE ACTS AND SAYINGS IN THE NEW TESTAMENT Gospels do not represent actual historical happenings. Decades after the death of Jesus, believers fabricated these words and deeds—including the story of the Resurrection—to fit the needs of their communities.

Before the session

■ Write your own paraphrase of the fourth conspiracy:

_____

_____

■ Suppose that, in future years, someone wrote your biography. How would the writer of that volume know what stories and quotes are true and accurate?

_____

_____

Gather paper and writing instruments for the study group to use during a brainstorming session.

During the session

Take two minutes and tell a partner your own story of learning the truth about Santa or some other mythical icon. What do you most remember about that discovery?

■ Consider this Gospel fiction conspiracy from the viewpoint of a supporter of these claims. What barriers would make it hard to accept the view that the acts and the sayings in the New Testament Gospels do represent actual historical happenings?

_____

_____

_____

■ Brainstorm in pairs or small groups. Produce a list of possible needs that—according to supporters of this conspiracy—might have caused early Christians to fabricate Jesus's words or deeds.

_____

_____

■ In your opinion, if Jesus had been only a powerful human teacher, would that be sufficient to sustain your faith? What if He had been an apocalyptic prophet but nothing more? Predict what a twenty-first-century church would teach if it held one of these views.

_____

_____

■ Clue number one describes the oral cultures of the first and second centuries as a contributing factor to the valid preservation of the scriptural texts. What technologies do you use that assist you in preserving messages and ensuring they are not tampered with? Compare these technologies with tools that were available in an oral culture.

■ The oral histories about Jesus recorded in Paul's writings give us clear clues about how the words of the New Testament first circulated. Identify one of the two examples from Paul's letters that the author uses to support his argument in clue number two.

_____

_____

■ The author concludes that there are three major "cracks" in the Gospel fiction conspiracy. Explain why he believes it is highly unlikely that the Gospel truth was turned into fiction before the Gospels were even written.

_____

_____

After the session

■ Perhaps you believe that there are cracks in the Gospel fiction conspiracy, or maybe you continue to believe that the New Testament is filled with fiction. After reading this chapter, discussing it with your study group, and considering your own thoughts, what evidence would be required to convince you of the viewpoint that's the opposite of your own viewpoint?

_____

_____

■ Write down questions or concerns that require further explanation and study.

_____

_____

_____

_____

_____

The MYSTERIOUS CASE of the MYTHICAL MESSIAH

WHAT'S the CONSPIRACY?

JESUS NEVER EXISTED AT ALL. DECADES AFTER THE DEATH OF JESUS, believers fabricated the Gospel stories from pagan myths.

Before the session

■ Many classic moral stories include protagonists who never existed, yet these stories teach valuable lessons. Why does it matter to you whether Jesus the Messiah was real?

_____

_____

During the session

■ Have you ever been confronted by an individual who, like the man in the coffee shop described in this chapter, believed in this conspiracy? What were the positive aspects of your interaction with this individual? Was there any particular part of your conversation that you wish you could change after reading this chapter?

_____

_____

■ The author writes that in the eyes of the Christ-myth crowd, "Jesus never lived, and Jesus never died—because Jesus never even existed" (page 100). Distinguish between this myth and the idea from the previous chapter— that the Jesus of the New Testament was a real person but that the New Testament doesn't tell the truth about Him.

_____

_____

■ Although persons in the learning group may share similar beliefs, it is possible that some participants are still struggling with an individual decision about how they view this conspiracy. Organize the group into two smaller groups. Assign to each smaller group one of the viewpoints below. Direct each smaller group to support their assigned viewpoint by using clues from *Conspiracies and the Cross* and other literature of which they may be aware.

"To fully understand whether the Jesus described in the Bible was a literal historical person..."

   ■ Viewpoint one: "...we should see if there are similarities between the New Testament's descriptions of Jesus and some previous pagan practices."

   ■ Viewpoint two: "...we should investigate to see if the events described in the New Testament actually occurred."

Identify three proofs to which people appeal when they claim that Jesus never existed.

_____

_____

_____

■ Choose one of the three clues that the author uses to crack the conspiracy. Reconstruct an outline of the author's argument that supports that clue.

_____

_____

_____

■ If you have a particularly ambitious group, organize the group into subgroups of three people and spend a few minutes role-playing a confrontation and a response regarding this issue. Use the outlines that were completed in the previous activity as a basis for your responses.

■ What factors do you believe can be instrumental in converting a "mythical Messiah believer" to the belief that Jesus did truly exist? You may not encounter individuals who embrace this conspiracy on a regular basis. If that's the case, the author's engagement with a skeptic in the coffee shop is a case to consider. However, if you do frequently engage people in conversations on topics of this sort, you may want to consider a specific instance from your own experience as you answer the question.

_____

_____

_____

_____

_____

After the session

■ Would you be willing to apply the term "literalist Christian" to yourself? What implications do you think this term might have?

_____

_____

_____

Conspiracy Number Seven Learning Session

CODES IN THE GOSPELS, SECRETS IN THE SCROLLS

WHAT'S the CONSPIRACY?

THE DEAD SEA SCROLLS AND PERHAPS even THE NEW TESTAMENT books include encoded secrets about Jesus—information that, if properly understood, could completely change everything that Christians believe.

Before the session

■ Do your own research to discover some recent news about the Dead Sea Scrolls.

■ Some people may readily dismiss the codes conspiracy, yet this conspiracy is widely believed among many best-selling writers. Conduct a cursory survey of books or movies that deal with Bible codes, encryptions, or secrets. What is your reaction to these findings?

■ Gather and prepare supplies for developing a simple chart on which to record responses that will be shared with the class. Depending on your setting, you may use paper and marker, whiteboard, overhead projector, or a computer with an LCD projector.

During the session

■ The 1947 discovery of long-lost scrolls near the Dead Sea was a revolutionary find. After the discovery, a panel of experts gained exclusive access to these scrolls. What benefits were probably intended by this arrangement? What was the danger?

_____

_____

_____

_____

■ Identify three "facts" from the Qumran community that are often used in attempts to disprove Christian teaching and beliefs.

■ Describe the "pesher method" developed by Barbara Thiering, as if you were talking to a good friend who is interested in the topic of this book.

■ By now, you should have a good understanding of the viewpoints some scholars have used to support the notion that the New Testament is encoded with secret messages. Each of these speculations shares a common problem. What is the common problem in each one?

■ Evidence presented from both sides demonstrates this fact: the teachings of the Qumran community, as found in the Dead Sea Scrolls, provide important insight into the context in which Christianity was born. Use a simple two-column chart to compare the case made by secular scholars to debunk Christianity with the author's rebuttal in clue number one.

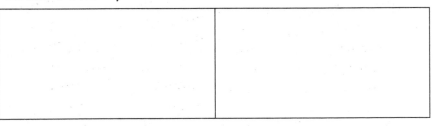

■ Three claims from the code conspiracy are either shown to be questionable or they are disproven completely in this chapter. Summarize those claims in the space below.

■ Identify the author's conclusions on the matter of the code conspiracy. What is your conclusion?

After the session

■ Record some new understandings that have emerged as you read and studied this chapter.

_____

_____

_____

_____

JESUS, MARY, AND THE HOLY GRAIL

WHAT'S the CONSPIRACY?

ESUS MARRIED MARY MAGDALENE AND FOUNDED A PHYSICAL DYNASTY, and this long-suppressed information may be entwined with the legend of the Holy Grail.

Before the session

■ After reading the chapter, draw a simple diagram of how Jesus, Mary, and the Holy Grail seem to be related in the minds of some conspiracy theorists.

During the session

■ Why do you think Jesus's marital status is a big concern for some people? What would the marriage of Jesus add to your faith? What would it remove from your faith?

_____

_____

_____

_____

■ The author names at least three things that have been identified as "the Holy Grail." Name these, as well as any others that you may find.

_____

_____

_____

_____

■ Has your name ever caused you to be mixed up with someone else? Explain how you were finally able to clear up the matter and set things straight. Compare your circumstance with attempts to identify family names inscribed on first-century ossuaries.

_____

_____

■ Many of Jesus's contemporaries had good reasons to care about Jesus's crucified body and His resurrected body. Working together, make a list of these groups or individuals. Be aware that the authorities who had Jesus crucified would have been interested in making certain that no one could claim that Jesus was alive. If they could have quieted the first followers of Jesus by publicly displaying the dead body of Jesus, they would have done so.

_____

_____

■ Much has been made of a supposed liaison between Mary Magdalene and Jesus. Analyze why some scholars hold so tightly to a "sexualized definition of *koinonos*" as they have built their case for this relationship.

_____

_____

■ In your experience, what movies and/or books have been "faith shaking"? Which ones have built up your faith? Why?

_____

_____

■ What aspects of Christianity would fall apart if Jesus's bones were found?

_____

_____

■ Identify the single most important reason the author gives that "the marriage of Jesus didn't become part of the church's story of Jesus."

_____

_____

After the session

■ The author contends that "even if they don't desire to admit it, every person longs to make contact with something that comes from God" (page 150). Perhaps this is a truth that you have yet to recognize. Reflect and record a brief description of where you find yourself with regard to this possibility. Have you experienced the Spirit of God through faith in Jesus Christ as your Lord and God?

_____

_____

■ Write down questions or concerns that require further explanation and study. Was there anything in this chapter that you did not understand?

_____

_____

THE DOGS BENEATH THE CROSS

WHAT'S the CONSPIRACY?

J ESUS WAS NEVER BURIED, AND HE WAS NEVER RAISED FROM THE DEAD. Dogs and other wild animals consumed His body.'

Before the session

- What has been the single most important question posed in your life up to this point in time? Illustrate the importance of this question by tracing the direct impact from that point until now.

  _____

  _____

  _____

During the session

- The labels "foolishness," "insanity," and "idiocy" do not paint the most flattering picture of Christianity. Modify the series of three descriptors to describe Christianity the way you would like it to be viewed. Do your descriptions adequately account for the death and resurrection of Jesus as the centerpiece of Christianity?

  _____

  _____

  _____

- Of the evidences that are often given in support of the carrion conspiracy, which one do you feel has the most credibility? Which one has the least?

  _____

  _____

  _____

- Hypothesize about what motive would lead someone like Michael Baigent to promote a fake letter. Do you think that perhaps he himself believed that the letters were real? Was he duped, or is he attempting to dupe others?

_____

_____

_____

After the session

■ Identify the single most important question in Christianity as identified by the author. Explain to a friend why this is such an important question. Summarize for your friend the author's argument for why it is virtually certain that Jesus's body was buried.

_____

_____

_____

NO PLACE FOR THE EVIDENCE

WHAT'S the CONSPIRACY?

HISTORY DEALS WITH WHAT PROBABLY HAPPENED. SINCE MIRACLES ARE always improbable, the resurrection of Jesus cannot be considered a historical event, regardless of how much historical evidence supports the Resurrection.

Before the session

■ As you read the chapter, compile a list of five independent witnesses named in the text that witness to the crucifixion, burial, and resurrection of Jesus.

_____

_____

_____

_____

During the session

■ What action after Jesus died could have conclusively put an end to rumors that Jesus had been resurrected?

_____

_____

■ Debate the following statement: "History deals with what probably happened." Is this a statement that you can support? Or do you disagree?

_____

_____

■ Reconstruct three or more supports for the following possibilities:

■ Jesus's followers had "hopeful hallucinations" after His death.

_____

_____

■ Jesus's disciples stole the body of Jesus.

_____

_____

■ Someone simply moved Jesus's body.

_____

_____

■ Jesus really rose from the dead.

_____

_____

■ "Shouldn't the resurrection of Jesus be considered as one very probable possibility?" Why, according to the author, should the Resurrection be considered "very probable"? Use your list of five independent witnesses to defend the probability of the Resurrection.

_____

_____

_____

_____

After the session

■ Using the materials in this book, prepare and memorize the information that you would need to answer this question: How do you know that Jesus was really raised from the dead?

_____

_____

_____

_____

Concluding Learning Session

A PLACE FOR THE EVIDENCE IN YOUR LIFE

T HIS FINAL STUDY GUIDE IS DESIGNED TO FACILITATE PERSONAL INTRO-
spection and affirmation.

Study group leader, consider sharing some of your personal story and overview the message below during your last session.

Study group participants, contemplate personal responses that will promote spiritual growth.

■ This book is a collection of evidence, much like files and forensic evidence collected in support of a criminal trial. At the end of such a trial, various outcomes ensue, but in each case, one thing is inevitable: action is taken! Stop for a moment and thoughtfully identify what action you should take on the basis of the evidence presented in this book.

■ The common thread weaving through each response to the conspiracies is this: The death, burial, and resurrection of Jesus Christ should be considered as historical events, impacting the lives of women and men now and for eternity. This common thread was present among believers in Jesus from the very beginning. Remember the oral history recorded by Paul?

> For I passed on to you what I also received:
> That the Messiah *died* on behalf of our sins according to the
>   Scriptures,
> And that He was *buried*,
> And that He *rose* on the third day according to the Scriptures,
> And that He was *seen* by Cephas,
> Then the Twelve;
> Then He was seen by more than five hundred brothers at once…
> Then He was seen by James,
> Then by all the apostles.
>
> —1 Corinthians 15:3–7

■ Several New Testament verses describe the process of applying the gospel in the context of our individual lives. Investigate each of these scriptures, and look for the common themes in each one.

- John 1:12

_____

_____

- Acts 16:31

_____

_____

- Romans 10:9–10

_____

_____

- Ephesians 2:8–9

_____

_____

- Have you found a place for the evidence in your life? You began this study by considering where you found yourself on the spectrum between "thoughtful trust" and "blind belief." After reading the evidences presented, write a final reflection on these two approaches to faith. Perhaps these questions will help you as you write your reflection:

    - What personal beliefs have changed as a result of this study?

    _____

    _____

    - How have I grown?

    _____

    _____

    - In what areas do I want to study more?

    _____

    _____

    - What is the next step of faith that I need to take?

    _____

    _____

- If you desire additional assistance in understanding the message that has been presented in this book or in moving forward as a Christian, seek the counsel of a local Bible-believing church, or e-mail the author at timothy@ timothypauljones.com

Bibliography

"1 Clement 41:1–3." *The Apostolic Fathers I.* Loeb Classical Library. Edited by Kirsopp Lake. Cambridge, MA: Harvard University Press, 1985.

Adamik, Tamás. "The Baptized Lion in the Acts of Paul." Viewed at http://keur .eldoc.ub.rug.nl/FILES/wetenschappers/11/584/c4.pdf.

Allert, Craig, *A High View of Scripture?* (Grand Rapids, MI: Baker Academic, 2007).

Attridge, Harold and George MacRae. "Gospel of Truth." *The Nag Hammadi Library* rev. ed. Edited by J. Robinson. Leiden, The Netherlands: Brill, 1990.

Avigad, Nahman, and Yigael Yadin. *A Genesis Apocryphon.* Jerusalem, Israel: Magnes Press, 1956.

Baigent, Michael. *The Jesus Papers: Exposing the Greatest Cover-Up in History.* New York: HarperSanFrancisco, 2007.

Baigent, Michael, and Richard Leigh. *The Dead Sea Scrolls Deception.* New York: Touchstone, 1991.

Bailey, Kenneth. "Informal Controlled Oral Tradition and the Synoptic Gospels." *Asia Journal of Theology* 5 (1991).

Bahrdt, Karl F. *Ausführung des Plans und Zwecks Jesu*, 11 volumes. Reprint edition. Berlin, Germany: Walter de Gruyter, 1784–1792.

Bauckham, Richard. *Jesus and the Eyewitnesses.* Grand Rapids, MI: Eerdmans, 2006.

Bauer, Walter. *Orthodoxy and Heresy in Earliest Christianity.* Translated by R. A. Kraft and G. Krodel. London: SCM Press, 1971.

Baur, F. C. *Die christliche Gnosis oder die christliche Religions-Philosophie in ihrer geschichtlichen Entwicklung.* Tübingen, Germany: Osiander, 1835.

———. *The Church History of the First Three Centuries.* Edited and translated by A. Menzies. London and Edinburgh: Williams and Norgate, 1879.

———. *Paulus der Apostel Jesu Christi, Sein Leiben und Wirken, seine Briefe und seine Lebre.* Stuttgart, Germany: Becher and Muller, 1845.

Beasley-Murray, George R. *Baptism in the New Testament.* Grand Rapids, MI: Eerdmans, 1962.

Beck, Roger. *Planetary Gods and Planetary Orders in the Mysteries of Mithras.* London, UK: Brill, 1988.

———. *The Religion of the Mithras Cult in the Roman Empire.* New York: Oxford University Press, 2006.

Blomberg, Craig L. *Matthew.* Nashville, TN: Broadman and Holman, 1992.

Bock, Darrell. *The Missing Gospels.* Nashville, TN: Thomas Nelson, 2006.

Borg, Markus. *Meeting Jesus Again for the First Time.* New York: HarperSanFrancisco, 1995.

Borg, Markus, and Thomas Moore. *The Lost Gospel Q.* Berkeley, CA: Ulysses Press, 1999.

Bovon, François. "The Tomb of Jesus." SBL Forum (2007). Viewed at http://www.sbl-site.org/Article.aspx?ArticleId=656.

Brown, Dan. *The Da Vinci Code.* New York: Doubleday, 2003.

Brown, Dan, and Matt Lauer. "Video: The Today Show (Host: Matt Lauer)," June 9, 2003. The Da Vinci Code Official Web Site. Viewed at http://www.danbrown.com/novels/davinci_code/breakingnews.html.

Brown, R. *The Death of the Messiah: From Gethsemane to the Grave: A Commentary on the Passion Narratives in the Four Gospels.* Volume 2. New York: Doubleday, 1994.

Bruce, F. F. *The Canon of Scripture.* Downers Grove, IL: InterVarsity, 1988.

———. *The New Testament Documents: Are They Reliable?* Downers Grove, IL: InterVarsity, 1967.

Bultmann, Rudolph. "Is Exegesis Without Presuppositions Possible?" *Existence and Faith: Shorter Writings of Rudolf Bultmann.* Translated by S. M. Ogden. Cleveland, OH: The World Publishing Company, 1960.

———. *Jesus Christ and Mythology.* Reprint edition. Englewood Cliffs, NJ: Prentice Hall, 1997.

Burrows, Millar, ed. *The Dead Sea Scrolls of St. Mark's Monastery.* Volumes 1 and 2. New Haven, CT: Yale University, 1950.

Campbell, Joseph. *Occidental Mythology.* New York: Penguin, 1964.

Cameron, Ron, ed. *The Other Gospels: Non-Canonical Gospel Texts.* Philadelphia, PA: Westminster, 1982.

Carlson, Stephen F. *The Gospel Hoax.* Waco, TX: Baylor University Press, 2005.

Clauss, Manfred. *The Roman Cult of Mithras.* Translated by R. Gordon. New York: Routledge, 2000.

Clement of Alexandria. *Stromata.* Viewed at http://www.earlychristianwritings.com/text/clement-stromata-book3.html.

CNN.com. "One Year Later, Heaven's Gate Suicide Leaves Only Faint Trail," March 25, 1998. Viewed at http://www.cnn.com/US/9803/25/heavens.gate/.

Cohen, Henri. *Medailles imperials VII.* London: 1888.

Collins, Raymond F. *First Corinthians.* Collegeville, MN: Liturgical, 1999.

Corpus Iuris Civilis. *Pandectae [Digesta] 48.24.1–3.* Viewed at http://web.upmf-grenoble.fr/Haiti/Cours/Ak/.

Craig, William Lane, and Bart Ehrman. "Is There Historical Evidence for the Resurrection of Jesus? A Debate Between William Lane Craig and Bart Ehrman," March 28, 2006. Viewed at http://www.holycross.edu/departments/crec/website/resurrection-debate-transcript.pdf.

Craig, William Land, and Shabir Ally. "Did Jesus of Nazareth Physically Rise from the Dead?" Debate with William Lane Craig, University of Toronto, March 4, 2003. Viewed at http://www.youtube.com/watch?v=DrS5lRLi0uI.

"Creed of Constantinople—381 (Nicene Creed), The." Viewed at http://www .earlychurchtexts.com/main/constantinople/creed_of_constantinople.shtml.

Cross, Colin. *Who Was Jesus?* New York: Atheneum, 1970.

Cross, F. L., et al. "Grail, the Holy." *The Oxford Dictionary of the Christian Church*. Third edition. Oxford, UK: Oxford University Press, 1997.

Cross, Frank M. *The Ancient Library of Qumran and Modern Biblical Studies*. Garden City, NY: Doubleday, 1958.

Crossan, John Dominic. *The Birth of Christianity*. New York: HarperCollins, 1998.

———. *The Historical Jesus: The Life of a Mediterranean Jewish Peasant*. Reprint. New York: HarperSanFrancisco, 1993.

———. *Jesus: A Revolutionary Biography*. New York: HarperCollins, 1994.

———. *Who Killed Jesus?* New York: Harper, 1996.

Crossan, John Dominic, and Jonathan L. Reed. *Excavating Jesus: Beneath the Stones, Behind the Texts*. New York: HarperCollins, 2001.

Dawkins, Richard. *The God Delusion*. Boston: Houghton Mifflin, 2006.

De Morgan, Sophia. "Gnostic Gnonsense: A Critical Review of The Gnostic Gospels by Elaine Pagels." *Answering Infidels*. Viewed at http://www.answeringinfidels .com/index.php?option=content&task=view&id=42.

Deedat, Ahmed. *Christ in Islam*. Durban, South Africa: Islamic Propagation Centre, 1985. Viewed at http://www.jamaat.net/cis/christintro.html.

———. *Crucifixion or Cruci-Fiction?* Jeddah, Saudi Arabia: Abul-Qasim, 1984. Viewed at http://www.jamaat.net/crux/crucifixion.html.

———. *Was Jesus Crucified?* Chicago, IL: Kazi, 1992.

Drews, Arthur. *The Christ Myth*. Reprint. Amherst, NJ: Prometheus Books, 1998.

Dungan, David. *Constantine's Bible: Politics and the Making of the New Testament*. Minneapolis, MN: Fortress Press, 2007.

Ehrman, Bart. *Jesus: Apocalyptic Prophet of the New Millennium*. Oxford, UK: Oxford University Press, 1999.

———. *Lost Christianities*. New York: Oxford University Press, 2003.

———. *The Lost Gospel of Judas Iscariot*. New York: Oxford University Press, 2006.

———. *Misquoting Jesus: The Story Behind Who Changed the Bible and Why*. New York: HarperSanFrancisco, 2005.

———. *Peter, Paul, and Mary Magdalene: The Followers of Jesus in History and Legend*. New York: Oxford University Press, 2006.

Ehrman, Bart, and RBL. "Q&A: Bart Ehrman: Misquoting Jesus." *Religion BookLine*, January 25, 2006. Viewed at http://www.publishersweekly.com/article/ CA6301707.html?q=Q%26A+bart+ehrman.

Ehrman, Bart, and Stephen Colbert. "Bart Ehrman," *The Colbert Report*, June 20, 2006. Viewed at http://www.comedycentral.com/motherload/player .jhtml?ml_video=70912&ml_collection=&ml_gateway=&ml_gateway_id=&ml_

comedian=&ml_runtime=&ml_context=show&ml_origin_url=%2Fmotherload
%2Findex.jhtml%3Fml_video%3D70912&ml_playlist=&lnk=&is_large=true.

Eisenman, Robert. *The Dead Sea Scrolls and the First Christians.* Rockport, MA: Element, 1996.

———. *James the Brother of Jesus.* New York: Viking, 1996.

———. *James the Just in the Habakkuk Pesher.* Leiden: Brill, 1986.

———. *The New Testament Code.* London: Watkins, 2006.

Eisenman, Robert, and Michael O. Wise. *The Dead Sea Scrolls Uncovered.* New York: Penguin, 1992.

Eusebius of Caesarea. *Ecclesiastical History.* Volumes 1 and 2. Loeb Classical Library. Edited by Kirsopp Lake. Cambridge, MA: Harvard University Press, 1980.

———. *The Life of the Blessed Emperor Constantine.* Viewed at http://www.fordham .edu/halsall/basis/vita-constantine.html.

Evans, Craig A. *Fabricating Jesus.* Downers Grove, IL: InterVarsity Press, 2006.

———. "Jewish Burial Traditions and the Resurrection of Jesus." Viewed at http://www .craigaevans.com/Burial_Traditions.pdf.

———. "Vita Constantini." *Ecclesiastical History.* Volume 2. Loeb Classical Library. Edited by Kirsopp Lake. Cambridge, MA: Harvard University Press, 1980.

Falk, Harvey. *Jesus the Pharisee.* Eugene, OR: Wipf and Stock, 2003.

Ferguson, Everett. *Backgrounds of Early Christianity.* Third edition. Grand Rapids, MI: William B. Eerdmans, 2003.

———, ed. *Encyclopedia of Early Christianity.* New York: Garland, 1990.

Feuerverger, Audrey. "Dear Statistical Colleagues," March 12, 2007. Viewed at http:// fisher.utstat.toronto.edu/andrey/OfficeHrs.txt.

Fitzmyer, J. A. "4Qpap Tobitaar," *Qumran Cave 4: VIII Parabiblical Texts 2.* Oxford, UK: Clarendon, 1995.

Freke, Timothy, and Peter Gandy. *The Jesus Mysteries: Was the "Original Jesus" a Pagan God?* New York: Random House, 1999.

———. *The Laughing Jesus: Religious Lies and Gnostic Wisdom.* New York: Three Rivers, 2006.

Frend, W. H. C. *The Rise of Christianity.* Philadelphia, PA: Fortress, 1984.

Funk, Robert. *The Five Gospels: What Did Jesus Really Say? The Search for the Authentic Words of Jesus.* New York: HarperSanFrancisco, 1997.

———. *Honest to Jesus.* New York: HarperSanFrancisco, 1996.

———. "The Once and Future Jesus," *The Once and Future Jesus.* Edited by G. Jenks. Santa Rosa, CA: Polebridge, 2000.

Funk, Robert, et al. *The Acts of Jesus: The Search for the Authentic Deeds of Jesus.* New York: HarperSanFrancisco, 1999.

Gamble, Harry Y. *Books and Readers in the Early Church.* New Haven, CT: Yale University, 1995.

Gerhardsson, Birger. *The Origins of the Gospel Traditions.* London, UK: SCM, 1979.

———. *Memory and Manuscript* Grand Rapids, MI: Eerdmans, 1998.

"God Who Wasn't There, The." Viewed at http://www.thegodmovie.com/.

Goguel, Maurice. "Recent French Discussion of the Historical Existence of Jesus Christ." *The Harvard Theological Review* 19 (April 1926): 115–142.

Golb, Norman. *Who Wrote the Dead Sea Scrolls?* New York: Scribners, 1995.

Gordon, Richard. *Image and Value in the Greco-Roman World.* Aldershot, UK: Variorum, 1996.

Gorka, Terry. "Atheists & Agnostics Take Aim at Christians," June 11, 2007. Viewed at http://www.barna.org/FlexPage.aspx?Page=BarnaUpdate&BarnaUpdateID= 272.

"Gospel of Judas, The." ABC, June 25, 2006. Viewed at http://abc.net.au/tv/guide/ netw/200606/programs/ZY8369A001D25062006T193000.htm.

Gospel of Peter 1:1, 23, 25. Viewed at http://www.earlychristianwritings.com/peter -greek.html.

Gundry, Robert Horton. *Mark: A Commentary on His Apology for the Cross.* Grand Rapids, MI: Eerdmans, 1993.

———. *Matthew: A Commentary on His Handbook for a Mixed Church Under Persecution.* Grand Rapids, MI: Eerdmans, 1994.

Haas, Nicu. "Anthropological Observations on the Skeletal Remains from Giv'at ha-Mivtar." *Israel Exploration Journal* 20 (1970): 38–59.

Habermas, Gary. "Experiences of the Risen Jesus: The Foundational Historical Issue in the Early Proclamation of the Resurrection," *Dialog: A Journal of Theology* 45 (Fall 2006): 288–297.

Harpur, Tom. *The Pagan Christ.* Toronto, Ontario: Thomas Allen, 2004.

Harris, William. *Ancient Literacy.* Cambridge, MA: Harvard University Press, 1989.

Hart, J. "Was Jesus Gay? No, But Morton Smith Thought So." *Dartmouth Review* (May 18, 2007..

Head, Peter M. "The Date of the Magdalen Papyrus of Matthew." *Tyndale Bulletin* 46 (1995): 251–285.

Hengel, Martin. *Crucifixion in the Ancient World and the Folly of the Message of the Cross.* Revised edition. Minneapolis, MN: Augsburg Fortress, 1977.

———. *The Four Gospels and the One Gospel of Jesus Christ.* Translated by John Bowden. Harrisburg, PA: Trinity Press, 2000.

Hezser, Catherine. *Jewish Literacy in Roman Palestine.* Tübingen: Mohr (Siebeck), 2001.

Hippolytus of Rome. *Kata Pason Haireseon Elengchos, Hippolyti opera graece et latine.* Volume 1, *Patrologiae Cursus Completus, Series Graeco-Latina.* Reprint edition edited by J. Fabricius. Paris: Lutetiae Parisiorum, 1857–1866.

———. *Philosophoumena. Patrologiae Cursus Completus, Series Graeco-Latina.* Reprint edition edited by J. Fabricius. Paris: Lutetiae Parisiorum, 1857–1866.

Hitchens, Christopher. *God Is Not Great: How Religion Poisons Everything.* New York: Hachette Book Group, 2007.

Hohlwein, N. "Le vétéran Lucius Bellienus Gemellus, gentleman-farmer au Fayoum."

Études de Papyrologie 8 (1957): 69–91.

Howard, George. *Hebrew Gospel of Matthew.* Macon, GA: Mercer University, 1995.

Hull, A. J. T., et al. "Radiocarbon Dating of Scrolls and Linen Fragments from the Judean Desert." *Radiocarbon* 37 (1995): 1–19.

Hultgren, Arland J. *The Rise of Normative Christianity.* Minneapolis, MN: Fortress, 1994.

Ilan, Tal. *Lexicon of Jewish Names in Late Antiquity.* Part 1. Tübingen, Germany: Mohr, 2002.

Irenaeus of Lyons. *Sancti Irenæi espiscopi Lugdunensis et martyris Detectionis et eversionis falso cognominatæ agnitionis, seu, Contra hæreses libri quinque, Patrologiae Cursus Completus, Series Graeco-Latina.* Reprint edition edited by J. P. Migne. Paris: Lutetiae Parisiorum, 1857.

Jenkins, Philip. *Hidden Gospels.* New York: Oxford University Press, 2001.

Jeremias, Joachim. *The Eucharistic Words of Jesus.* New York: Scribner, 1966.

Jerome. *On Illustrious Men.* Translated by T. P. Halton, in Fathers of the Church Series. Washington DC: The Catholic University of America Press, 1999.

Jones, Jim. "Jonestown Audiotape Q928," March 2007. Viewed at http://jonestown .sdsu.edu/.

Jones, Timothy. *Hullabaloo.* Colorado Springs, CO: David C. Cook, 2007.

———. *Misquoting Truth.* Downers Grove, IL: InterVarsity Press, 2007.

Josephus, Flavius. *Antiquitates Judaica* 17:10. Viewed at http://www .earlychristianwritings.com/text/josephus/josephus.htm.

———. *Antiquities of the Jews.* Viewed at http://www.earlychristianwritings.com/ text/josephus/ant-18.htm.

———. *The Jewish War.* Loeb Classical Library. Edited by H. St. J. Thackeray. Cambridge, MA: Harvard University Press, 1927.

———. *Contra Apionem* [The Life Against Apion]. Loeb Classical Library. Edited by H. St. J. Thackeray. Cambridge, MA: Harvard University, 1926.

———. *The War of the Jews.* Viewed at http://www.earlychristianwritings.com/text/ josephus/josephus.htm.

Juvenal. *Satires.* Viewed at http://www.curculio.org/Juvenal/s14.html.

Katz, Ian. "When Christopher Met Peter," *The Guardian,* May 31, 2005.

Keener, Craig S. *A Commentary on the Gospel of Matthew.* Grand Rapids, MI: Eerdmans, 1999.

Kelley, Nicole. *Knowledge and Religious Authority in the Pseudo-Clementines.* Tubingen, Germany: Mohr Siebeck, 2006.

Kennedy, George. "Classical and Christian Source Criticism." *The Relationships Among the Gospels.* Edited by W. O. Walker. San Antonio, TX: Trinity University, 1978.

Klausner, Joseph. *Jesus of Nazareth.* Boston, MA: Beacon, 1925.

Kloner, Amos. "A Tomb with Inscribed Ossuaries in East Talpiyot, Jerusalem." *Atiquot* 29 (1996): 15–22.

Koester, Helmut. "Apocryphal and Canonical Gospels." *Harvard Theological Review* 73 (1980): 105–130.

Kostenberger, Andreas. "Baptism in the Gospels," *Believer's Baptism: Sign of the New Covenant in Christ*. Edited by T. Schreiner and S. Wright. Nashville, TN: Broadman and Holman, 2006.

Kruger, M. "Review of Misquoting Jesus: The Story Behind Who Changed the Bible and Why (Bart Ehrman)," *Journal of the Evangelical Theological Society* 49 (June 2006): 389.

Lalleman, Pieter. "Polymorphy of Christ." *The Apocryphal Acts of John*. Kampen, The Netherlands: Kok Pharos, 1995.

Lawrence, Jonathan D. *Washing in Water: Trajectories in Ritual Bathing in the Hebrew Bible and Second Temple Literature*. Atlanta, GA: Scholars, 2006.

Leloup, Jean-Yves. *The Gospel of Mary Magdalene*. Rochester, VT: Inner Traditions, 2002.

Lemaire, Andre. "Burial Box of James the Brother of Jesus." *Biblical Archaeology Review* 28 (November–December 2002): 24–33.

Lewis, C. S. *God in the Dock: Essays on Theology and Ethics*. Edited by Walter Hooper. Grand Rapids, MI: William B. Eerdmans, 1970.

Lieberman, Saul. *Hellenism in Jewish Palestine*. New York: JTS, 1962.

Llewelyn, Stephen R., ed. *New Documents Illustrating Early Christianity*. Volume 8. Grand Rapids, MI: Eerdmans, 1998.

Lombatti, Antonio. "Inscriptions of the ossuaries of Dominus Flevit," June 27, 2007. Viewed at http://www.antoniolombatti.it/B/Blog/3BF5DF28-60DF-4E90 -BB09-478530685A32.html.

Lord, Albert B. "The Gospels as Oral Traditional Literature." *The Relationships Among the Gospels*. Edited by W. Walker. San Antonio, TX: Trinity University Press, 1978.

"Lost Gospel of Judas, The." *National Geographic*, May 2006.

Lucero, Sarah. "Preacher Claims to Be Christ." *San Antonio Express-News*, February 27, 2007.

Lüdemann, Gerd. *The Resurrection of Jesus*. London: SCM Press, 1994.

Lüdemann, Gerd, with Alf Özen. *What Really Happened? A Historical Approach to the Resurrection*. London, UK: SCM, 1995.

Mack, Burton L. *The Lost Gospel: The Book of Q and Christian Origins*. New York: HarperOne, 1994.

———. *Who Wrote the New Testament? The Making of the Christian Myth*. New York: HarperSanFrancisco, 1995.

MacGregor, Kirk. "1 Corinthians 15:3b–6a, 7 and the Bodily Resurrection of Jesus." *Journal of the Evangelical Theological Society* 49 (June 2006): 225–234.

Martyr, Justin. *Dialogus cum Tryphone. Patrologiae Cursus Completus, Series Graeco-Latina*. Reprint edition edited by J. P. Migne. Paris: Lutetiae Parisiorum, 1857–1866.

————. *Apologia Prima. Patrologiae Cursus Completus, Series Graeco-Latina*. Reprint edition edited by J. P. Migne. Paris: Lutetiae Parisiorum, 1857–1866.

————. *The First Apology*. Viewed at http://www.ccel.org/ccel/schaff/anf01.viii.ii.lxvi .html.

Meier, John. *A Marginal Jew*. New York: Doubleday, 1991.

Metzger, Bruce. *The Canon of the New Testament: Its Origin, Development, and Significance*. Oxford, UK: Oxford University, 1987.

————. *Manuscripts of the Greek Bible*. New York: Oxford University Press, 1981.

Metzger, Bruce, and Bart Ehrman. *The Text of the New Testament: Its Transmission, Corruption, and Restoration*. New York: Oxford University Press, 2005.

Meyer, Marvin. *Gnostic Discoveries*. New York: HarperOne, 2006.

Meyer, Marvin, and Elaine Pagels. "Introduction." *The Nag Hammadi Scriptures*. New York: HarperOne, 2007.

Milik, J. T. *Ten Years of Discovery in the Wilderness of Judea*. Naperville, IL: Allenson, 1959.

Milik, J. T., and D. Barthelemy. *Discoveries in the Judean Desert*. Volume 1. Oxford, UK: Oxford University Press, 1955.

Millard, A. R. *Reading and Writing in the Time of Jesus*. New York: New York University Press, 2000.

Miller, Robert, ed. *The Complete Gospels*. Revised edition. Santa Rosa, CA: Polebridge Press, 1994.

Morgan, Teresa. *Literate Education in the Hellenistic and Roman Worlds*. Cambridge, UK: Cambridge University Press, 1999.

"Muratorian Canon, The." View at http://www.earlychristianwritings.com/text/ muratorian-latin.html/.

Neusner, Jacob. *Are There Really Tannaitic Parallels to the Gospels?* Atlanta, GA: Scholars Press, 1993.

"Nicæno-Constantinopolitan Creed, The." Viewed at http://www.ccel.org/ccel/ schaff/creeds2.iv.i.ii.html.

Nolland, John. *Luke 9:1–18:34*. Dallas, TX: Word, 1993.

Nongbri, Brent. "The Use and Abuse of P52." *Harvard Theological Review* 98 (2005): 23–52.

Origen of Alexandria. *Contra Celsum. Patrologiae Cursus Completus, Series Graeco-Latina*. Reprint edition edited by J. P. Migne. Paris: Lutetiae Parisiorum, 1857–1866.

Osiek, Carol. "An Early Tale That Almost Made It Into the New Testament." *Bible Review* (October 1994): 49–54.

Pagels, Elaine. *Beyond Belief: The Secret Gospel of Thomas*. New York: Random House, 2003.

————. *The Gnostic Gospels*. New York: Random House, 1979.

Pagels, Elaine, and Helmut Koester. "Report on the Dialogue of the Savior." *Nag Hammadi and Gnosis*. Edited by R. Wilson. Leiden, The Netherlands: Brill, 1978.

Paterculus, Valleius. "The Roman History." Viewed at http://penelope.uchicago.edu/Thayer/E/Roman/Texts/Velleius_Paterculus/home.html.

Patton, Judd. "The Jefferson Bible." *Jefferson's Bible: The Life and Morals of Jesus of Nazareth*. Reprint edition edited by J. Patton. Grove City, PA: ABD, 1997.

Paulus, H. E. G. *Das Leben Jesu als Grundlage einer reinen Geschichte des Urchristentums*. Heidelberg, Germany: E. F. Winter, 1828.

Pearson, Birger A. *Gnosticism and Christianity in Roman and Coptic Egypt*. London: T & T Clark, 2004.

Pelikan, Jaroslov. "Maasai Creed." *American Public Media*, May 18, 2006.

Pellegrino, Charles, and Simcha Jacobovici. *The Jesus Family Tomb*. New York: HarperSanFrancisco, 2007.

Perrin, Nicholas. *Thomas, the Other Gospel*. Louisville, KY: Westminster John Knox, 2007.

Philo of Alexandria. *Flaccus*. Viewed at http://www.earlychristianwritings.com/yonge/book36.html.

———. *Hypothetica*. Volume IX. Loeb Classical Library. Edited by F. H. Colson. Cambridge, MA: Harvard University, 1941.

———. *In Flaccus*. Loeb Classical Library. Edited by F. H. Colson. Cambridge, MA: Harvard University, 1941.

———. *On the Contemplative Life*. Volume IX. Loeb Classical Library. Edited by F. H. Colson. Cambridge, MA: Harvard University, 1941.

———. *On the Embassy to Gaius*. Volume X. Loeb Classical Library. Edited by F. H. Colson. Cambridge, MA: Harvard University, 1962.

———. *On Providence*. Volume IX. Loeb Classical Library. Edited by F. H. Colson. Cambridge, MA: Harvard University, 1941.

Picknett, L., and C. Prince. *The Templar Revelation: Secret Guardians of the True Identity of Christ*. New York: Bantam, 1997.

Pliny the Younger. *Letters, II, Books 8–10. Panegyricus*. Loeb Classical Library. Edited by B. Radice. Cambridge, MA: Harvard University, 1969.

"Pray Before the Head of 'Bob.'" Viewed at http://www.resort.com/~banshee/Misc/8ball/.

Pryor, John W. "Papyrus Egerton 2." *Australian Biblical Review* 37 (1989): 1–13.

Roberts, C. H. "An Unpublished Fragment of the Fourth Gospel in the John Rylands Library." *Bulletin of the John Rylands Library* 20 (1936): 45–55.

———. *Greek Literary Hands*. Oxford, UK: Clarendon, 1955.

Robinson, James M., ed. *The Coptic Gnostic Library*. Volumes 1 and 2. Leiden, The Netherlands: Brill, 2000.

Robinson, James M., and Helmut Koester, *Trajectories Through Early Christianity* (Philadelphia, PA: Fortress, 1971).

Robinson, Thomas A. *The Bauer Thesis Examined*. Lewiston, NY: Mellen, 1988.

Schneider, Paul. *The Mystery of the Acts of John*. San Francisco, CA: Mellen Research University Press, 1991.

Schonfield, Hugh J. *The Passover Plot*. New York: Random House, 1965.

Seneca. *De consolatione ad Marciam. Volume II: Moral Essays*. Loeb Classical Library. Edited by J. Basore. Cambridge, MA: Harvard University, 1932.

Schneemelcher, Wilhelm, ed. *New Testament Apocrypha*. Translated by R. Wilson. Louisville, KY: John Knox, 1992.

Schiffman, Lawrence. *Who Was a Jew?* Hoboken, NJ: KTAV, 1985.

Schweitzer, Albert. *The Quest of the Historical Jesus*. Viewed at http://www .earlychristianwritings.com/schweitzer/chapter20.htm.

Shanks, Hershel, and Ben Witherington III. *The Brother of Jesus*. New York: HarperSanFrancisco, 2003.

Shedinger, R. F. "The Textual Relationship Between P45 and Shem Tob's Hebrew Matthew," *New Testament Studies* 43 (1997): 58–71.

Sherwin-White, A. N. *Roman Society and Roman Law in the New Testament*. Oxford, UK: Clarendon, 1963.

Smith, Morton. *Clement of Alexandria and a Secret Gospel of Mark*. Cambridge, MA: Harvard University Press, 1973.

———. *The Secret Gospel*. London, UK: Gollancz, 1974.

———. *Tannaitic Parallels to the Gospels*. Philadelphia, PA: Society of Biblical Literature, 1951.

Smith, Paul. "Priory of Sion Fake Parchments: History of a Hoax." Viewed at http:// priory-of-sion.com/posd/pdchparchments.html.

Snyder, Tom. *Myth Conceptions*. Grand Rapids, MI: Baker Academic, 1995.

Spong, John Selby. *A New Christianity for a New World*. New York: HarperSanFrancisco, 2000.

Stanton, Graham. *Gospel Truth?* Valley Forge, PA: Trinity Press, 1995.

Stoyanov, Yuri. *The Hidden Tradition in Europe*. London, UK: Penguin, 1994.

Sukenik, E. L. *The Dead Sea Scrolls of the Hebrew University*. Jerusalem, Israel: Magnes Press, 1955.

Tabor, James. *The Jesus Dynasty*. New York: Simon and Schuster, 2006.

Tacitus, Cornelius. "Annales." Viewed at http://www.perseus.tufts.edu/.

Terian, A., ed. *Philonis Alexandrini De Animalibus*. Chico, CA: Scholars Press, 1981.

Tertullian of Carthage. "Adversus Marcionem." Viewed at http://www.tertullian .org.

———. "De baptismo." Viewed at http://www.tertullian.org.

———. "De carne Christi." Viewed at http://www.tertullian.org/.

———. "De Praescriptione Haereticorum." Viewed at http://www.tertullian.org/.

Thiede, Carsten Peter. *The Earliest Gospel Manuscript?* Exeter, UK: Paternoster, 1992.

Thiering, Barbara. *Jesus and the Riddle of the Dead Sea Scrolls*. New York: HarperCollins, 1992.

————. *Jesus the Man*. Toronto: Corgi Books, 1993.

Tranquillus, Suetonius. "De Vita Caesarum." Viewed at http://www.perseus.tufts .edu/.

Trever, John C. *The Dead Sea Scrolls: A Personal Account*. Grand Rapids, MI: Eerdmans, 1979.

Tuckett, Christopher. "Synoptic Traditions in Some Nag Hammadi and Related Texts." *Vigiliae Christianae* 36 (1982): 173–190.

Turcan, Robert. *The Cults of the Roman Empire*. Translated by A. Nevill. Malden, MA: Blackwell, 1996.

Tzaferis, V. "Crucifixion–the Archaeological Evidence: Remains of a Jewish Victim of Crucifixion Found in Jerusalem." *Biblical Archaeology Review* 11 (January– February 1985): 44–53.

van Biema, David. "A Different Jesus to Believe In?" *TIME*, May 9, 2007.

————. "The Gospel Truth?" *TIME*, April 8, 1996.

————. "Rewriting the Gospels," *TIME*, March 2, 2007.

van Voorst, Robert. *Jesus Outside the New Testament*. Grand Rapids, MI: Eerdmans, 2000.

————. *The Ascents of James*. Atlanta, GA: Scholars Press, 1989.

Vermes, Geza. *The Complete Dead Sea Scrolls in English*. New York: Penguin, 1997.

Voragine, Jacubus de. "Readings From the Golden Legend." Translated by W. Caxton. Viewed at http://www.aug.edu/augusta/iconography/goldenLegend/index.html.

Wallace, Daniel. "The Gospel According to Bart." *Journal of the Evangelical Theological Society* 49 (June 2006): 327–349.

Walls, A. F. "Papias and Oral Tradition." *Vigiliae Christianae* 21 (1967): 137–140.

Wells, George Albert. *The Jesus Myth*. Peru, IL: Open Court, 1999.

White, James. *From Toronto to Emmaus*. Vestavia Hills, AL: Solid Ground, 2007.

Wilford, John Noble. "Computer Breaks Monopoly on Study of the Dead Sea Scrolls." *New York Times*, September 5, 1991.

Witherington III, Ben. *The Acts of the Apostles: A Socio-Rhetorical Commentary*. Grand Rapids, MI: Eerdmans, 1998.

Wright, N. T. *The Challenge of Jesus: Rediscovering Who Jesus Was and Is*. Downers Grove, IL: InterVarsity Press, 1999.

————. *The Resurrection of the Son of God*. Philadelphia, PA: Fortress, 2003.

————. *Who Was Jesus?* London, UK: SPCK, 1992.

Yamauchi, Edwin. *Pre-Christian Gnosticism*. Grand Rapids, MI: Baker Book House, 1983.

Yzermans, Vincent. *Wonderworker: The True Story of How Saint Nicholas Became Santa Claus*. Chicago, IL: ACTA, 1994.

Notes

IN THE TEXT OF *CONSPIRACIES AND THE CROSS*, THE AUTHOR HAS TRANS-lated Hebrew, Aramaic, Greek, and Latin texts from primary source materials. For English renderings of the Dead Sea Scrolls, see Geza Vermes, *The Complete Dead Sea Scrolls in English* (New York: Penguin, 1997). For an English rendering of the Mishnah, see Jacob Neusner, *The Mishnah: A New Translation* (New Haven, Connecticut: Yale University Press, 1988). For an English rendering of the Quran, see http://www.muslim.org/english-quran/search/index.htm.

INTRODUCTION: The Trouble With Jesus

1. N. T. Wright, *The Challenge of Jesus: Rediscovering Who Jesus Was and Is* (Downers Grove, IL: InterVarsity Press, 1999), 18.
2. R. Funk et al., *The Acts of Jesus: The Search for the Authentic Deeds of Jesus* (New York: HarperSanFrancisco, 1999), 104–105, 161, 473.
3. N. T. Wright, *The Five Gospels: What Did Jesus Really Say? The Search for the Authentic Words of Jesus* (New York: HarperSanFrancisco, 1997), 549–553.
4. J. D. Crossan, as quoted in D. Van Biema, "The Gospel Truth?" *TIME* (April 8, 1996): (http://www.time.com/). In statements such as this one, one of the crucial differences among Jesus Seminar fellows becomes clear: While John Dominic Crossan views Jesus as a reactionary peasant, the other fellows—including Robert Funk—have seen Jesus as an itinerant sage. Despite these differing visions, however, nearly all the fellows agree on a reductionistic view of Jesus, assuming that the Gospels are not primarily historical documents.
5. M. Lauer and D. Brown, "Video: The Today Show (Host: Matt Lauer)," http://www.danbrown.com/novels/davinci_code/breakingnews.html (accessed November 5, 2007).
6. M. Baigent, R. Leigh, and H. Lincoln, *Holy Blood, Holy Grail* (New York: Dell, 1983); L. Picknett and C. Prince, *The Templar Revelation: Secret Guardians of the True Identity of Christ* (New York: Bantam, 1997); M. Baigent and R. Leigh, *The Dead Sea Scrolls Deception* (London: Jonathan Cape, 1992); J. D. Crossan, *The Historical Jesus: The Life of a Mediterranean Jewish Peasant* (New York: HarperSanFrancisco, 1991).
7. D. Van Biema, "The Gospel Truth?" *TIME*, April 8, 1996, http://www.time.com/time/magazine/article/0,9171,984367,00.html (accessed November 5, 2007).
8. D. Brown, *The Da Vinci Code* (New York: Doubleday, 2003), 233.
9. D. Van Biema, "Rewriting the Gospels," *TIME*, March 2, 2007, http://www.time.com/time/magazine/article/0,9171,1595238,00.html (accessed November 5, 2007).
10. M. Maudlin, as quoted in Van Biema, "Rewriting the Gospels," *TIME*, March 2, 2007, http://www.time.com/time/magazine/article/0,9171,1595238,00.html (accessed November 5, 2007).
11. M. Baigent, *The Jesus Papers: Exposing the Greatest Cover-Up in History* (New York:

HarperSanFrancisco, 2007), 245–274.

12. B. Ehrman, *Misquoting Jesus: The Story Behind Who Changed the Bible and Why* (New York: HarperSanFrancisco, 2005), 41–52, 133–149.

13. "The Lost Gospel of Judas," *National Geographic*, May 2006, http://www .nationalgeographic.com/lostgospel/ (accessed November 5, 2007).

14. "The God Who Wasn't There," http://www.thegodmovie.com/ (accessed November 5, 2007).

15. T. Freke and P. Gandy, *The Jesus Mysteries: Was the "Original Jesus" a Pagan God?* (New York: Random House, 1999); T. Harpur, *The Pagan Christ* (Toronto, ON: Thomas Allen, 2004).

16. S. Lucero, "Preacher Claims to Be Christ," *San Antonio Express-News*, February 27, 2007, http://www.mysanantonio.com/news/metro/stories/MYSA022607 .secondcomingpreacher.KENS.1864300a.html (accessed November 5, 2007); D. Van Biema, "A Different Jesus to Believe In?" *Time*, May 9, 2007, http://www.time.com/ time/nation/article/0,8599,1618968,00.html (accessed November 5, 2007).

17. C. Pellegrino and S. Jacobovici, *The Jesus Family Tomb* (New York: HarperSanFrancisco, 2007).

18. D. Van Biema, "Rewriting the Gospels," *TIME*, April 8, 1996, http://www.time.com/ time/magazine/article/0,9171,1595238,00.html (accessed November 5, 2007).

19. I. Katz, "When Christopher Met Peter," in *The Guardian*, May 31, 2005, http://books .guardian.co.uk/hay2005/story/0,,1496348,00.html (accessed November 5, 2007).

20. C. Hitchens, *God Is Not Great: How Religion Poisons Everything* (New York: Hachette Book Group, 2007), 110.

21. R. Dawkins, *The God Delusion* (Boston: Houghton Mifflin, 2006), 31.

22. Dawkins, *The God Delusion*, 250, 253.

23. "The proportion of atheists and agnostics increases from 6% of Elders (ages 61+) and 9% of Boomers (ages 42-60), to 14% of Busters (23-41) and 19% of adult Mosaics (18-22). When adjusted for age and compared to 15 years ago, each generation has changed surprisingly little over the past decade and a half. Each new generation entered adulthood with a certain degree of secular fervor, which appears to stay relatively constant within that generation over time. This contradicts the popular notion that such generational differences are simply a product of people becoming more faith-oriented as they age" (T. Gorka, "Atheists & Agnostics Take Aim at Christians," June 11, 2007, http://www.barna.org/FlexPage.aspx?Page=BarnaUpdate&BarnaUpdateID=272 (accessed November 5, 2007).

24. M. Maudlin, as quoted in Van Biema, "Rewriting the Gospels," *Time*, March 2, 2007, http://www.time.com/time/magazine/article/0,9171,1595238,00.html (accessed November 5, 2007).

25. Dawkins, *The God Delusion*, 36.

26. "Allah…has revealed to you [Muhammad] this Scripture as Truth" (*Surat 'ali Imran* [3], 2–3).

27. "They neither killed nor crucified him [Messiah Jesus, the prophet of Allah]. It was only made to appear that way…they did not kill him—no, Allah lifted him up to himself" (*Surat An-Nisa* [4], 157–159). In all likelihood, the Quran did *not* originally deny the death of Jesus on the cross; this interpretation emerged later. This viewpoint has, however, become the dominant view among many Muslims. For details, see A. McRoy's text *For Nicaea: An Answer to the Muslim Propaganda Book 'Before Nicaea'* (forthcoming, provided to the author through personal communication).

28. It is interesting to consider how close this idea—held by many conservative believers in Jesus—stands to more liberal views of scholars such as Albert Schweitzer. In

Schweitzer's work *The Quest of the Historical Jesus*, the present reality of Jesus was—in the end, with Jesus having been stripped of the historical reality of anything beyond his supposed place as a failed apocalyptic messenger—reduced to the existential experience of the individual: "He comes to us as One unknown, without a name, as of old, by the lake-side, he came to those men who knew Him not.... To those who obey,... *they shall learn in their own experience Who He is*," (A. Schweitzer, *The Quest of the Historical Jesus*, http://www.earlychristianwritings.com/schweitzer/chapter20.html (accessed November 5, 2007), emphasis added.

29. J. Jones, Jonestown Audiotape Q 928, March 2007, http://jonestown.sdsu.edu/ (accessed November 5, 2007).

30. CNN.com, "One Year Later, Heaven's Gate Suicide Leaves Only Faint Trail," March 25, 1998, http://www.cnn.com/US/9803/25/heavens.gate/ (accessed November 5, 2007).

31. "Pray Before the Head of 'Bob,'" http://www.resort.com/~banshee/Misc/8ball/ (accessed November 5, 2007).

32. H. Schonfield, *The Passover Plot* (New York: Random House, 1965).

33. Baigent et al., *Holy Blood, Holy Grail*; M. Baigent, R. Leigh, and H. Lincoln, *The Messianic Legacy* (New York: Henry Holt, 1987).

34. C. S. Lewis, "Answers to Questions on Christianity" and "Myth Became Fact," in *God in the Dock: Essays on Theology and Ethics,* ed. Walter Hooper (Grand Rapids, MI: William B. Eerdmans, 1970), 58, 66.

35. B. Metzger, *The Canon of the New Testament: Its Origin, Development, and Significance* (Oxford, UK: Oxford University, 1987); idem, *The Text of the New Testament: Its Transmission, Corruption, and Restoration* (Oxford, United Kingdom: Oxford University, 1964).

36. F. F. Bruce, *The Canon of Scripture* (Downers Grove, IL: InterVarsity, 1988); idem, *The New Testament Documents: Are They Reliable?* (Downers Grove, IL: InterVarsity, 1967).

37. B. Thiering, *Jesus and the Riddle of the Dead Sea Scrolls* (New York: HarperCollins, 1992).

38. K.F. Bahrdt, *Ausführung des Plans und Zwecks Jesu* 11 vols., repr. ed. (Berlin, Germany: Walter de Gruyter, 1784–1792); H.E.G. Paulus, *Das Leben Jesu als Grundlage einer reinen Geschichte des Urchristentums* (Heidelberg, Germany: E. F. Winter, 1828).

39. Some Muslim scholars contend that, according to the Quran, Jesus survived crucifixion. Others contend the Quran teaches that Jesus was never crucified at all. See, e.g., S. Ally, "Did Jesus of Nazareth Physically Rise from the Dead?" debate with William Lane Craig, University of Toronto, March 4, 2003, http://www.youtube.com/watch?v=DrS5l RLi0uI; A. Deedat, *Christ in Islam* (Durban, South Africa: Islamic Propagation Centre, 1985), http://www.jamaat.net/cis/christintro.html (accessed November 5, 2007); idem, *Crucifixion or Cruci-Fiction?* (Jeddah, Saudi Arabia: Abul-Qasim, 1984), http://www.jamaat.net/crux/crucifixion.html (accessed November 5, 2007); idem, *Was Jesus Crucified?* (Chicago, IL: Kazi, 1992).

CONSPIRACY NUMBER ONE: No One Knows Who Wrote the Gospels

1. B. Ehrman, *Lost Christianities* (New York: Oxford University Press, 2003), 3, 235. In fact, the John's Gospel *does* include several "we" statements that were intended to identify the source of the Gospel as a companion of Jesus; cf. R. Bauckham, *Jesus and the Eyewitnesses: The Gospels as Eyewitness Testimony* (Grand Rapids, MI: William B. Eerdmans, 2006), 369–383.

2. B. Ehrman, *Jesus: Apocalyptic Prophet of the New Millennium* (New York: Oxford University Press, 1999), 44, 46.

3. T. Freke and P. Gandy, *The Laughing Jesus: Religious Lies and Gnostic Wisdom* (New York: Three Rivers, 2006), 69.

4. See B. Metzger, *Manuscripts of the Greek Bible* (New York: Oxford University Press, 1981), 49–51, 102, for medieval dating methods. The first dated manuscript of the New Testament seems to be the minuscule manuscript of the Gospels known by the number 461. This manuscript was copied in A.D. 835.

5. Tertullian of Carthage made it clear that the autographs (original manuscripts) of Paul's letters were still available in A.D. 200. As such, it is not inconceivable that some of the earliest Gospel fragments were copied from original manuscripts. See Tertullian of Carthage, *De Praescriptione Haereticorum*, 36.1, October 6, 2007, http://www.tertullian .org/ (accessed November 5, 2007).

6. For a more skeptical approach to P52, see B. Nongbri, "The Use and Abuse of P52," *Harvard Theological Review* 98 (N.p.: 2005), 23–52. However, Nongbri fails to account adequately for the close correspondence between P52 and PFay110. For the first references to P52 after its discovery, see C. Roberts, "An Unpublished Fragment of the Fourth Gospel in the John Rylands Library," *Bulletin of the John Rylands Library* 20 (N.p.: 1936), 45–55.

7. C. Roberts, *Greek Literary Hands* (Oxford, UK: Clarendon, 1955), 11.

8. Image of P387: http://www.columbia.edu/cgi-bin/dlo?obj=columbia.apis.p387&size=300 &face=f&tile=0 (accessed November 5, 2007). See transcription of text at http://perseus .tufts.edu (accessed November 5, 2007); for more information about the Gemellus correspondence, see N. Hohlwein, "Le vétéran Lucius Bellienus Gemellus, gentleman-farmer au Fayoum," *Études de Papyrologie* 8 (N.p.: 1957), 69–91.

9. In the 1990s, C. P. Thiede contended that P64 and P67 should be dated in the first century A.D. These contentions—as well as Thiede's claims that fragment 7Q5 from the Dead Sea Scrolls is part of Mark's Gospel and that the *Titulus Crucis* kept at the Church of Santa Croce in Rome actually came from the cross of Jesus—have been widely regarded as gross overstatements of the historical evidences. (Cf. C. P. Thiede, *The Earliest Gospel Manuscript?* [Exeter, United Kingdom: Paternoster, 1992]). See, e.g., P. Head, "The Date of the Magdalen Papyrus of Matthew," *Tyndale Bulletin* 46 (N.p.: 1995), 251–285. Unfortunately, many well-intended Christian apologists continue to treat Thiede's claims as uncontested truth.

10. The most similar letter formations to the ones in this manuscript seem to be the ones found in Papyrus Oxyrhynchus 2498, a late second- or early third-century fragment of the works of Hesiod. See image of POxy2498, http://163.1.169.40/gsdl/collect/POxy/ index/assoc/HASH0128/2ec86d20.dir/POxy.v0028.n2498.a.01.hires.jpg (accessed November 5, 2007).

11. Irenaeus seems to suggest that Papias knew the apostle John. See Irenaeus of Lyons, *Sancti Irenæi espiscopi Lugdunensis et martyris Detectionis et eversionis falso cognominatæ agnitionis, seu, Contra hæreses libri quinque*, Patrologiae Cursus Completus, Series Graeco-Latina, repr. ed. J. P. Migne (Paris: Lutetiae Parisiorum, 1857), 5:33:4—hereafter cited as, e.g., Irenaeus, *Contra haereses*, 5:33:4.

12. For a thorough examination of the place of Papias and of the general authenticity of his claims, see Bauckham's *Jesus and the Eyewitnesses*, 12–38, 202–239.

13. Eusebius of Caesarea, *Ecclesiastical History* vol. 1, Loeb Classical Library, ed. K. Lake (Cambridge, MA: Harvard University Press, 1980), 3:39—hereafter cited as, e.g., Eusebius, 3:39.

14. Eusebius places Papias—with Clement of Rome—in Trajan's reign, before the martyrdom of Ignatius in A.D. 107 (Eusebius, 3:36). See R. Gundry, *Matthew: A Commentary on His Handbook for a Mixed Church Under Persecution* (Grand Rapids,

MI: Eerdmans, 1994), 610–611; idem, *Mark: A Commentary on His Apology for the Cross* (Grand Rapids, MI: Eerdmans, 1993, 2000), 1027–1029.

15. Bauckham, *Jesus and the Eyewitnesses*, 17–18.

16. Irenaeus, *Contra haereses*, 3:1:1. Some have questioned the authenticity of Irenaeus's recollections from his years with Polycarp. However, Irenaeus's entire letter to Florinus—a friend who had joined a movement that denied the authentic humanity of Jesus Christ—testifies to his time with Polycarp: "O Florinus…when I was a boy, I watched you in lower Asia with Polycarp, moving in splendor in the royal court, and trying to gain his approval. I remember the events of that time even more clearly than those of recent years. Whatever it is that boys learn, as they grow in their minds, merges permanently with their minds. That's why I can still describe the very spot in which blessed Polycarp sat as he taught; I can still describe how he exited and entered, his habits of life, his expressions, his teachings among the people, and the accounts he gave of his interaction with John and with others who had seen the Lord. As he remembered their words—what he heard from them about the Lord and about his miracles and teachings, having received them from the eyewitnesses of the 'Word of Life'—Polycarp related all of it in harmony with the Scriptures.…Continually, by God's grace, I still recall them in faith. I testify before God that, if the blessed and apostolic elder heard any such thing [as the beliefs that Florinus had recently embraced], he would have cried out, placed his fingers in his ears—as was his habit—and exclaimed, 'Good God! To what sort of time have you spared my life that should have to endure such things as this?'" (Eusebius, 5:20:4–8). The tone and content of this letter strongly corroborates Irenaeus's connection to Polycarp. If Irenaeus was *not* in fact a disciple of Polycarp, such a letter as this one would have proved meaningless to Florinus and would have provided fodder for the arguments of Irenaeus's opponents.

17. The influential work of J. D. Crossan merits special mention at this point. Crossan places the following idiosyncratic dates on the New Testament Gospels: Secret Gospel of Mark and Mark's Gospel as it has survived to us, he places between A.D. 60 and 80, even though Secret Gospel of Mark is almost certainly a twentieth century hoax. Matthew's and Luke's Gospels are dated in the 90s, as well as a first edition of John's Gospel. The surviving edition of John's Gospel—according to Crossan—does not emerge until the early to mid-second century. Simultaneously, Crossan places the "lost Gospels" far earlier than most biblical scholars. See J. D. Crossan, *The Historical Jesus*, 427–434. Even such scholars as Bart Ehrman—far from an evangelical in his view of the Gospels!—dates Mark's Gospel in the 60s, Matthew's and Luke's Gospels in the 70s or 80s if not earlier, and John's Gospel no later than the 90s (Ehrman, *Lost Christianities*, 19–20).

18. Eusebius, 5:20:4–8.

19. In the Gospels according to Mark and Luke, the tax collector is called "Levi." Although many commentators have viewed "Levi" and "Matthew" as different names for the same individual, this is highly unlikely (see Bauckham, *Jesus and the Eyewitnesses*, 109–111). Given the open-ended and formulaic nature of this account, it is more likely that the individual who rendered the Greek version of the Gospel according to Matthew— knowing that Matthew, the apostolic eyewitness behind the teachings of Jesus preserved in this Gospel, had once been a tax collector—adapted Mark's description of the calling of Levi the tax collector to describe the apostle Matthew. Levi was, it appears, the brother of the apostle known as "James son of Alphaeus" (Mark 2:14; 3:18). There is no reason why Matthew and Levi, both tax collectors, could not have been called in the same manner; after all, Simon, Andrew, James, and John appear to have been called in two different encounters in nearly identical ways (Mark 1:16–20).

20. A. R. Millard, *Reading and Writing in the Time of Jesus* (New York: New York University Press, 2000), 28–29. Some scholars have argued that the apostles were literate and that they would have carried *pinakes* and noted significant sayings of Jesus. It seems to me, however, that this assumes a higher rate of literacy in Galilee and Judea—especially among persons in trades such as fishing—than the available evidence can sustain. For discussion and references, see B. Gerhardsson, *The Origins of the Gospel Traditions* (London, UK: SCM, 1979), 68–161; S. Lieberman, *Hellenism in Jewish Palestine* (New York: JTS, 1962), 203.

21. The abundance of surviving Roman taxation receipts, written in Greek, clearly demonstrates this fact. The epigraphical evidence includes not only brief receipts that follow simple formulas—for examples, see the numerous pieces of Elephantine and Egyptian ostraca in U. Wilken, *Griechische Ostraka aus Aegypten und Nubien* (Manchester, NH: Ayer, 1979); F. Preisigke et al., *Sammelbuch griechischer Urkunden aus Aegypten* (Berlin: Walter de Gruyter, 1974)—but also more lengthy and complex receipts on papyrus, such as POxy 51:3609.

22. A. R. Millard, *Reading and Writing in the Time of Jesus* (New York: New York University Press, 2000), 31, 170. See the taxation documentation from the pre-Christian era and from the first and second centuries A.D. found in the Oxyrhynchus papyri POxy 49:3461; POxy 62:4334; POxy 24:2413; POxy 45:3241; and, POxy 66:4527, as well as more extensive contractual agreements such as the third-century POxy 43:3092.

23. B. Ehrman and W. Craig, "Is There Historical Evidence for the Resurrection of Jesus?: A Debate between William Lane Craig and Bart Ehrman," March 28, 2006, http://www .holycross.edu/departments/crec/website/resurrection-debate-transcript.pdf (accessed November 6, 2007).

24. Ehrman, *Lost Christianities*, 235.

25. In the New Testament world, a new concept about authorship and authority had been emerging for some time, the requirement that a trustworthy work be reliably connected to a specific author. Otherwise, the work was subject to suspicion as a forgery. See D. Dungan, *Constantine's Bible: Politics and the Making of the New Testament* (Minneapolis, MN: Fortress Press, 2007), 34–35, 47.

26. Three second-century New Testament papyri—P46, P52, and P90—seem to have originated in at least two, perhaps three, different areas of Egypt (Fayyum, Busiris, and Oxyrhynchus). For New Testament manuscripts to have achieved this degree of distribution in central Egypt—nearly one thousand miles from Rome and more than five hundred miles from Jerusalem—by the early to mid-second century, the Gospels had probably reached most, if not all, primary population centers of the Roman Empire by this time.

27. The Easter controversy makes it clear that no universally recognized authority figure existed in the second century. Two bishops of Rome—Anicetus and Victor—tried at different times in the second century A.D. to standardize the date of Easter celebrations among Christians. Yet churches in the eastern half of the Roman Empire—primarily Asia Minor—persisted in celebrating Easter at a different time than the churches around Rome. The matter was still not settled in the fourth century A.D., as is clear from the proceedings of the Council of Nicea. For various accounts of this controversy, see Raniero Cantalamessa et al., *Easter in the Early Church: An Anthology of Jewish and Early Christian Texts* (Collegeville, MN: Liturgical Press, 1993), 34–37; Eusebius, 5:23–28; Francis A. Sullivan, *From Apostles to Bishops: The Development of the Episcopacy in the Early Church* (Mahwah, NJ: Paulist Press, 2001), 140–153.

28. This merging of Matthew's recollections with Mark's Gospel while translating Matthew's recollections might not have been viewed as the creation of a new work.

It would have been viewed as an expanded translation. For more on ancient authors' understanding of "translation," see G. Kennedy, "Classical and Christian Source Criticism," in *The Relationships Among the Gospels*, ed. W. O. Walker (San Antonio, TX: Trinity University, 1978), 144.

29. George Howard argues that the earlier, Hebraic form of the Gospel according to Matthew may be found in the writings of a Jewish scholar named Shem Tov Ben Isaac, author of a fourteenth-century refutation of the Christian Gospels. See G. Howard, *Hebrew Gospel of Matthew* (Macon, GA: Mercer University, 1995); R. F. Shedinger, "The Textual Relationship Between P45 and Shem Tob's Hebrew Matthew," in *New Testament Studies* 43 (N.p.: 1997), 58–71.

30. It seems, as with the Gospel according to Matthew, that the Greek and Aramaic versions were independent documents while still sharing the same content. See M. Hengel, *The Four Gospels and the One Gospel of Jesus Christ*, trans. J. Bowden (Harrisburg, PA: Trinity Press, 2000), 74.

31. J. A. Fitzmyer, "4Qpap Tobitaar," in *Qumran Cave 4: VIII Parabiblical Texts 2* (Oxford, UK: Clarendon, 1995), 1–76.

CONSPIRACY NUMBER TWO: How the Lost Gospels Got Lost

1. E. Pagels, *Beyond Belief: The Secret* Gospel of Thomas (New York: Random House, 2003), 32.

2. This is, for example, how some critics read Gospel of Thomas, with its lack of miracle stories or affirmations of Jesus's divinity (see, e.g., M. Meyer, *Gnostic Discoveries* [New York: HarperOne, 2006], 81).

3. In *Acts of John* 93, for example, Jesus's feet did not leave prints on the earth; in this context, these words are placed in the mouth of the apostle John: "Sometimes, when I felt him, the essence was without physical substance and without a body, as if it were not existing at all." This phenomenon of "polymorphy" appears in several apocryphal acts (P. Lalleman, "Polymorphy of Christ," in *The Apocryphal Acts of John* [Kampen, The Netherlands: Kok Pharos, 1995], 97–100). P. Schneider contends that such a docetic view was intended to address unique concerns of believers who were facing potential persecution, attempting to proselytize orthodox Christians on behalf of the Valentinians (P. Schneider, *The Mystery of the Acts of John* [San Francisco, CA: Mellen Research University Press, 1991], 142–222).

4. E. Pagels, *The Gnostic Gospels* (New York: Random House, 1979), xiii–xiv.

5. Freke and Gandy, *The Laughing Jesus*, 4.

6. It is hoped that the reader recognizes that in their original context, these passages had deeper meanings than these attempts at levity may signify. In fact, they provide support for dating Gospel of Thomas in the second (rather than the first) century. Ialdabaoth, a deity in mid to late second century Gnosticism, had the head of a lion. The imagery of Jesus in wood and stone has to do with the identification of the living Jesus within all things—again, an idea most typical of mid-second century Gnosticism. See P. Jenkins, *Hidden Gospels* (New York: Oxford University Press, 2001), 70–71.

7. M. Meyer and E. Pagels, "Introduction" *The Nag Hammadi Scriptures* (New York: HarperOne, 2007), 9. For H. Koester's seminal article defending early dates for apocryphal Gospels, see H. Koester, "Apocryphal and Canonical Gospels," *Harvard Theological Review* 73 (N.p.: 1980), 105–130. Koester contends that Gospel of Thomas, Gospel of Peter, *Apocryphon of James*, *Dialogue of the Savior*, and Papyrus Egerton 2 come from the same era as the New Testament Gospels. I have excluded *Apocryphon of James* from focused consideration in this chapter because—as even J. D. Crossan

admits—this document has been so heavily edited that any coherent first- or second-century remnant is irrecoverable, even if such a stratum once existed (J. D. Crossan, *The Historical Jesus*, 432). Despite Crossan's claims to the contrary, the same is probably true of *Dialogue of the Savior*. For discussion, see R. Cameron, ed., *The Other Gospels: Non-Canonical Gospel Texts* (Philadelphia, PA: Westminster, 1982), 38–48; E. Pagels and H. Koester, "Report on the Dialogue of the Savior," in *Nag Hammadi and Gnosis*, ed. R. Wilson (Leiden, The Netherlands: Brill, 1978), 66–74. It is possible that some authentic sayings of Jesus have survived in *Dialogue of the Savior* and *Apocryphon of James*; however, the surviving forms of these texts reflect the historical realities of the mid to late second century A.D. As such, the results of any attempt to discover a first-century stratum remain purely conjectural.

8. Meyer, *Gnostic Discoveries*, 81.
9. Brown, *The Da Vinci Code*, 245–246.
10. M. Borg and T. Moore, *The Lost Gospel* Q (Berkeley, CA: Ulysses Press, 1999), 13, 17, 27–28.
11. B. Mack, *Who Wrote the New Testament?: The Making of the Christian Myth* (New York: HarperSanFrancisco, 1995), 47.
12. Brown, *The Da Vinci Code*, 231, 234, 256.
13. "The Lost Gospel of Judas," *National Geographic*, May 2006, http://www.nationalgeographic.com/lostgospel/ (accessed November 6, 2007).
14. Even some atheists squeezed their way onto the Gospel of Judas bandwagon. In *The God Delusion*, Richard Dawkins has this to say about Gospel of Judas: "A manuscript purporting to be the lost Gospel of Judas has recently been translated and has received publicity in consequence.... Whoever the author was, the gospel is seen from the point of view of Judas Iscariot and makes the case that Judas betrayed Jesus only because Jesus asked him to play that role. It was all part of the plan to get Jesus crucified so that He could redeem humankind. Obnoxious as that doctrine is, it seems to compound the unpleasantness that Judas has been vilified ever since." Dawkins, *The God Delusion*, 252–253.
15. M. Borg, *Meeting Jesus Again for the First Time* (New York: HarperSanFrancisco, 1995), 46, 119.
16. Pagels, *Beyond Belief*, 34.
17. Crossan, *The Historical Jesus*, 72–88; cf. B. Mack, *The Lost Gospel: The Book of* Q *and Christian Origins* (New York: HarperCollins, 1993), 41–49.
18. Freke and Gandy, *The Laughing Jesus*, 4.
19. While I have attempted to cover the most significant "lost Gospels," the list provided here is not exhaustive. For a more thorough treatment of the "lost Gospels," see D. Bock, *The Missing Gospels* (Nashville, TN: Thomas Nelson, 2006).
20. For the Gospel of the Ebionites and *the* Gospel of the Nazoreans as deriving some traditions from the Gospel according to Matthew and Luke, see R. Cameron, ed., *The Other Gospels* (Philadelphia, PA: Westminster, 1982), 97–106.
21. For the Gospel of Philip and the Gospel of Mary as deriving some traditions from the New Testament Gospels, see C. Tuckett, "Synoptic Traditions in Some Nag Hammadi and Related Texts," in *Vigiliae Christianae* 36 (N.p.: 1982), 173–190. The Gospel of Philip also seems to presuppose a Valentinian Christology, which would place the text in the mid to late second century (W. Schneemelcher, ed., *New Testament Apocrypha*, trans. R. Wilson [Louisville, KY: John Knox, 1992], 179–208). With reference to Dialogue of the Savior, see B. Ehrman, *Lost Scriptures* (New York: Oxford University Press, 2003), 52.
22. Cf. reference to the Valentinian movement in Irenaeus, *Contra haereses*, 3:11:9. The

Valentinian affinities in Gospel of Truth would seem to place the Gospel in the mid to late second century (H. Attridge and G. MacRae, "Gospel of Truth," *The Nag Hammadi Library* rev. ed., ed. J. Robinson [Leiden, The Netherlands: Brill, 1990], 38; J. Robinson, ed., *The Coptic Gnostic Library* vol. 1 [Leiden, The Netherlands: Brill, 2000], 76–81).

23. J. Robinson, ed., *The Coptic Gnostic Library* vol. 2, 38.

24. Clement of Alexandria, *Stromata*, 3:92, http://www.earlychristianwritings.com/text/clement-stromata-book3.html (accessed November 6, 2007). Interestingly, while Clement seemed to recognize Gospel of the Egyptians as including some valid information about Jesus's sayings (idem, 3:45; 3:63; 3:64; 3:66), he also viewed the content of this Gospel as suspect and as subordinate to the Gospel according to Matthew, Mark, Luke, and John. Immediately after the quotation cited here, Clement was quick to add, "Now notice, first of all, that we don't find this saying in the four Gospels that have been passed down to us—only in *Gospel of the Egyptians*" (idem, 3:93).

25. For reference to Cainites in the church fathers, see Irenaeus, *Contra haereses,* 1:31:1. With characteristic emphasis on the apocalyptic elements of Jesus's message—a refreshing corrective to the diminution of Jesus by the Jesus Seminar to an itinerant sage, divorced from Jewish culture and from apocalyptic expectations—Bart Ehrman adds the suggestion that the community in which Gospel of Judas emerged was struggling to incorporate Jewish heritage in the aftermath of failed Jewish apocalyptic expectations (*The Lost Gospel of Judas Iscariot* [New York: Oxford University Press, 2006], 115-180). Ehrman questions whether the "Cainites" actually existed or if the sect was merely a rhetorical invention of second-century Christians. While it is possible that the *term* "Cainites" was created for the sake of rhetorical invective, it seems that Irenaeus (as well as Tertullian and Hippolytus, who also mentioned the Cainites) referred to *some* real sect that reworked biblical narratives, turning apparent villains into heroes. Even with his skepticism about the Cainite sect, Ehrman dates the Gospel of Judas around the same date as evangelical scholars, well into the second century (ibid., 3, 54-65). The alternative reconstruction has been proposed by A. DeConick, *The Thirteenth Apostle* (New York: Continuum, 2007).

26. "The Gospel of Judas," *ABC*, June 25, 2006, http://abc.net.au/tv/guide/netw/200606/programs/ZY8369A001D25062006T193000.htm (accessed November 6, 2007).

27. Translated from Gospel of Peter 1:1, 23, 25, www1.uni-bremen.de/~wie/texteapo/GPeter-Greek.html (accessed October 2006).

28. In *The Complete Gospels*, a member of the Jesus Seminar makes a startling statement, considering the serious and substantive questions about this supposed Gospel fragment: "There is almost unanimous agreement among Clementine scholars that the letter is authentic" (R. Miller, ed., *The Complete Gospels*, rev. ed. [Santa Rosa, CA: Polebridge Press, 1994], 408).

29. M. Smith, *The Secret Gospel* (London, UK: Gollancz, 1974), 10–21.

30. Translated from M. Smith, *Clement of Alexandria and a Secret Gospel of Mark* (Cambridge, MA: Harvard University Press, 1973), 97–152.

31. S. Carlson, *The Gospel Hoax* (Waco, TX: Baylor University Press, 2005), 58–64.

32. Smith makes the intriguing comment on page 21 of his book on the subject: "Fake or not, the puzzle was going to be fun" (Smith, *The Secret Gospel*, 21). The homoerotic overtones of the supposed additional paragraph would seem to coincide with Smith's own character. According to a supportive colleague and former student of Smith's— someone with no motivation to defame Smith's character—"Morton Smith did not conceal his 'sexual orientation.' Several Columbia students complained to me about his aggressive behavior, and one student, a particularly handsome young man in the preppy genre, told me he had even dropped one of Smith's courses on that account" (J. Hart,

"Was Jesus Gay? No, But Morton Smith Thought So," in *The Dartmouth Review*, May 18, 2007, http://dartreview.com/archives/2007/05/18/was_jesus_gay_no_but_morton_smith_thought_so.php [accessed November 6, 2007]).

33. See Hippolytus of Rome, *Philosophoumena*, Patrologiae Cursus Completus, Series Graeco-Latina, repr., ed. J. Fabricius (Paris: Lutetiae Parisiorum, 1857–1866), 5:7. It is possible that this reference is not to Gospel of Thomas but to a later text known as Infancy Gospel of Thomas, which recounts supposed incidents from Jesus's childhood.

34. C. Evans, *Fabricating Jesus* (Downers Grove, IL: InterVarsity Press, 2006), 64, 70–71.

35. In N. Perrin, *Thomas, the Other Gospel* (Louisville, KY: Westminster John Knox, 2007), arguments have been advanced for a late second-century Syriac origin for the surviving form of Gospel of Thomas. While a few of Perrin's arguments may be overstated, I find the whole of his case to be convincing. At the same time, it must be taken seriously that a large portion of Gospel of Thomas—at least half, probably more—does stem from the first century A.D.

36. It appears that the author of Papyrus Egerton 2 was aware of John's Gospel (J. Pryor, "Papyrus Egerton 2" *Australian Biblical Review* 37 [N.p: 1989], 11–13), also suggesting a second-century date for this papyrus fragment.

37. The fragment refers to a high priest as a "Pharisee"; high priests were, however, from Sadducaic backgrounds. Such a historical blunder suggests a date after the first century and a province removed from Judea.

CONSPIRACTY NUMBER THREE: It Was All About Power

1. Most recent scholarship implies that between 85 percent and 90 percent of people in the first century A.D. were functionally illiterate. See W. Harris, *Ancient Literacy* (Cambridge, MA: Harvard University Press, 1989); T. Morgan, *Literate Education in the Hellenistic and Roman Worlds* (Cambridge: Cambridge University Press, 1999); C. Hezser, *Jewish Literacy in Roman Palestine* (Tübingen: Mohr [Siebeck], 2001). See especially pages 326–331 in Harris's book. For a more optimistic perspective than one finds in these texts, see A. R. Millard, *Reading and Writing in the Time of Jesus* (New York: New York University Press, 2000), 154–85.

2. Brown, *The Da Vinci Code*, 233–234.

3. Pagels, *Beyond Belief*, 31–32.

4. "The doctrine of 'one God' confirms, for orthodox Christians, the emerging institution of the 'one bishop' as monarch ('sole ruler') of the church" (Pagels, *The Gnostic Gospels* [New York: Random House, 1979], 47).

5. "The orthodox teaching on resurrection…legitimized a hierarchy of persons through whose authority all others must approach God" (Pagels, *The Gnostic Gospels*, 27).

6. "The orthodox pattern…describes God in exclusively masculine terms.…This translates into social practice:…the orthodox community came to accept the domination of men over women as the divinely ordained order, not only for social and family life, but also for the Christian churches" (Pagels, *The Gnostic Gospels*, 66).

7. Pagels, *The Gnostic Gospels*, 34.

8. In its larger context, the quotation reads: "Let each of you, brothers, in his own order give thanks unto God, maintaining a good conscience and not transgressing the appointed rule of his service, but acting carefully in every way. Not in every place, brothers, are the continual daily sacrifices offered, or the freewill offerings or the sin offerings or the trespass offerings, but only in Jerusalem. Even there the offering is not made just anywhere, but in front of the holy place in the court of the altar; and this too through the high priest and previously mentioned servants, after the victim to be

offered has been inspected for blemishes. So, they who do anything contrary to his careful ordinance of will receive death as the penalty" (1 Clement 41:1–3, *The Apostolic Fathers I*, Loeb Classical Library, ed. K. Lake [Cambridge, MA: Harvard University Press, 1985]). Clement of Rome does use this careful process of sacrifice as an example of how carefully Christians should guard their beliefs about Jesus, but at no level does he suggest that the death penalty should be dealt to heretics.

9. Cf. Pagels, *The Gnostic Gospels*, 7–8, 11, 14.

10. This is an adaptation of Walter Bauer's classic hypothesis as modified in light of correctives from Helmut Koester and J. M. Robinson. Although I am familiar with Bauer's approach as well as its flaws and strengths, a critique of Bauer's work stands beyond the scope of this study. For the underlying basis of Pagels's perspective, see W. Bauer, *Orthodoxy and Heresy in Earliest Christianity*, trans. R. A. Kraft and G. Krodel (London: SCM Press, 1971); J. M. Robinson and H. Koester, *Trajectories Through Early Christianity* (Philadelphia, PA: Fortress, 1971). For critiques, see A. J. Hultgren, *The Rise of Normative Christianity* (Minneapolis, MN: Fortress, 1994); B. A. Pearson, *Gnosticism and Christianity in Roman and Coptic Egypt* (London: T & T Clark, 2004); T. A. Robinson, *The Bauer Thesis Examined* (Lewiston, N.Y.: Mellen, 1988).

11. See, e.g., Ignatius of Antioch, *Pros Philadelpheis, The Apostolic Fathers*, trans. and ed. J. Lightfoot, J. R. Harmer, and M. Holmes (Grand Rapids, MI: Baker Book House, 1992), 180–181, hereafter cited as, e.g., Ignatius, *Pros Romaious*, 166.

12. Baigent, *The Jesus Papers*, 70.

13. "No one before Irenaeus had ever claimed that there were only four genuine Gospels." (Freke and Gandy, *The Laughing Jesus*, 69.)

14. Dawkins, *The God Delusion*, 95.

15. B. Mack, *Who Wrote the New Testament?: The Making of the Christian Myth* (New York: HarperSanFrancisco, 1995), 287.

16. Baigent, *The Jesus Papers*, 84.

17. Brown, *The Da Vinci Code*, 231, 233.

18. Ehrman, *Misquoting Jesus*, 36.

19. This is not to say that—if Pagels were correct—the *existence of belief* (whether veridical or delusory) in Jesus's bodily resurrection wouldn't have preceded the controversy. It is to say that given Pagels's reconstruction, belief in the *essentiality* of bodily resurrection should have emerged during or after the controversies over the power of certain bishops.

20. Two bishops of Rome—Anicetus and Victor—tried at different times in the second century A.D. to standardize the date of Easter celebrations among Christians, yet churches in the eastern half of the Roman Empire—primarily Asia Minor—persisted in celebrating Easter at a time different from the time that it was celebrated by the churches around Rome. The matter was still not settled in the fourth century A.D., as is clear from the proceedings of the Council of Nicaea. For various accounts of this controversy, see R. Cantalamessa et al., *Easter in the Early Church: An Anthology of Jewish and Early Christian Texts* (Collegeville, MN: Liturgical Press, 1993), 34–37; Eusebius, 5.23–28; F. Sullivan, *From Apostles to Bishops: The Development of the Episcopacy in the Early Church* (Mahwah, NJ: Paulist Press, 2001), 140–53.

21. The overall tone of a letter from Clement—overseer of the Roman church—to the Corinthian church, written around A.D. 96, suggests that the Roman overseer anticipated some deference from other congregations in the late first century. Irenaeus's declaration near the end of the second century that "every church should agree with [the Roman] church" (Irenaeus, *Contra haereses*, 3:3:2) certainly represents earlier tradition. (Ignatius of Antioch's reference to the Roman church as the place where divine love "presides" can hardly be taken as an indication of perceived primacy of the

Roman church or the Roman overseer; this is laudatory terminology of the sort that stands at the beginning of many ancient letters. For text of letter, see Ignatius, *Pros Romaious*, 166–171.) However, the controversy of A.D. 155 makes it clear that this power was not viewed as universal among early Christians; most important, the fact that the first controversy over overseers' power didn't occur until the mid-second century—while belief in bodily resurrection was deemed essential in the first century—invalidates Elaine Pagels's argument, which would require the essentiality of belief in the bodily resurrection to arise in the midst of or soon after such controversy.

22. See B. Witherington III, *The Acts of the Apostles: A Socio-Rhetorical Commentary* (Grand Rapids, MI: Eerdmans, 1998), 61–63, for evidence of a date of composition between A.D. 75 and 85.

23. Despite Pagels's attempts to depict the New Testament texts as presenting multiple understandings of resurrection—bodily resurrection as well as spiritual immortality experienced through visions—the most natural meaning of *egeiro* ("raise") with *ek nekron* ("from out of [the] dead") in Galatians 1:1 entails an actual reviving and restoration of the physical body. It appears that Paul's phrase *tou egeirantos auton ek nekron* should be taken as an adaptation of the second of the Eighteen Benedictions (*Shemoneh Esrei*) from the Jewish synagogue liturgy. In this benediction, God is referred to as "Raiser of the Dead" (*mehayyeh hammetim*), a clear reference to the expectation of bodily resurrection.

24. For discussion of the 1 Corinthians 15 text as well as other issues related to early traditions of the Resurrection, see G. Habermas, "Experiences of the Risen Jesus: The Foundational Historical Issue in the Early Proclamation of the Resurrection," *Dialog: A Journal of Theology* 45 (Fall 2006): 288–97; G. Lüdemann, *The Resurrection of Jesus* (London: SCM Press, 1994), 38; Funk et al., *The Acts of Jesus*, 454.

25. A few scholars—including Gerd Lüdemann, Marcus Borg, and John Shelby Spong— have claimed that 1 Corinthians 15 may not point to bodily resurrection (see, e.g., J. Spong, *A New Christianity for a New World* [New York: HarperSanFrancisco, 2000], 87, 102). However, several scholars have provided convincing evidence that this is indeed what Paul described in this text. See K. MacGregor, "1 Corinthians 15:3b–6a, 7 and the Bodily Resurrection of Jesus," *Journal of the Evangelical Theological Society* 49 (June 2006): 225–34; N. T. Wright, *The Resurrection of the Son of God* (Minneapolis, MN: Augsburg Fortress, 2003), 83ff.

26. Simon Peter seems to have been in Rome during the reign of Emperor Nero. See Irenaeus, *Contra haereses*, 3:1:1, as well as a comment in Ignatius, *Pros Romaious*, 170–171, where it is implied that Peter and Paul once provided personal guidance to the Roman church.

27. The Gospel according to Mark was written after the deaths of Peter and Paul. See Irenaeus, *Contra haereses*, 3:1:1: "After [the] departure [of Peter and Paul], Mark—Peter's follower and translator—handed down to us in writing what had been preached by Peter."

28. Ignatius, *Pros Smyrnaious*, 186–187.

29. S. De Morgan, "Gnostic Gnonsense: A Critical Review of The Gnostic Gospels by Elaine Pagels," *Answering Infidels*, http://www.answeringinfidels.com/index.php?option =content&task=view&id=42 (accessed November 7, 2007).

30. See Tertullian of Carthage, *De carne Christi*, 5 (October 6, 2007), http://www .tertullian.org/ (accessed November 7, 2007).

31. For primary sources for "the body as prison house of the soul," see the works of Plato— e.g., Plato, *Phaedo*, Loeb Classical Library, trans. H. Fowler (Cambridge, MA: Harvard University Press, 1982), sec. 67. Here, Socrates states in his dialogue with Simmias: "*Ten*

psychen…ekluomenen hosper ek desmon ek tou somatos;"—"The soul…loosed out of the prison, out of the body."

32. E. Yamauchi's classic *Pre-Christian Gnosticism* (Grand Rapids, MI: Baker Book House, 1983) remains a solid defense of the thesis that Gnosticism emerged *within* rather than *previous to* Christianity. Though Yamauchi likely underestimated the degree to which the *foundations of* and the *tendency toward* gnosticized thinking may have been present prior to the first century A.D., his primary point still stands.

33. Translated from "The Muratorian Canon," http://www.earlychristianwritings.com/text/muratorian-latin.html/ (accessed November 7, 2007).

34. Ibid.

35. For the text of the Muratorian Fragment, see Bruce M. Metzger, *The Canon of the New Testament* (Oxford: Clarendon Press, 1987), 305–307. For analysis of the Muratorian Fragment, see G. M. Hahneman, *The Muratorian Fragment and the Development of the Canon* (New York: Oxford University Press, 1992).

36. C. Osiek, "An Early Tale That Almost Made It Into the New Testament," *Bible Review* (October 1994): 49–54.

37. Dungan, *Constantine's Bible*, 15.

38. The phrase "looking back on the church's history" indicates recognition of the anachronism of speaking of a "Christian canon" in the first, second, or third centuries. The discussion concerning which books could be connected to apostolic eyewitnesses continued well into the fourth century A.D., and—previous to the emergence of the canon—books that never became canonical were regularly cited as "Scripture." (It is worthwhile to recognize at this point that the word *Scripture* means simply "That Which Is Written" and could often, in ancient Christian usage, refer to any writing widely recognized as truthful.) What was closed in the fourth century was *not* the canon—that was closed by implication, though not in any official sense, with the deaths of the apostolic eyewitnesses—but the *discussion*. For a worthwhile discussion from a somewhat different perspective, see C. Allert, *A High View of Scripture?* (Grand Rapids, MI: Baker Academic, 2007), 48–86, 177–188.

39. Eusebius, 3:25:6.

40. For discussion, see Dungan, *Constantine's Bible*, 71–92.

41. Eusebius, 6:12:2.

42. In addition to Gospel of Peter, there seems to have been a harmonized Gospel—primarily drawn from the New Testament Gospels, but perhaps also utilizing some other traditions—that Justin Martyr utilized (Allert, *A High View of Scripture?*, 114). This Gospel too, lacking clear connections to an apostolic eyewitness, eventually passed into disuse.

43. *Papyrus Cairo* 10759.

44. Tertullian of Carthage, *De baptismo*, 17 (October 6, 2007), http://www.tertullian.org (accessed November 7, 2007).

45. Paraphrased from Acts of Paul, trans. E. Goodspeed, as quoted in T. Adamik, "The Baptized Lion in the Acts of Paul," http://keur.eldoc.ub.rug.nl/FILES/wetenschappers/11/584/c4.pdf (accessed November 7, 2007).

46. Eusebius of Caesarea, "Vita Constantini," *Ecclesiastical History* vol. 2, Loeb Classical Library, ed. K. Lake (Cambridge, MA: Harvard University Press, 1926), 3:64. In the Thirty-Ninth Festal Letter, Athanasius cited 2 Corinthians 7:1—"let us cleanse ourselves from every defilement of flesh and spirit"—in his exhortation to rely on the books that he had listed as canonical. It is possible that this rhetoric led to suppression or destruction of some noncanonical texts.

CONSPIRACTY NUMBER FOUR: Who Misquoted Jesus?

1. "Age iam, qui uoles curiositatem melius exercere in negotio salutis tuae, percurre ecclesias apostolicas apud quas ipsae adhuc cathedrae apostolorum suis locis praesident, apud quas ipsae *authenticae litterae* eorum recitantur sonantes uocem et repraesentantes faciem uniuscuiusque" (Tertullian of Carthage, *De Praescriptione Haereticorum*, 36:1, October 6, 2007, http://www.tertullian.org [accessed November 7, 2007]). Although *authenticae* could mean "complete copies," it would not make sense for Tertullian to have told his readers to travel to Rome, Thessalonica, Ephesus, or Corinth to see these copies; by A.D. 200, complete copies of Paul's letters could have been found throughout the Roman Empire in the cities of the very persons to whom Tertullian was writing. The most natural reading of the term in this context is as a reference to the autographs of these letters.
2. Millard, *Reading and Writing in the Time of Jesus*, 33–34.
3. Brown, *The Da Vinci Code*, 234.
4. B. Ehrman and RBL, "Q & A: Bart Ehrman: *Misquoting Jesus*," in *Religion BookLine*, January 25, 2006, http://www.publishersweekly.com/article/CA6301707.html?q =Q%26A+bart+ehrman; B. Ehrman and S. Colbert, "Bart Ehrman," *The Colbert Report*, June 20, 2006, http://www.comedycentral.com/motherload/player.jhtml?ml_video =70912&ml_collection=&ml_gateway=&ml_gateway_id=&ml_comedian=&ml_ runtime=&ml_context=show&ml_origin_url=%2Fmotherload%2Findex.jhtml%3Fml _video%3D70912&ml_playlist=&lnk=&is_large=true (accessed November 7, 2007).
5. Ehrman, *Misquoting Jesus*, dust jacket, hardcover edition.
6. Ibid., 132.
7. Ibid., 7, 10.
8. Ibid., 11.
9. Ibid., 7.
10. Ibid., dust jacket, hardcover edition.
11. S. Jacobovici and C. Pellegrino, *The Jesus Family Tomb: The Discovery, the Investigation, and the Evidence that Could Change History* (New York: HarperSanFrancisco, 2007), x.
12. D. Wallace, "The Gospel according to Bart," *Journal of the Evangelical Theological Society* 49 (June 2006): 330.
13. Two additional examples of Mark's presentation of Jesus as a passionate prophet would include the use of the verbs *epitimao* (also used to describe silencing of demons) and *phimoo* (more commonly used to describe the muzzling of a wild beast) to describe Jesus' calming of the storm in Mark 4:39.
14. These clear attributions of deity to Jesus Christ run contrary to Ehrman's claim that the New Testament "rarely, *if ever*" attributes deity to Jesus (*Misquoting Jesus*, 114, emphasis added). Although the attributions of deity to Jesus may be—arguably—rare, it is hardly fair to imply that there may be *no* such cases ("if ever").
15. Metzger and Ehrman, *The Text of the New Testament*, 88.
16. Ehrman, *Misquoting Jesus*, 80–83.
17. Ehrman, *Misquoting Jesus*, 69.
18. Mack, *Who Wrote the New Testament?*, 8, 243.
19. See, for example, Evans, *Fabricating Jesus*, 7; C. Blomberg, *Matthew* (Nashville, TN: Broadman and Holman, 1992), 43–44; C. Keener, *A Commentary on the Gospel of Matthew* (Grand Rapids, MI: Eerdmans, 1999), 39–40.
20. Ehrman, *Misquoting Jesus*, 62.
21. M. Kruger, "Review of *Misquoting Jesus: The Story Behind Who Changed the Bible and Why* (Bart Ehrman)," *Journal of the Evangelical Theological Society* 49 (June 2006): 389.

22. Ehrman, *Misquoting Jesus*, 208, 211.

23. Ibid., 177.

24. Ibid., 52.

25. Ibid., 56.

26. Ibid., 81.

27. Ibid., 65.

28. Ibid., 142–143.

29. Ibid., 166–167.

30. Ibid., 67.

31. Metzger and Ehrman, *The Text of the New Testament*, 327.

32. Ehrman, *Misquoting Jesus*, 98.

33. Ehrman, *Misquoting Jesus*, 168–170.

34. Brown, *The Da Vinci Code*, 234.

35. Bruce, *The Canon of Scripture*, 203–205.

36. B. Ehrman, *Misquoting Jesus: The Story Behind Who Changed the Bible and Why* (New York: HarperCollins, 2005) 69.

CONSPIRACY NUMBER FIVE: Gospel Truth or Gospel Fiction?

1. During the reign of Diocletian, Nicholas of Myra was apparently imprisoned. Before Nicholas was martyred, however, Diocletian died, and Nicholas was released. See V. Yzermans, *Wonderworker: The True Story of How Saint Nicholas Became Santa Claus* (Chicago, IL: ACTA, 1994), 6–7.

2. This story may be found in T. Jones, *Hullabaloo* (Colorado Springs, CO: David C. Cook, 2007), 118–120.

3. Crossan, *The Historical Jesus*, xxx.

4. Mack, *Who Wrote the New Testament?*, 46.

5. B. Ehrman, *Peter, Paul, and Mary Magdalene: The Followers of Jesus in History and Legend* (New York: Oxford University Press, 2006), 259.

6. Pagels, *Beyond Belief*, 44.

7. In books entitled *The Jesus Legend* and *The Jesus Myth*, a professor named G. A. Wells has proposed another variation of this process: Wells claims that for Paul, Jesus was a vague, supernatural figure who existed at an indefinite point in the past, not a historical person who lived, died, and rose again at a particular place and time. In the late first century, the authors of the New Testament Gospels merged the memory of a popular teacher with Paul's mythical deity to create the figure that Christians today identify as Jesus (G. A. Wells, *The Jesus Myth* [Peru, IL: Open Court, 1999], 55–95).

8. R. Funk, "The Once and Future Jesus," in *The Once and Future Jesus*, ed. G. Jenks (Santa Rosa, CA: Polebridge, 2000), 7; R. Funk, *Honest to Jesus* (New York: HarperSanFrancisco, 1996), 306.

9. J. Patton, "The Jefferson Bible," in *Jefferson's Bible: The Life and Morals of Jesus of Nazareth* reprint, ed. J. Patton (Grove City, PA: ABD, 1997), A21.

10. So profound was the influence of Strauss's work that, according to Albert Schweitzer, New Testament studies can be divided into the era *before* Strauss and the era *after* Strauss (A. Schweitzer, *The Quest of the Historical Jesus*, http://www .earlychristianwritings.com/schweitzer/chapter1.html [accessed November 8, 2007]). For a brief analysis of Strauss's influence, see Ehrman, *Jesus: Apocalyptic Prophet of the New Millennium*, 27–29.

11. R. Bultmann, *Jesus Christ and Mythology*, repr. ed. (Englewood Cliffs, NJ: Prentice Hall, 1997), 16.

12. B. Ehrman, "Is There Historical Evidence for the Resurrection of Jesus? A Debate Between William Lane Craig and Bart Ehrman," March 28, 2006, http://www.holycross.edu/departments/crec/website/resurrection-debate-transcript.pdf (accessed November 8, 2007).

13. Ehrman, *Jesus: Apocalyptic Prophet of the New Millennium*, 31.

14. Ibid., 47.

15. Jacobovici and Pellegrino, *The Jesus Family Tomb*, ix.

16. Some scholars have argued that the apostles would have carried *pinakes*—wooden tablets coated with beeswax on which notes were scratched using a stylus—and noted significant sayings of Jesus. It seems to me, however, that this presumes a higher rate of literacy in Galilee and Judea than the available evidence can sustain. For discussion and references, see B. Gerhardsson, *The Origins of the Gospel Traditions* (Philadelphia, PA: Fortress Press, 1979), 67–91; S. Lieberman, *Hellenism in Jewish Palestine*, 203.

17. T. Jones, *Misquoting Truth* (Downers Grove, IL: InterVarsity Press, 2007), 87.

18. J. D. Crossan, *Jesus: A Revolutionary Biography* (New York: HarperCollins, 1994), 58.

19. See discussion in J. D. Crossan, *The Birth of Christianity* (New York: HarperCollins, 1998), 49–93. A fundamental flaw in Crossan's approach is his use of *modern examples that occurred in a written culture* to make claims about *premodern realities that occurred in an oral culture*.

20. Funk et al., *The Acts of Jesus*, 6.

21. B. Gerhardsson, *Memory and Manuscript* (Grand Rapids, MI: Eerdmans, 1998), 123.

22. Even though Paul was completely capable of writing in Greek (Galatians 6:11; Philemon 1:19–21), scribes penned Paul's letters for him (Romans 16:22; compare 1 Peter 5:12).

23. Ken Bailey has separated oral history and oral traditioning into three categories—*informal uncontrolled oral tradition* (what one would commonly call "rumor"), *informal controlled oral tradition* (in which the community serves as a collective guardian of the history), and *formal controlled oral tradition* (in which a specific individual or group of individuals guards the integrity of the story). (See K. Bailey, "Informal Controlled Oral Tradition and the Synoptic Gospels," *Asia Journal of Theology* 5 [1991]: 34–51.) I disagree with Bailey's assertion that accounts of Jesus's life were transmitted as *informal controlled traditions*. The eyewitnesses of events remained the authoritative guardians of these stories until their deaths, by which time the Gospels were being written; thus, these accounts constituted *formal controlled oral traditions*. Still, Bailey's distinctions remain noteworthy.

24. Philo of Alexandria, *On the Contemplative Life* vol. IX, Loeb Classical Library, ed. F.H. Colson (Cambridge, MA: Harvard University, 1941), 75–77.

25. Gerhardsson, *Memory and Manuscript* (Grand Rapids, MI: Eerdmans, 1998), 135. This text, of course, speaks of the *ideal* among rabbis, perhaps not the actual practice. However, the ideal makes it clear how highly repetition and memorization were valued.

26. Quoted in Eusebius, 3:39. Papias was not attempting to replace or to disregard the written Gospels. Rather, recognizing the value of oral tradition, he sought to ascertain the best oral witnesses to receive alongside the Gospels. See H. Y. Gamble, *Books and Readers in the Early Church* (New Haven, CT: Yale University, 1995), 30–31; A. F. Walls, "Papias and Oral Tradition," *Vigiliae Christianae* 21 (1967): 137–140.

27. N. T. Wright, *The Resurrection of the Son of God*, 318–319. See also J. Jeremias, *The Eucharistic Words of Jesus* (New York: Scribner, 1966), 100–102; and the reference to the Hebrew *qibbel* in R. Collins, *First Corinthians* (Collegeville, MN: Liturgical, 1999), 426, 431.

28. Even scholars from the Jesus Seminar do not completely deny the early emergence of this tradition. See G. Lüdemann, *The Resurrection of Jesus*, 38; Funk et al., *The Acts of Jesus*, 454.

29. This is most likely why Paul occasionally introduced a statement with the phrase, "Not I, but the Lord" (1 Corinthians 7:10–12). He was recounting a truth that was rooted in the teachings of Jesus Himself.

30. For further thoughts on the hypothesis of a reliably maintained oral tradition, see A. B. Lord, "The Gospels as Oral Traditional Literature," in *The Relationships Among the Gospels*, ed. W. Walker (San Antonio, TX: Trinity University Press, 1978), 33–91.

31. A. N. Sherwin-White has noted that two generations are too short of a time for legend to replace a significant core of oral history (A. N. Sherwin-White, *Roman Society and Roman Law in the New Testament* [Oxford, UK: Clarendon, 1963], 190).

32. J. Martyr, *Dialogus cum Tryphone*, Patrologiae Cursus Completus, Series Graeco-Latina, repr., ed. J. P. Migne (Paris: Lutetiae Parisiorum, 1857–1866), 103:8; 106:3.

33. Tertullian of Carthage, *Adversus Marcionem*, 4:2, October 6, 2007, http://www .tertullian.org (accessed November 8, 2007).

34. For further exposition of the importance of eyewitness testimony among early Christians, see M. Hengel, *The Four Gospels and the One Gospel of Jesus Christ*, trans. J. Bowden (Harrisburg, PA: Trinity Press, 2000), 141–168.

CONSPIRACY NUMBER SIX: The Mysterious Case of the Mythical Messiah

1. M. Goguel, "Recent French Discussion of the Historical Existence of Jesus Christ," *The Harvard Theological Review* 19 (April 1926): 115–117; A. Drews, *The Christ Myth* repr. ed. (Amherst, NJ: Prometheus Books, 1998), 8.

2. Drews, *The Christ Myth* repr. ed., 7–9.

3. R. van Voorst, *Jesus Outside the New Testament* (Grand Rapids, MI: Eerdmans, 2000), 8–10.

4. Wells, *The Jesus Myth*. In his earlier works, G. A. Wells denied that anyone such as Jesus ever existed. In later work, Wells admits that there *may* have been a historical teacher named Jesus. Paul, however, treated Jesus in vague and ahistorical terms, separated from any particular point in history: "[Paul] does not give this crucifixion even a setting in time and place, nor mention any of its attendant circumstances" (55). The New Testament Gospels, Wells contends, fused the historical teacher with Paul's otherworldly Redeemer and rooted this fusion in a particular historical time and place. However, Galatians 1 makes it clear that Paul *did* connect Jesus to a specific time, place, and people: Paul returned to a specific *place* where he interviewed Cephas—Aramaic for "Peter"—and obtained eyewitness testimony about Jesus. He also encountered *specific persons* who knew or were related to Jesus. At the *time* when Paul wrote his letter, these persons were still alive. Earl Doherty has made similar arguments—though with far more frequent lapses of logic—in E. Doherty, *The Jesus Puzzle: Did Christianity Begin With a Mythical Christ? Challenging the Existence of an Historical Jesus* (Age of Reason Publications, 2005).

5. *The God Who Wasn't There*, http://www.thegodmovie.com/dvd.php (accessed November 8, 2007).

6. Freke and Gandy, *The Laughing Jesus*, 4, 61.

7. Ibid., 65.

8. Freke and Gandy, *The Jesus Mysteries*, 9.

9. Freke and Gandy, *The Laughing Jesus*, 55.

10. Ibid., 65–66.

11. For defense of essential physicality of resurrection, see N. T. Wright, *The Resurrection of the Son of God*.

12. Origen of Alexandria, *Contra Celsum*, Patrologiae Cursus Completus, Series Graeco-Latina, repr., ed. J. P. Migne (Paris: Lutetiae Parisiorum, 1857–1866), 37. Interestingly,

it does not appear that Celsus objected to the idea of virgin birth *per se*; his primary objection seems to have been that such an event could account for the origins of someone as lowly as Jesus.

13. See, e.g., Freke and Gandy, *The Laughing Jesus*, 55–57; Drews, *The Christ Myth* repr. ed., 101, 242–243.

14. See, e.g., discussion of winter solstice in R. Beck, *The Religion of the Mithras Cult in the Roman Empire* (New York: Oxford University Press, 2006), 209–210. Also significant is the birth of the god Aion on January 6, the date that Christians later celebrated as Epiphany (M. Clauss, *The Roman Cult of Mithras,* trans. R. Gordon [New York: Routledge, 2000], 165)—but, once again, this date was connected to Jesus hundreds of years after the Gospels were written.

15. Freke and Gandy, *The Laughing Jesus*, 61.

16. For further exploration of the discontinuity between the sacrifice of Jesus and the sacrifices of pagan deities, see B. Metzger, "Methodology in the Study of the Mystery Religions and Early Christianity," in *Historical and Literary Studies: Pagan, Jewish, and Christian* (Grand Rapids, MI: Eerdmans, 1968). See, e.g., the description of Dionysian worship in R. Turcan, *The Cults of the Roman Empire,* trans. A. Nevill (Malden, MA: Blackwell, 1996), 313.

17. Clauss contends that the attendants at the rock birth of Mithras should not even be identified as shepherds (Clauss, *The Roman Cult of Mithras,* trans. R. Gordon, 68–70).

18. The supposed connection between Mithras and virgin birth may be found, e.g., in J. Campbell, *Occidental Mythology* (New York: Penguin, 1964), 261. The two dominant images of Mithras are the slaying of the bull and his birth from solid stone. See the discussion of the *mithraeum* in Clauss, *The Roman Cult of Mithras,* trans. R. Gordon, 42–61.

19. J. Tabor, *The Jesus Dynasty* (New York: Simon and Schuster, 2006), 60.

20. Tom Snyder suggests and provides evidence that most parallels between Christianity and mystery religions may be readily—and more plausibly—explained as pagan attempts to incorporate elements of Christianity, as Christianity became a dominant minority religion in the Roman Empire. See T. Snyder, *Myth Conceptions* (Grand Rapids, MI: Baker Academic, 1995).

21. C. S. Lewis, "Answers to Questions on Christianity" and "Myth Became Fact," in *God in the Dock: Essays on Theology and Ethics*, ed. W. Hooper (Grand Rapids, MI: William B. Eerdmans, 1970), 58, 66.

22. R. Beck, *Planetary Gods and Planetary Orders in the Mysteries of Mithras* (London, UK: Brill, 1988), 26.

23. Justin Martyr, *Apologia Prima, Patrologiae Cursus Completus,* Series Graeco-Latina, repr., ed. J. P. Migne (Paris: Lutetiae Parisiorum, 1857–1866), chapter 66.

24. R. Gordon, *Image and Value in the Greco-Roman World* (Aldershot, UK: Variorum, 1996), 96.

25. Freke and Gandy, *The Laughing Jesus*, 58.

26. Beck, *The Religion of the Mithras Cult in the Roman Empire*, 217.

27. See Flavius Josephus, *The Jewish War,* Loeb Classical Library, ed. H. St. J. Thackeray (Cambridge, MA: Harvard University Press, 1927), books 5–7.

28. R. Beck, *Beck on Mithraism* (Aldershot, UK: Ashgate Publishing, 2004), 87.

29. For more information about Paterculus, as well as the Latin text of his history, see Valleius Paterculus, "The Roman History," http://penelope.uchicago.edu/Thayer/E/Roman/Texts/Velleius_Paterculus/home.html (accessed November 8, 2007).

30. "Iudaeos impulsore Chresto assidue tumultuantis Roma expulit" (Suetonius Tranquillus, *De Vita Caesarum* 25:4, http://www.perseus.tufts.edu/ [accessed November 8, 2007]).

31. "Ergo abolendo rumori Nero subdidit reos et quaesitissimis poenis adfecit quos per
    flagitia invisos vulgus Christianos appellabat. auctor nominis eius Christus Tiberio
    imperitante per procuratorem Pontium Pilatum supplicio adfectus erat; repressaque in
    praesens exitiabilis superstitio rursum erumpebat, non modo per Iudaeam, originem
    eius mali, sed per urbem etiam quo cuncta undique atrocia aut pudenda confluunt
    celebranturque" (Cornelius Tacitus, *Annales,* 15:44, http://www.perseus.tufts.edu/
    [accessed November 8, 2007]).

32. A few scholars have denied the authenticity of Tacitus's account on two primary
    bases: (1) He refers to Jesus Christ as "Christus," technically a *title* rather than a
    name. However, the motive of Tacitus at this point seems to have been to account for
    the origins of the name "Christianos." "Christus" functioned as a means of making
    a connection between this name and the name of the sect (Christianos). (2) He
    incorrectly designated Pontius Pilate as *procuratorem* ("procurator") when Pilate was
    actually *praefectum* ("prefect"). However, in provinces such as Judea and Galilee, little—
    if any—distinction would have existed between procurators and prefects (J. Meier, *A
    Marginal Jew* [New York: Doubleday, 1991], 100). The speeches found in the first book
    of Tacitus's *Annales* (see 1:81, for example) clearly suggest that Tacitus had access to
    imperial archives. As such, this record could have come from an imperial account of
    Jesus's trial that has since been lost, though it is also possible that Tacitus received this
    information from Christians.

33. Pliny the Younger, *Letters, II,* books 8–10. *Panegyricus,* Loeb Classical Library, ed.
    B. Radice (Cambridge, MA: Harvard University, 1969), 10:96–97.

34. Freke and Gandy, *The Laughing Jesus,* 59.

35. Philo described his appearance before Caligula in Philo of Alexandria, *On the Embassy
    to Gaius* vol. X, Loeb Classical Library, ed. F. H. Colson (Cambridge, MA: Harvard
    University, 1962), 75–77. In *De Animalibus* 58, he referred to a horse race that may
    have occurred in A.D. 47. This uncertain date represents the latest datable reference in
    his works; he would have been well into his seventies by this time. See A. Terian, ed.,
    Philonis Alexandrini De Animalibus (Chico, CA: Scholars Press, 1981), section 58.

36. Philo's visit to Jerusalem, which survives in an Armenian recension, is documented in
    Philo of Alexandria, *On Providence* vol. IX, Loeb Classical Library, ed. F. H. Colson
    (Cambridge, MA: Harvard University, 1941), 2:64.

37. Flavius Josephus, *Antiquitates Judaica,* 18:63–64, http://www.perseus.tufts.edu (accessed
    November 8, 2007).

38. Ibid., 20:200.

39. J. Meier provides compelling evidence that the second reference in Josephus refers back
    to the first, affirming the authenticity of some earlier reference to Jesus (J. Meier, *A
    Marginal Jew* [New York: Doubleday, 1991], 57–59).

40. It should be noted that some proponents of the Christ myth hypothesis claim this
    citation from Justin the Martyr's dialogue with the Jew Trypho to prove that some
    Jews did not accept the existence of a historical Jesus: "The Messiah—if he has been
    born and if he exists anywhere—is not known, perhaps not even knowing himself,
    and remains powerless until Elijah arrives to anoint him.... You, having accepted
    a groundless message, have invented a Messiah for yourselves" (Justin Martyr,
    Dialogus cum Tryphone, Patrologiae Cursus Completus, Series Graeco-Latina, repr.,
    ed. J. P. Migne [Paris: Lutetiae Parisiorum, 1857–1866], chapter 8). Yet what Trypho
    describes here is the *office* or *function* of the Jewish "Christ" or "Messiah," not the
    historicity of Jesus, whom Trypho recognizes as a historical person but rejects as the
    Jewish Messiah. Trypho's claim does *not* have to do with the nonexistence of Jesus; his
    claim has to do with his refusal to recognize Jesus as the Jewish Messiah and with his

belief that the Messiah had not yet been revealed to humanity. This claim from Christ-myth proponents demonstrates a failure to recognize that "Christ" or "Messiah" was not part of Jesus's name; it was a title, simultaneously ascribed to Him by Christians but rejected by Jewish persons.

41. See, e.g., J. Klausner, *Jesus of Nazareth* (Boston, MA: Beacon, 1925), 18–47.

CONSPIRACY NUMBER SEVEN: Codes in the Gospels, Secrets in the Scrolls

1. Some discrepancies exist with reference to reports of the date of this discovery. See J. Trever, *The Dead Sea Scrolls: A Personal Account* (Grand Rapids, MI: Eerdmans, 1979) for discussion of the early statements from the Bedouin.
2. See, e.g., N. Avigad and Y. Yadin, *A Genesis Apocryphon* (Jerusalem, Israel: Magnes Press, 1956); M. Burrows, ed., *The Dead Sea Scrolls of St. Mark's Monastery*, vol. 1 (New Haven, CT: Yale University, 1950); M. Burrows, ed., *The Dead Sea Scrolls of St. Mark's Monastery*, vol. 2 (New Haven, CT: Yale University, 1951); F. Cross, *The Ancient Library of Qumran and Modern Biblical Studies* (Garden City, NY: Doubleday, 1958); J. Milik, *Ten Years of Discovery in the Wilderness of Judea* (Naperville, IL: Allenson, 1959); J. Milik and D. Barthelemy, *Discoveries in the Judean Desert*, vol. 1 (Oxford, UK: Oxford University Press, 1955); E. Sukenik, *The Dead Sea Scrolls of the Hebrew University* (Jerusalem, Israel: Magnes Press, 1955).
3. G. Vermes, *The Complete Dead Sea Scrolls in English* (New York: Penguin, 1997), 7.
4. J. Wilford, "Computer Breaks Monopoly On Study of the Dead Sea Scrolls," in *The New York Times*, September 5, 1991, http://query.nytimes.com/gst/fullpage.html?res=9D0CEFD81630F936A3575AC0A967958260&n=Top/Reference/Times%20Topics/Subjects/D/Dead%20Sea%20Scrolls (accessed November 8, 2007).
5. B. Thiering, *Jesus the Man* (Toronto: Corgi Books, 1993), 363.
6. Baigent and Leigh, *The Dead Sea Scrolls Deception*, 136.
7. Ibid., 136–137.
8. 1QS, 7; 4Q258.
9. Josephus, *The Jewish War*, 6:8:1–6:9:2.
10. For typical comparisons and claims, see, e.g., M. Baigent and R. Leigh, *The Dead Sea Scrolls Deception*, 130–135, 174; B. Thiering, *Jesus the Man*, 13–14. According to Robert Eisenman—whose view is, in all fairness, far more knowledgeable and nuanced than Baigent, Leigh, or Thiering—first-century "Christianity" was synonymous with Essenism, Ebionism, and the Zealot movement. It was only in the early second century that Christianity became distinguishable from the general movement of Jewish Messianism. See R. Eisenman, *The New Testament Code* (London: Watkins, 2006), 3–4; R. Eisenman and M. Wise, *The Dead Sea Scrolls Uncovered* (New York: Penguin, 1992), 11.
11. When discussing persons excluded from the Qumran covenant, the Community Rule declares, "They shall not enter the water to partake in the pure meal of the saints, for they shall not be cleansed unless they repent of their wickedness" (1QS, 5:12–14).
12. Damascus Document (4Q266) 10:11–14.
13. 1QSa=1Q28a, 18–24. Cf. Thiering, *Jesus the Man*, 13–14.
14. Baigent and Leigh, *The Dead Sea Scrolls Deception*, 177.
15. Baigent and Leigh find this reference in a fragment of 4Q285, also known as the *Serekh Ha Milchamah* ("Rule of the War") document.
16. 4Q246.
17. Baigent and Leigh, *The Dead Sea Scrolls Deception*, 66, 132, 136, 137.
18. Ibid., 181, 182.
19. Tabor, *The Jesus Dynasty*, 247, 261.

20. Eisenman, *The New Testament Code*, xxvi, 32–35.
21. Baigent and Leigh, *The Dead Sea Scrolls Deception*, 195–197.
22. Eisenman, *The New Testament Code*, 21, 32.
23. Ibid., 6.
24. Ibid., xxvi–xxvii, 6.
25. Ibid., 167, 763.
26. Ibid., 9.
27. Ibid., 6.
28. Ibid., 16.
29. Eisenman, *James the Brother of Jesus*, xvii.
30. 1QpHab.
31. See, e.g., Septuagint renderings of 1 Maccabees 1:1 where "Kittim" refers to Greeks, of 1 Maccabees 8:5 where the term refers to Macedonians, and of Daniel 11:30 where it refers to Romans.
32. Laurence Gardner refers to Thiering's *Jesus the Man* as "the finest work for describing precisely how the Essene scribal codes work in practice—written by Dr. Thiering who discovered and perfected the process" (L. Gardner, *The Magdalene Legacy: The Jesus and Mary Bloodline Conspiracy* (New York: Barnes & Noble, 2005), 315.
33. Thiering, *Jesus the Man*, 275.
34. Ibid., 47–59.
35. Ibid., 329.
36. Ibid., 334.
37. Ibid., 363.
38. Ibid., 154.
39. Ibid., 154.
40. For tenuous but intriguing suggestions depicting Paul as a politically powerful Herodian, see R. Eisenman, *The Dead Sea Scrolls and the First Christians* (Rockport, MA: Element, 1996), 226–246.
41. Partly because of the relatively low frequency of definitively dated manuscripts—especially in Hebrew and Aramaic—from the two centuries before the time of Jesus and for the first century A.D., the paleographic practice of searching for similarities in handwriting is not particularly helpful in dating the Qumran scrolls. The potential range of dates for the scrolls seems to extend from the latter decades of the second century A.D. to A.D. 70.
42. A. J. T. Hull et al., "Radiocarbon Dating of Scrolls and Linen Fragments from the Judean Desert," *Radiocarbon* 37 (1995): 16–18. For an alternative view of possible dates for the Habakkuk pesher released prior to the carbon 14 tests, see R. Eisenman, *James the Just in the Habakkuk Pesher* (Leiden: Brill, 1986), 75–86.
43. In establishing a first century A.D. date for some or all of the scrolls, one of the more promising hypotheses may be found in N. Golb, *Who Wrote the Dead Sea Scrolls?* (New York: Scribners, 1995).
44. Baigent and Leigh, *The Dead Sea Scrolls Deception*, 137.
45. *Berakhot Tannaim* 3:7; *Mekilta* 13:19. For other examples, see M. Smith, *Tannaitic Parallels to the Gospels* (Philadelphia, PA: Society of Biblical Literature, 1951). Though many parallels cited by Smith are strained, this dissertation remains a worthwhile survey of *potential* parallels. J. Neusner, *Are There Really Tannaitic Parallels to the Gospels?* (Atlanta, GA: Scholars Press, 1993) corrects some portions of Smith's research, but Neusner's work is, unfortunately, driven by his personal falling-out with his former mentor ~~Morton Smith~~.
46. J. Lawrence, *Washing in Water: Trajectories in Ritual Bathing in the Hebrew Bible and*

Second Temple Literature (Atlanta, GA: Scholars, 2006) examines the Jewish background of ritual bathing and baptism, demonstrating that Jews viewed *miqveh* not only in terms of ritual purity but also in terms of an initiation rite. It has been disputed whether Jewish proselyte baptism actually preceded the proclamation of John the Baptist (see, e.g., A. Kostenberger, "Baptism in the Gospels," in *Believer's Baptism: Sign of the New Covenant in Christ*, ed. T. Schreiner and S. Wright [Nashville, TN: Broadman and Holman, 2006], 11–12). However, it seems likely that Jewish proselyte baptism provided the primary foundation for John's proclamation, on the basis of: (1) traditions in the Mishnah that attribute disputes over Jewish proselyte baptism to the first-century rabbis Hillel and Shammai (*Mishnah Pesahim* 8:8; *Mishnah Eduyoth* 5:2) and (2) the unlikely scenario of Jews borrowing a practice from Christians, coupled with the entirely likely scenario of the inverse occurrence (L. Schiffman, *Who Was a Jew?* [Hoboken, NJ: KTAV, 1985], 26; G.R. Beasley-Murray, *Baptism in the New Testament* [Grand Rapids, MI: Eerdmans, 1962], 18–31).

47. In the Dead Sea Scrolls, the title could refer to a messianic figure or to a messianic pretender; the context is too fragmented to be certain. The text from 4Q246 reads, "He will declare himself 'Son of God,' and they will call him 'Son of the Most High.'"

48. Baigent and Leigh, *The Dead Sea Scrolls Deception*, 177.

49. Suggestions for the identity of "the Righteous Teacher" have included a Maccabean priest (Onias III and Mattathias have been suggested), the rabbi Hillel, Menahem the Zealot, James the brother of Jesus, and John the Baptist, among others.

50. 4Q285.

51. [...] indicates a hole—or "lacuna"—in the fragment that cannot be reconstructed.

52. For discussion of the nature of peshers, see N. T. Wright, *Who Was Jesus?* (London, UK: SPCK, 1992), 21–27.

53. C.P. Thiede, *The Earliest Gospel Manuscript?* (Exeter, UK: Paternoster, 1992).

54. C. Roberts, "On Some Presumed Papyrus Fragments of the New Testament from Qumran," *Journal of Theological Studies* 23 (1972): 446–447; G. Stanton, *Gospel Truth?* (Valley Forge, PA: Trinity Press, 1995).

55. For a succinct—well, succinct for Eisenman, anyway—summary of this hypothesis, see Eisenman, *The Dead Sea Scrolls and the First Christians*, 332–351.

56. 4Q268.

57. This range of dates would allow for the possibility that Rabbi Hillel, who died in 19 B.C., was the Righteous Teacher—a possibility that has yet to be sufficiently explored. For an initial survey of this possibility, see H. Falk, *Jesus the Pharisee* (Eugene, OR: Wipf and Stock, 2003).

58. In *The Jesus Dynasty*, James Tabor has suggested that Clopas married Mary the mother of Jesus after the death of Joseph in keeping with Jewish levirate laws (Matthew 22:24). Although some of Tabor's interpretations depend on his nonsupernaturalistic assumptions about Scripture, many portions of *The Jesus Dynasty* remain plausible, even for individuals who do not share Tabor's assumptions. Supposing that John 19:25 was, at some point, incorrectly copied and should read, "His mother Mary wife of Clopas and His mother's sister and Mary Magdalene" (Mary's sister may have been named Salome [Mark 15:40; 16:1; also compare the order of Jesus's siblings in Mark 6:3 with Mary the mother of James in Mark 15:40; Matthew 27:56], the following scenario could represent a reasonable reconstruction: Mary married Clopas after the death of Joseph; *Clopas*, which means "replacement," could have served as his title as Joseph's replacement. His actual name—based in part on references in Eusebius to family members of Jesus who led the Jerusalem church—may have been Alphaeus. If this were the case, his previous son James or his son James with Mary—that is, the stepbrother or half brother of

Jesus—may have been one of the twelve apostles (Matthew 10:3; Mark 3:18; Luke 6:15; Acts 1:13). It is even possible that the apostle named Judas—not Iscariot—was the son of James and grandson of Clopas (Luke 6:15–16; Acts 1:13). Some might object to this scenario on the basis of Matthew 12:46–49, Mark 3:31–34, and Luke 8:20–21; these texts do not, however, require that *all* Jesus's brothers came to take Him away; the texts simply affirm that more than one brother came with Mary His mother to deal with Jesus. For further references to the family of Jesus and to the possible dynastic aspects of the church's leadership in Jerusalem, see Eusebius, 3:11, 19, 32; 4:22.

59. Eusebius, 2:23:4–7.

60. Based on several renderings and reconstructions of *The Ascents of James*, including one located in R. van Voorst, *The Ascents of James* (Atlanta, GA: Scholars Press, 1989), 73–75.

61. In many ways, Eisenman's hypothesis represents a reworking of F. C. Baur's nineteenth-century hypothesis regarding the Ebionites and Paul, as found in F. C. Baur, *Paulus der Apostel Jesu Christi, Sein Leiben und Wirken, seine Briefe und seine Lebre* (Stuttgart, Germany: Becher and Muller, 1845) and in idem., *Die christliche Gnosis oder die christliche Religions-Philosophie in ihrer geschichtlichen Entwicklung* (Tübingen, Germany: Osiander, 1835). For a more accessible version of Baur's ideas, see idem, *The Church History of the First Three Centuries*, ed. and trans. A. Menzies (London and Edinburgh: Williams and Norgate, 1879), http://books.google.com (accessed November 12, 2007).

62. K. MacGregor, "1 Corinthians 15:3b-6a, 7 and the Bodily Resurrection of Jesus," *Journal of the Evangelical Theological Society* 49 (June 2006): 225–234; G. Habermas, "Experiences of the Risen Jesus: The Foundational Historical Issue in the Early Proclamation of the Resurrection," *Dialog: A Journal of Theology* 45 (Fall 2006): 288–97. Even scholars who deny the historicity of the Resurrection admit that this summation probably preceded Paul's proclamation. See Lüdemann, *The Resurrection of Jesus*, 38; Funk et al., *The Acts of Jesus*, 454.

63. See the testimony of Papias in Eusebius, 3:39.

64. For an excellent survey of the life of James coupled with a treatment of the James Ossuary that may have been a bit too optimistic, see H. Shanks and B. Witherington III, *The Brother of Jesus* (New York: HarperSanFrancisco, 2003).

65. Even texts beyond the New Testament refer to James with reverence. In Gospel of Thomas 12, Jesus declares, "It is to James the Righteous One that you shall go." In Gospel of the Hebrews, James was one of the first witnesses of the Resurrection (Jerome, *On Illustrious Men*, trans. T. P. Halton, Fathers of the Church Series [Washington DC: The Catholic University of America Press, 1999], 7–10). Josephus the Jewish historian attributed the fall of Jerusalem, in part, to the execution of James in A.D. 62 at the hands of the high priest Ananus (Josephus, *Antiquitates Judaica,* 20: 200–201, http://www.perseus.tufts.edu [accessed November 12, 2007]).

66. For further study of *Ascents of James* and of *Pseudo-Clementine Recognitions*, two dissertations are recommended: van Voorst, *The Ascents of James* and N. Kelley, *Knowledge and Religious Authority in the Pseudo-Clementines* (Tübingen, Germany: Mohr Siebeck, 2006).

CONSPIRACY NUMBER EIGHT: Jesus, Mary, and the Holy Grail

1. Translated from "The Creed of Constantinople—381 (Nicene Creed)," http://www.earlychurchtexts.com/main/constantinople/creed_of_constantinople.shtml (accessed November 12, 2007); "The Nicæno-Constantinopolitan Creed," http://www.ccel.org/ccel/schaff/creeds2.iv.i.ii.html (accessed November 12, 2007).

2. Brown, *The Da Vinci Code*, 245.

3. R. Brown. *The Death of the Messiah: From Gethsemane to the Grave: A Commentary on the*

Passion Narratives in the Four Gospels vol. 2 (New York: Doubleday, 1994), 1092–1093.

4. Baigent, *The Jesus Papers*, 113.
5. Brown, *The Da Vinci Code*, 244.
6. Ibid., 125, 309.
7. Baigent, *The Jesus Papers*, xiii. Cf. Baigent, Leigh, and Lincoln, *Holy Blood, Holy Grail*, 290–298.
8. Gardner, *The Magdalene Legacy*, 152.
9. Ibid., 9–13.
10. Baigent, *The Jesus Papers*, 107.
11. M. Starbird, *Mary Magdalene, Bride in Exile* (Rochester, VT: Bear, 2005), 89.
12. Brown, *The Da Vinci Code*, 247.
13. Gospel of Mary 5:5. For Coptic text, see *Papyrus Berolinensis 8502, 1 and 4. Vol. III. The Coptic Gnostic Library*, ed. J. Robinson.
14. Gospel of Philip 59:6–11. For Coptic text, see *Nag Hammadi Codex II, 2–7: Together With XIII, 2*, Brit. Lib. Or. 4926(1), and P.Oxy. 1, 654, 655. Vol. I. The Coptic Gnostic Library*, ed. J. Robinson.
15. See, e.g., Starbird, *Mary Magdalene, Bride in Exile*, 74–76.
16. F. L. Cross et al., "Grail, the Holy," in *The Oxford Dictionary of the Christian Church* 3rd ed. (Oxford, UK: Oxford University Press, 1997), 700.
17. If these references make no sense to you, it would be helpful for you to purchase T. Jones, dir., *Monty Python and the Holy Grail* (Sony Pictures, 1975, 2001) as soon as possible.
18. J. de Voragine, "Readings From the Golden Legend," trans. W. Caxton, http://www.aug .edu/augusta/iconography/goldenLegend/index.html (accessed November 12, 2007).
19. Starbird, *Mary Magdalene, Bride in Exile*, xii, 93–102.
20. In the book and documentary film *The Jesus Family Tomb*, the attempt is made to suggest that Jesus's resurrection may have been *spiritual* and, therefore, that the discovery of Jesus's body would be irrelevant for Christian faith. John Dominic Crossan, who explicitly denies the possibility of resurrection, and an otherwise unknown Roman Catholic priest named Mervyn Fernando are cited in support of this hypothesis. However, despite contrary suggestions throughout the book and film, Paul's description of Jesus's resurrection assumes the reemergence of physical life in a previously deceased body, and early Christian traditions uniformly testify to the discovery of an empty tomb.
21. Though I have not quoted J. White, *From Toronto to Emmaus* (Vestavia Hills, AL: Solid Ground, 2007), this text did point me toward some resources that are cited in this section.
22. Tables have been compiled utilizing data from T. Ilan, *Lexicon of Jewish Names in Late Antiquity*, part 1 (Tübingen, Germany: Mohr, 2002); Bauckham, *Jesus and the Eyewitnesses*.
23. I have merged statistics from "Martha" and "Mara," because *Mara* seems to have been a diminutive form of Martha. Although on men's ossuaries, it appears that the Aramaic *Mara* meant "master," it is also the case that on one woman's ossuary, Mara is specifically said to be the same as Martha. Given the clearly female name Mariamne, it seems more likely that the inscription "Mariamenou Mara" refers either to "Mariamne also known as Mara" or, perhaps more likely, "Mariamne's Mara," that is, Mara, the daughter of Mariamne. See the reference to the fourth Mara in T. Ilan, *Lexicon of Jewish Names in Late Antiquity*, part 1, 422–423.
24. In *The Jesus Family Tomb*, this name is changed to Joses though the text would be more accurately transliterated as Joseh or Josah.
25. According to *The Jesus Family Tomb*, the name Mary appears in its Latin spelling Maria written in Hebrew letters. This phenomenon is presented as a rare Latinized spelling and as potential proof that this Mary was the blessed Virgin Mary. In the first place,

the spelling is more likely Greek than Latin. More important, out of the forty-two known ossuaries that bear forms of the name Mary, this precise pattern appears on nine of them, more than one-fifth of the relevant ossuaries! See Pellegrino and Jacobovici, *The Jesus Family Tomb*, 16–17.

26. In Jacobovici's own words about himself, "I'm an Orthodox Jew who grew up in a secular home and is better versed in Marxism than rabbinics" (Pellegrino and Jacobovici, *The Jesus Family Tomb*, 136). If Mara and Martha are taken as two separate names—which *is* plausible, even though it remains highly unlikely that *Mara* meant "Master" in this context—the order of frequency would stand as follows: Mary, 21.3 percent; Salome, 17.7 percent; Shelam-Zion, 7.3 percent; Martha, 6.1 percent; Joanna, 3.7 percent; Sapphira, 3.7 percent; Bernice, 2.4 percent; Imma, 2.1 percent; Mara, 2.1 percent.

27. Pellegrino and Jacobovici, *The Jesus Family Tomb*, 62, 95–96, 102.

28. Ibid., 172.

29. Ibid., 111.

30. Ibid., 45.

31. François Bovon identifies the Mariamne found in Acts of Philip as Mary Magdalene: "the Mariamne of the *Acts of Philip* is part of the apostolic team with Philip and Bartholomew; she teaches and baptizes.... This portrayal of Mariamne fits very well with the portrayal of Mary of Magdala in the Manichean Psalms, the Gospel of Mary, and Pistis Sophia." (F. Bovon, "The Tomb of Jesus," *SBL* Forum (2007), http://www.sbl-site.org/Article.aspx?ArticleId=656 [accessed November 12, 2007]).

32. Names similar to Mariamne (e.g., Mariamme) appear in the writings of Origen of Alexandria, Epiphanius of Salamis, and Hippolytus of Rome; however, with the possible exception of a third-century reference in the writings of Hippolytus, even these references never clearly connect the name with Mary Magdalene. See, e.g., Origen of Alexandria, *Contra Celsum*, Patrologiae Cursus Completus, Series Graeco-Latina, repr., ed. J. P. Migne (Paris: Lutetiae Parisiorum, 1857–1866), 5:61; Hippolytus of Rome, *Kata Pason Haireseon Elengchos, Hippolyti opera graece et latine*, vol. 1, Patrologiae Cursus Completus, Series Graeco-Latina, repr., ed. J. Fabricius (Paris: Lutetiae Parisiorum, 1857–1866), 5:7:1; 10:9:3.

33. A. Kloner, "A Tomb with Inscribed Ossuaries in East Talpiyot, Jerusalem," *Atiquot* 29 (1996), 15–22.

34. A. Lemaire, "Burial Box of James the Brother of Jesus," *Biblical Archaeology Review* 28 (November–December 2002), 24–33.

35. The statistical model presented in *The Jesus Family Tomb* seems to include an assumption that invalidates any resultant probabilities: *It assumes that one of the family tombs around Jerusalem is indeed the family tomb of Jesus.* In other words, all that the statistical relationship proves is that if one of the extant family tombs around Jerusalem *is* the tomb of Jesus, this tomb is probably the one. If, however, *none* of the extant family tombs is the tomb of Jesus, the statistics contribute nothing to any conclusions about the tomb. The statistical model also appears to take for granted that Mariamne was indeed Mary Magdalene—another questionable assumption. Audrey Feuerverger, the statistician consulted for the program, has distanced himself from the conclusions of *The Jesus Family Tomb*. See A. Feuerverger, "Dear Statistical Colleagues," March 12, 2007, http://fisher.utstat.toronto.edu/andrey/OfficeHrs.txt accessed November 12, 2007).

36. For a catalog of the *Dominus Flevit* inscriptions and photographs of the ossuaries, see A. Lombatti, "Inscriptions of the ossuaries of Dominus Flevit," June 27, 2007, http://www.antoniolombatti.it/B/Blog/3BF5DF28-60DF-4E90-BB09-478530685A32.html (accessed November 12, 2007).

37. For F. Bovon's critique of Jacobovici's claims, see F. Bovon, "The Tomb of Jesus," *SBL*

Forum (2007), http://www.sbl-site.org/Article.aspx?ArticleId=656 (accessed November 12, 2007). Bovon states, in part, "When I was questioned by Simcha Jacobovici and his team the questions were directed toward the *Acts of Philip* and the role of Mariamne in this text. I was not informed of the whole program and the orientation of the script....I do not believe that Mariamne is the real name of Mary of Magdalene. Mariamne is, besides Maria or Mariam, a possible Greek equivalent, attested by Josephus, Origen, and the *Acts of Philip*, for the Semitic Myriam."

38. Baigent, *The Jesus Papers*, xiii.

39. The function of the Greek word *kaleo* ("call") is not readily apparent in many English translations; it is frequently paraphrased as "invited" or "bidden."

40. Ancient feasts included two "calls" issued to guests. The potential guest would respond to the initial calling by informing the host that he or she would be present on that day. Partly because meal preparations were less predictable and because ancient culture placed less of a premium on promptness and exact timing of events, a second call was issued when the meal was completed. This call went out only to persons who had already vowed to be at the feast. An example of this pattern may be found in Esther 5:8 and 6:14, as well as in the writings of later rabbis, the Jewish philosopher Philo and Apuleius. See J. Nolland, *Luke 9:1—18:34* (Dallas, TX: Word, 1993), 755.

41. Philo of Alexandria, *Hypothetica*, vol. IX, Loeb Classical Library, ed. F.H. Colson (Cambridge, MA: Harvard University, 1941), 8:11.

42. Brown, *The Da Vinci Code*, 247.

43. J. Y. Leloup, *The Gospel of Mary Magdalene* (Rochester, VT: Inner Traditions, 2002), 5–6.

44. "Gospel of Philip" in *Encyclopedia of Early Christianity*, ed. E. Ferguson (New York: Garland, 1990); cf. Starbird, *Mary Magdalene, Bride in Exile*, 74.

45. Gospel of Philip 59:6–11. Some translations render *companion* as "consort" and add "upon the mouth" to the second phrase. These renderings are possible, but they are far from certain.

46. Starbird, *Mary Magdalene, Bride in Exile*, 74. Cf. L. Gardner, *The Magdalene Legacy*, 129–130; Brown, *The Da Vinci Code*, 246. Dan Brown confuses languages and refers to the text as having been written in Aramaic rather than Coptic or Greek—even though no surviving form of Gospel of Philip ever existed in Aramaic and no known Aramaic term means both "companion" and "spouse"!

47. Baigent, *The Jesus Papers*, 8.

48. For a discussion of Plantard's retraction see P. Smith, "Priory of Sion Fake Parchments: History of a Hoax," http://priory-of-sion.com/posd/pdchparchments.html (accessed November 13, 2007). Much of the false history created by Pierre Plantard was plagiarized from the documents of an esoteric group known as the Order of the Rose-Croix of the Temple of the Grail. These documents were also the source from which Plantard discovered the myth of the French priest Saunière.

49. Brown, *The Da Vinci Code*, 245.

50. Other evidences of the supposed marriage of Jesus and Mary include some claims regarding the "Cathars," a group that arose within the Roman Catholic church in the tenth century and promoted a Gnostic view of God and of the world. Laurence Gardner claims, "In discussing the...historical records of the sect of Cathars in Southern France, Dondaine related that they believed 'Mary Magdalene was in reality the wife of Christ.'" (L. Gardner, *The Magdalene Legacy* [New York: Barnes & Noble, 2005], 110; cf. Y. Stoyanov, *The Hidden Tradition in Europe* [London, UK: Penguin, 1994], 222–223). Yet Cathar theology would seem to contradict this supposition: Cathars believed in two deities—one evil and one good. The evil deity (the Demiurge) created the physical world. According to Cathars, Jews worshiped the Demiurge. The good deity created the spiritual

world and sent Christ to provide a path of escape from the physical world. According to the Cathars, Jesus was a phantom—not God incarnate—which calls into serious question the claim that Cathars were persecuted because they viewed Jesus as the spouse of Mary Magdalene! Cathars lived simply, perhaps embracing celibacy, and spoke out against the corruption of medieval clergy. Several pseudohistorical sources, including *Holy Blood, Holy Grail*, have insinuated that the nineteenth-century priest Saunière found evidence in his church at Rennes le Chateau that the Cathars had been the keepers of the Holy Grail, which is to say, "the Cathar Treasure," the suppressed secret that Jesus married Mary Magdalene. Pope Innocent III declared the Albigensian Crusade in 1208 to eradicate the Cathari. The crusade lasted approximately from 1209 until 1229. The term *Albigensian* arose from the crusaders' assumption that the Cathari were concentrated in the village of Albi. No reliable evidence exists, however, to support the contention that this crusade was intended to maintain any long-suppressed secret about Jesus.

51. Brown, *The Da Vinci Code*, 309.
52. Clement of Alexandria, *Stromata*, 3:10, http://www.earlychristianwritings.com/text/clement-stromata-book3.html (accessed November 13, 2007).
53. According to *The Da Vinci Code*, the Roman Catholic church demonized human sexuality because "mankind's use of sex to commune directly with God posed a serious threat to the Catholic power base" (Brown, *The Da Vinci Code*, 309). It is true that, influenced by the same Platonism that inspired the Gnostics, a negative view of women and sexuality did grow among Christians throughout the ancient era. This perspective was not, however, sufficiently strong in the second century A.D. to provide a basis for a cover-up of Jesus's marriage to Mary Magdalene. Furthermore, because this process occurred after the first century A.D., this has nothing to do with the perspectives of the New Testament authors or the authenticity of their testimony.

CONSPIRACY NUMBER NINE: The Dogs Beneath the Cross

1. Throughout this chapter, I have drawn data from an outstanding article. (C. Evans, "Jewish Burial Traditions and the Resurrection of Jesus," http://www.craigaevans.com/Burial_Traditions.pdf (accessed November 13, 2007).
2. Seneca, *De consolatione ad Marciam*, in *Volume II: Moral Essays*, Loeb Classical Library, ed. J. Basore (Cambridge, MA: Harvard University, 1932), 20:3.
3. Examples are drawn from M. Hengel, *Crucifixion: In the Ancient World and the Folly of the Message of the Cross* rev. ed. (Philadelphia, PA: Fortress Press, 1977).
4. The graffito is grammatically incorrect—a plural form of "worship" (*sebete*) appears instead of the singular form required by the noun *Alexamenos*. Most likely, this represents a misspelling of the third person singular *sebetai* of the deponent verb *sebomai*. For more information regarding the Alexamenos Graffito, begin with E. Ferguson, *Backgrounds of Early Christianity* 3rd ed. (Grand Rapids, MI: William B. Eerdmans, 2003), 596–597.
5. J. D. Crossan, *Jesus: A Revolutionary Biography*, 127; J. D. Crossan and J. Reed, *Excavating Jesus: Beneath the Stones, Behind the Texts* (New York: HarperCollins, 2001), 289.
6. Josephus, *Antiquitates Judaica*, 17:10, http://www.perseus.tufts.edu (accessed November 13, 2007); idem, *The Jewish War*, 2:5.
7. Josephus, *The Jewish War*, 5:6; 5:11.
8. "*Illi eadem sumptis quaerunt animalia pinnis. Uoltur iumento et canibus crucibusque relictis ad fetus properat partemque cadaueris adfert*" (Juvenal, *Satires*, 14:77–78, http://www.curculio.org/Juvenal/s14.html [accessed November 13, 2007]).
9. Rerendered from S. R. Llewelyn, ed., *New Documents Illustrating Early Christianity*, vol.

8 (Grand Rapids, MI: Eerdmans, 1998), 1.

10. N. Haas, "Anthropological Observations on the Skeletal Remains from Giv'at ha-Mivtar," *Israel Exploration Journal* 20 (1970): 38–59.

11. J. D. Crossan, *Who Killed Jesus?* (New York: Harper, 1996), 188.

12. Crossan and Reed, *Excavating Jesus*, 290–291; Crossan, *Jesus: A Revolutionary Biography*, 153.

13. 11QT64:11–13; 4Q524; cf. 11QT48:10–14.

14. Tobit 1:18–20; 2:3–8; 4:3–4; 14:10–13. The Book of Tobit can be found in any Old Testament text that has been published for use in Roman Catholic or Orthodox Churches.

15. Josephus, *The Jewish War*, 4:5; cf. Philo of Alexandria, *In Flaccus*, Loeb Classical Library, ed. F.H. Colson (Cambridge, MA: Harvard University, 1941), 10:81–85.

16. Flavius Josephus, *Contra Apionem* [The Life Against Apion], Loeb Classical Library, ed. H. St. J. Thackeray (Cambridge, MA: Harvard University, 1926), 2:30.

17. *Mishnah Sanhedrin* 6:4–6.

18. Regarding the report in Gospel of Peter, Crossan correctly notes, "The unspoken hope and the unspoken presupposition... is that Jesus would have been buried, out of piety, by the *Jews* who had crucified him. It never actually describes that burial, but it presumes that those who executed Jesus are totally in control of death, burial, and tomb." Crossan, *The Historical Jesus*, 392. In this, Crossan is partly correct: Gospel of Peter rightly assumes that someone from the Jewish ruling council took care of Jesus's burial, but this act was completed not only "out of piety" but also out of love for Jesus.

19. Josephus, *Contra Apionem* [The Life Against Apion], 2:6.

20. Philo of Alexandria, *In Flaccus*, 10.81–85. Flaccus was a contemporary of Pontius Pilate. Philo lists violation of this custom in his list of charges against Flaccus.

21. Josephus, *Antiquitates Judaica*, 18:5, http://www.perseus.tufts.edu (accessed November 13, 2007); cf. Mark 6:14–29.

22. *Corpus Iuris Civilis, Pandectae [Digesta]* 48.24.1–3, http://web.upmf-grenoble.fr/Haiti/Cours/Ak/ (accessed November 13, 2007).

23. G. Lüdemann with A. Özen, *What Really Happened?: A Historical Approach to the Resurrection* (London, UK: SCM, 1995), 23.

24. In Cornelius Tacitus, *Annales*, 6:29, http://www.perseus.tufts.edu/ (accessed November 13, 2007), it is reported how Pomponius Labeo of Moesia was accused of treasonous mismanagement and how—if crucified—he would not have received burial.

25. Hengel, *Crucifixion*, 37–38.

26. It is possible that other crucified bodies *have* survived. Casualties of crucifixion weren't always nailed to their execution stakes; often, they were *tied* to crosses instead. The skeletal remains of these victims would show no signs of being nailed to their crosses. It is also significant that the spike in the surviving skeletal remains of a crucified man remained in the heel because the sharp point had been bent, preventing its removal. No spikes or evidence thereof were found in the wrists. It's possible that, in other skeletal remains of crucified individuals, spikes were cleanly removed. For further discussion of the remains of this Jewish victim of crucifixion, see V. Tzaferis, "Crucifixion—The Archaeological Evidence: Remains of a Jewish Victim of Crucifixion Found in Jerusalem," *Biblical Archaeology Review* 11 (January–February 1985): 44–53.

27. Evans, *Fabricating Jesus*, 216.

CONSPIRACY NUMBER TEN: No Place for the Evidence

1. For the date of the tradition recorded in 1 Corinthians 15:3–7, see the discussion and references in Jones, *Misquoting Truth*, 90–94.

2. See, e.g., the report of Irenaeus in Eusebius, 5:8:2–4.

3. Josephus, *Antiquitates Judaica*, 20:200–201, http://www.perseus.tufts.edu (accessed November 13, 2007).

4. James Tabor advances this view, based on his presupposition that miracles cannot occur: "Historians are bound by their discipline to work within the parameters of a scientific view of reality.... Dead bodies don't rise—not if one is clinically dead—as Jesus surely was after Roman crucifixion and three days in a tomb. So if the tomb was empty the historical conclusion is simple—Jesus' body was moved by someone and likely reburied in another location" (Tabor, *The Jesus Dynasty*, 233–234).

5. It is certainly true that women were sometimes *allowed* to give testimony in court. Yet, from the perspectives of Jews and Romans alike, it remained unseemly for a woman to present evidence. See, e.g., *Corpus Iuris Civilis, Pandectae [Digesta]* 3:1:1:5, http://web .upmf-grenoble.fr/Haiti/Cours/Ak/ (accessed November 13, 2007), where women were forbidden to participate in criminal trials, though participation in civil cases was not clearly disallowed. Similarly, Josephus declared, "From women, let no evidence be accepted, because of the levity and temerity of their gender" (Josephus, *Antiquitates Judaica*, 4:219, http://www.perseus.tufts.edu [accessed November 13, 2007]). The pagan critic Celsus even ridiculed Christians because the initial witnesses at the empty tomb were women (Origen of Alexandria, *Contra Celsum*, ed. J. P. Migne, *Patrologiae Cursus Completus*, Series Graecae 11 [Paris: Lutetiae Parisiorum, 1857–1866], 2:59). It seems clear then that if someone were to fabricate a story—such as the Resurrection tradition—in which the first witness to a crucial event was specifically identified and named, the fabricator would *not* have placed a woman in that crucial role.

6. Ehrman, *Peter, Paul, and Mary Magdalene*, 226. Even as I disagree with many points from Bart Ehrman, I profoundly respect his fair-mindedness in this assessment. Contrast Ehrman's fair-minded weighing of actual historical evidences to Gerd Lüdemann's preposterous claims about Mary Magdalene: "The narratives of the visits to the tomb have been formed around Mary from the town of Magdala in Galilee.—Mary was certainly a follower of Jesus and went with him to Jerusalem.—But her visit to the tomb of Jesus is not historical: the source of the tradition is a legend which came into being at a late stage, directed against attacks by opponents, and this presupposes an already extant 'Christian' belief in the resurrection of Jesus" (Lüdemann with Özen, *What Really Happened?*, 79). The difficulty with this claim is that when the New Testament Gospels were written, Christianity had already spread throughout the Roman Empire. How did so many people, spread across so much space, fabricate such a unified "legend"? The Gospel according to Mark, the Gospel according to John, and Gospel of Peter—as well as, probably, the tradition now recorded in Mark 16:9–13— emerged in relative independence in the midfirst to late second centuries. Yet all three witnesses—four, if Mark 16:9–13 constitutes a separate tradition—agree that Mary Magdalene found the tomb empty. Three of the witnesses agree that Mary saw at least one angelic being around the tomb and that this being informed her that Jesus was no longer in the tomb.

7. Metzger and Ehrman, *The Text of the New Testament*, 327.

8. Skeptics frequently point out that at some levels, the Gospel accounts of the Resurrection seem inconsistent with one another. Colin Cross, for example, declares, "The disciples of Jesus believed that Jesus had been seen alive again after his crucifixion

but it is impossibletextual criticism to get to the bottom of the story. The accounts
in the gospels are different and inconsistent" (C. Cross, *Who Was Jesus?* [New
York: Atheneum, 1970], 109). What is ignored is that—even supposing that some
inconsistencies *do* exist between various accounts, which is questionable—the agreement
on the empty tomb discovered by Mary Magdalene on the third day in independent
traditions is inexplicable apart from an actual, historical event.

9. Wright, *Who Was Jesus?*, 63.

10. B. Ehrman and W. Craig, "Is There Historical Evidence for the Resurrection of Jesus?: A
Debate between William Lane Craig and Bart Ehrman," March 28, 2006, http://www
.holycross.edu/departments/crec/website/resurrection-debate-transcript.pdf (accessed
November 13, 2007).

11. Tabor, *The Jesus Dynasty*, 233–234. For a survey of the history of this supposed canon
of historical research, see P. Eddy and G. Boyd, *The Jesus Legend* (Grand Rapids, MI:
Baker, 2007), 40–49.

12. R. Bultmann, "Is Exegesis Without Presuppositions Possible?" in *Existence and Faith:
Shorter Writings of Rudolf Bultmann*, trans. S. M. Ogden (Cleveland, OH: The World
Publishing Company, 1960), 291–292.

13. What I am suggesting here in simplified form is the *open historical-critical method*
proposed in Eddy and Boyd, *The Jesus Legend*, 82–90.

14. J. Pelikan, "Maasai Creed," *American Public Media*, May 18, 2006, http://
speakingoffaith.publicradio.org/programs/pelikan/masai.shtml (accessed November 13,
2007)

Index

Acknowledgments

C ONSPIRACIES AND THE CROSS BEGAN AT JIM MISCH'S SPLENDID Starbucks at the corner of Sixty-first Street and Yale Avenue in Tulsa, Oklahoma. The book reached its conclusion at the Starbucks on Frankfort Avenue in Louisville, Kentucky. The patron potable for this project has been the venti iced coffee with six pumps of vanilla flavoring and room for cream. Thanks to the many managers at Starbucks who allowed me to remain in their dining areas long after my presence officially qualified as loitering.

Randy Stinson, dean of the School of Leadership and Church Ministry at The Southern Baptist Theological Seminary, has consistently created an environment that provides faculty members with the flexibility that is necessary to formulate works such as this one. Colleagues such as Robert Plummer, Tom Schreiner, Mark Coppenger, Bill Cook, and Shawn Wright responded to many questions that were specific to their fields of expertise. Research assistant Terry Braswell was responsible for the research that I developed into chapters 8 and 9. In the study guides, Kristi van Dyke—Garrett Fellow in the School of Leadership and Church Ministry—created an outstanding curriculum that will assist thousands of churches and small groups as they teach these materials.

Debbie Marrie at Strang Communications has proven to be a patient and gracious encourager throughout this project, even in the moments when this writer wasn't nearly as prompt as he ought to have been. Once again—as always—Mike Nappa of Nappaland Literary Agency has provided the finest possible literary representation, masterfully matching this project with precisely the right publisher.

What compelled me most strongly to complete this book as quickly as possible was not, however, any agent, editor, or publisher. It was the fact that God has gifted me with two beautiful girls—my wife, Rayann, and my daughter, Hannah—who welcome me home each night and who believe in me even when I fail to believe in myself. When I consider the two of you, words can no longer bear the weight of what I feel. There are no sentences to describe this love. There is only the catch in my throat each time I look into your eyes and the fathomless yearning in my heart that haunts every moment we are apart. Your love is a greater gift than I could ever imagine or deserve. Through you, I am ever reminded of the vastness of God's love and the goodness of the life that He has given to me. It is to you that I dedicate this book.

Still learning to live as a child,

—TIMOTHY PAUL JONES
Rosh Hashanah 2007

I N ADDITION TO BACHELOR'S AND MASTER'S DEGREES IN BIBLICAL literature and pastoral ministry, Timothy Paul Jones has earned the doctor of philosophy degree from The Southern Baptist Theological Seminary. His doctoral dissertation challenged the linguistic basis of Wilfred Cantwell Smith's argument for the possibility of a faith that requires no objective content as well as examining the statistical relationship between Christian formation and transreligious spiritual development.

Besides *Conspiracies and the Cross*, Dr. Jones has authored *Christian History Made Easy* (Rose Publishing); *Finding God in a Galaxy Far, Far Away* (Random House); *Answers to the Da Vinci Code* (Rose Publishing); *Prayers Jesus Prayed* (Servant Publications); *Praying Like the Jew, Jesus* (Messianic Jewish Publications); *Hullabaloo: Finding Glory in Everyday Life* (Cook Communications); and, *Misquoting Truth* (InterVarsity Press). His articles have appeared in *Discipleship Journal, Leading Adults, Preaching, Biblical Illustrator, Perspectives in Religious Studies, Religious Education, Christian Education Journal, Bibliotheca Sacra*, and *Midwestern Journal of Theology*. Dr. Jones also coauthored the bestselling *The Da Vinci Codebreaker* (Bethany House) and contributed more than two hundred entries to two popular reference works, *Nelson's New Christian Dictionary* and *Nelson's Dictionary of Christianity* (Thomas Nelson). More than a half million of his books and pamphlets are in print around the world.

Dr. Jones is the recipient of numerous awards for his research and writing, including the Baker Book House Award for excellence in theological studies and—for his doctoral work in the field of faith development—the North American Professors of Christian Education Scholastic Recognition Award. In 2003, *Christianity Today* Online selected *Christian History Made Easy* for its listing of the "Top Ten Entry Points to Christian History." In 2005, the readers of LifeWay.com selected *Finding God in a Galaxy Far, Far Away* as a Reader's Choice Best Book of the Year.

After fourteen years of pastoral experience in Missouri and Oklahoma, Timothy Paul Jones now serves as professor of leadership and church ministry at The Southern Baptist Theological Seminary in Louisville, Kentucky. He has also served Midwestern Baptist Theological Seminary and Oklahoma Baptist University's Seminary Extension program as adjunct professor of biblical languages.

Dr. Jones has been married to his wife, Rayann, since 1994. In 2003, they adopted Hannah, a seven-year-old girl from Romania. Hannah and her daddy spend their evenings playing Star Wars Miniatures in the recreation room and baking cookies. The Jones family resides in Louisville in a house owned by three cats—Martin Luther, Shadowfax, and Cho Chang—and a Siberian Husky named Remus Lupin.